St. Francis de Sales

CLASSICS OF THE CONTEMPLATIVE LIFE

General Editor

J. M. HUSSEY

ST. FRANCIS DE SALES: *Selected Letters*, translated with an introduction by Elisabeth Stopp.

ST. PETER DAMIAN: *Selected Writings on the Spiritual Life*, translated with an introduction by Patricia McNulty.

ST. JOHN CLIMACUS: *The Ladder of Divine Ascent*, translated by Archimandrite Lazarus with an introduction by M. Heppell.

MEISTER ECKHART: *Selected Treatises and Sermons*, translated from Latin and German with an introduction and notes by James M. Clark and John V. Skinner.

Edited by E. ALLISON PEERS:

*

BERNARDINO DE LAREDO: *The Ascent of Mount Sion*, being the third book of the treatise of that name translated with an introduction and notes by E. Allison Peers.

WALTER HILTON: *The Goad of Love*, an unpublished translation of the *Stimulus Amoris* formerly attributed to St. Bonaventura, now edited from MSS. by Clare Kirchberger.

HENRY SUSO: *Little Book of Eternal Wisdom* and *Little Book of Truth*, edited by James M. Clark.

BLESSED JAN VAN RUYSBROEK: *The Spiritual Espousals*, translated from the Dutch with an introduction by Eric Colledge.

RICHARD OF SAINT-VICTOR: *Selected Writings on Contemplation*, translated with an introduction and notes by Clare Kirchberger.

ST. FRANCIS DE SALES
Selected Letters

Translated with an Introduction by
ELISABETH STOPP

HARPER & BROTHERS

Publishers

NEW YORK

PRINTED IN GREAT BRITAIN BY LATIMER TREND AND CO LTD
PLYMOUTH. NIHIL OBSTAT JOANNES M. T. BARTON, S. T. D., L. S.
S. CENSOR DEPUTATUS. IMPRIMATUR: E MORROGH BERNARD. VIC.
GEN. WESTMONASTERII, DIE 28A APRILIS, 1960.

PATRI DILECTISSIMI

Contents

Illustrations

Translator's Preface

My thanks are due to the First Monastery of the Order of the Visitation at Annecy, the editors of the Annecy Edition of the works of St. Francis de Sales, for permission to use their definitive text for my selection and translation of his letters and to reproduce a facsimile of his handwriting. This year the Order of the Visitation commemorates the 350th anniversary of its foundation at Annecy in 1610; I should like this book to contribute in a small way towards this occasion.

I gratefully acknowledge the help and encouragement given to me by Professor J. M. Hussey, the Reverend Stephen Rigby, the Reverend Ferdinand Valentine, O.P.; and at all stages by my husband.

Since 1616, when the first translation of the *Introduction to a Devout Life* appeared, St. François de Sales has been called 'St. Francis de Sales' in English devotional literature. I have preferred to keep to this hybrid version of his name because it has been sanctioned by tradition.

ELISABETH STOPP

Cambridge
5 May 1960

Introduction

In a letter to a lady in Paris who had complained of his plain-speaking, Francis de Sales wrote: 'I am quite prepared to admit that my letter was not without a certain rustic forthrightness, but need you take offence at this? You know very well the kind of country that produced me: can you expect delicate fruit from a mountain tree, and such a poor tree at that?'[1] To the end of his life—this letter was written in 1621, the year before he died—Francis remained bound up with his homeland, the duchy of Savoy, the mountainous stretch of country placed between France, Switzerland and Italy, predominantly French in affinity but sharing to some extent in the culture of all three. He was born of an ancient noble family on 21 August 1567 at the castle of Thorens near Annecy, the little town on the lake which was the seat of the exiled bishop of Geneva and subject to the court of Piedmont at Turin. It was here that he spent most of his life; he was a 'mountain tree', deeply rooted in the land of his origin, and it is against a background of ordered, stable hierarchy of traditional loyalty to his Church, his sovereign and his people that he must be seen and judged. His charm and gentleness, the aspects of his personality most apparent in his writing and therefore most generally stressed, form an incomplete picture; the vigour and tenacity, the uncompromising realism and common sense which characterize his race may too easily be overlooked. So too may the life-long struggle which a man of exceedingly quick and strong reactions had to wage to overcome his naturally choleric temper. In the end the victory of grace was so complete in him that he now lives in the popular imagination as the most gentle of saints. But this judgement is superficial unless it is borne in mind that his was the

[1] Letter 122.

15

gentleness of a God-given and yet hard-won integration, continually vitalized by the struggle of opposites which, as he himself says, lasted until the day of his death.

Francis de Sales was the eldest of thirteen children and as the heir to the family name he was destined to a career in the service of the state. He went to school at the Capuchin college at Annecy and when he was fifteen he was sent to study in Paris where he was inscribed in the arts faculty at the Jesuit College of Clermont. For the next six years he led the ordinary life of a student and nobleman of the time. He was accompanied by his own servant and by a strict priest tutor to whom he remained devoted and obedient throughout. He lodged in a hostelry close to the college in the Rue Saint Jacques, and apart from the courses in rhetoric and philosophy which he attended he also had lessons in fencing and dancing and became an accomplished horseman. The college was famous not only for its exemplary moral discipline at a time of great disorder but also for the excellence of its literary and humanistic studies, for the stress laid on outer stylistic form as well as on inner thought content. Through his grounding in Latin and Greek, his training in the art of reasoning and writing according to newly developed principles of philology and criticism, Francis was heir to all that was best in the Renaissance renewal of the university of Paris. As a writer he owes much to this training. The humanist substitution of a pleasing and conversational method of argument for the formal, rigid statement of the scholastics, of Plato and Cicero as models instead of Aristotle, coloured the whole bent of his mind and had a decisive influence on his prose style which was, in turn, to lay the foundations for the great prose of the classical period in French literature.

As a person coming from a small provincial town Francis gained his first insight into life in a great capital which was both the seat of a powerful government and a centre of culture and learning. He was a welcome visitor in the homes of the nobility among whom his father had connections. Although he was always rather reserved and quiet it appears that he had a great power of attraction and made many friends, for he was prepossessing both in manner and in appearance. He was tall and well built, his dress and general bearing handsome in the style of a nobleman of the period. Hoffbauer's portrait[1] shows a striking face framed by a high collar and set off by a black velvet cap decorated with a plumed white feather. The features are well shaped and regular, he has a determined mouth, finely marked eyebrows and large grey-blue eyes set wide apart and looking out into the world in a thoughtful and somewhat withdrawn manner. Indeed, there is a look almost as if of suffering in his face, perhaps a reflection of the spiritual crisis he went through in Paris when, for a time, overwork and a confusion of ideas on the matter of predestination made him feel that his soul was doomed to eternal separation from God. The torment of despair came to a sudden end as he knelt in prayer in St. Etienne des Grés saying the Memorare before an ancient statue of Mary. This personal experience of temptation on what was one of the chief points at issue in controversy with the Calvinists of Savoy undoubtedly helped to equip him in a special way for his work later on.

In the spring of 1588 he went back to Savoy for the first time in six years and after a holiday at home among the mountains he took the road again with his tutor and servant to go to Italy, to the University of Padua, for his higher legal studies. Three years later he took a brilliant doctorate in law and in the same year, a combination not unusual at the time, a doctorate in theology. Throughout this period Francis had been reading theology over and above his other studies and, as it were, on sufferance, as his father saw no need for this. Knowing what a blow it would be to him Francis had kept his religious vocation a secret from all except his mother. But it had been developing steadily from his boyhood days and he had only continued with his legal studies in a spirit of obedience while his heart was elsewhere. On his return from Padua he managed to enlist his mother's help and gradually accustom Monsieur de Boisy to the idea of his eldest son's ordination to the priesthood. The

---

[1] A reproduction of this portrait may be found on the cover of A. Dufournet's *La Jeunesse de St. François de Sales*, 1567–1602, Paris 1942.

situation at home improved a little when an influential member of the family, himself a priest, secured for Francis the position of provost to the cathedral chapter of Geneva. This was the first step towards the bishopric, and while it pleased the father, it mortified the son who considered himself completely unfitted for such rapid preferment. After making over to his younger brother his rights of family succession and after a further period of study at home he was ordained. He celebrated his first mass on 21 December 1593 at Annecy.

The bishop, himself a man of deep spirituality, recognized his provost's capacity and extraordinary spiritual gifts and did the best thing possible for him at this stage: he appointed him to the hardest task his diocese had to offer, that of mission priest in charge of the Chablais. This was the district near the lake of Geneva which had recently been restored to Savoy but had become completely Calvinist during sixty years of alien occupation. Geneva itself whose name the see still bore, was hostile territory and the bishop and his representatives could only go there at the risk of imprisonment or even of life itself. It was a tough assignment for a young and inexperienced priest of twenty-six.

When Francis went there early in 1594, helped for the first few weeks by his priest cousin, there was not a single priest left in the area and only a handful of Catholics who had managed somehow to cling to their faith without the help of the mass and the sacraments. At first Francis lived in a fortress garrisoned by the Duke of Savoy's soldiers, worked to some extent under their protection under conditions of intolerable hardship and poverty, ridiculed, persecuted, attacked even physically, saying mass day by day in icy, half-ruined churches, preaching to empty pews. He persevered almost against hope. By the time he left his post four years later, after a triumphal celebration of the Forty Hours' devotion to the Blessed Sacrament in the church at Thonon, attended by the Duke and a papal legate, the majority of the inhabitants had returned to the Church. It was a triumph of faith and fortitude but also of practical organizing capacity of a high order backed by expert legal knowledge. This hard apprenticeship brought Francis into contact with the realities of life, giving his spirituality a basis of realism and rock-like strength.

His missionary activity also led to the writing of his first book. He could not reach his people, especially the most educated and influential among them, by his preaching, so he set about writing, printing and distributing a series of regular broadsheets on points of Catholic doctrine, covering in time every aspect of the faith. The *Controversies*[1] are written, as Francis said in the introductory pamphlet by which he launched the series, not in a rich, ornate style but in the language and the manner natural to Savoy. He wrote trenchantly, confidently, neatly rounding off the clear statement of the profoundest truths with all the energy needed for polemics, but always charitably, already showing that secret gift of persuasion which characterizes all his later work and most especially his letters. He had the gift of moving the will without any showy eloquence but by relying on God in a clear and disciplined presentation of what he himself so ardently believed. 'When I preach,' he confided one day many years later to St. Vincent de Paul, 'I feel something happening that I do not understand; I do not find the words as a result of my own efforts but by an impulse coming from God.' The *Controversies* were not known in Francis's lifetime except by those to whom the leaflets were addressed over a period of years; but when in 1923 Pope Pius XI proclaimed St. Francis de Sales the patron of Catholic writers and journalists, he gave a high place to this work which differs so greatly in content and form, though not in purpose, from his later writings. So during the hard years in the Chablais he also served his apprenticeship as a writer. When he was a student he had written brilliant essays and theoretical exercises in controversy, as can be seen from some of the neat manuscript notebooks which have been preserved; but during the course of his missionary work he was for the first time faced with the practical tussle for the right word and phrase

[1] A. I. (A=the Annecy edition of the works of St. Francis de Sales; see Bibliography, p. 307.

which was to persuade in real earnest and ultimately to save souls.

In 1598 Francis was nominated coadjutor to the See of Geneva, sent to Rome to represent his bishop in an *ad limina* visit to the Pope, and then in 1601 to Paris on a diplomatic mission concerning the restitution of ecclesiastical rights in territory which Savoy had yielded to Henry IV of France. The mission was not an unqualified success but during his six months' stay in the capital Francis gained high favour at court and in the city. He was in constant demand as a preacher and was asked to give the Lenten sermons at the Chapel Royal. 'A rare bird, this Monsieur de Genève,' said Henry IV who was famous for his apt summing-up of character, 'he is devout and also learned; and not only devout and learned but at the same time a gentleman. A very rare combination.' He became personally attached to Francis and tried to induce him to stay in Paris by offering a rich benefice; but though Francis appreciated all that Paris gave him in the course of his visit he was not to be tempted away from the comparative obscurity of his native Savoy. He gained experience, not always pleasant, of the conduct of affairs at the court and in high places, he got to know the devout life of the capital in its best aspect by meeting men and women of deep spirituality like Bérulle and Madame Acarie; he was admitted to their counsels on matters such as the introduction of St. Theresa's Carmelites into France and plans for the reforming of monasteries and convents. He was Madame Acarie's confessor for a time, was consulted on matters of conscience by persons at court and had his first experience of directing the souls of the kind of people he was to help later on. His first long letter of direction, to a superior who wanted to know how best to set about reforming her convent, dates from this time. It should perhaps be added that the morals at court reflected in general those of the king which were notoriously bad; and that religious life in communities was at a low ebb, though there was a strong counter movement of enlightened piety afoot, especially among the educated laity. The effect that Francis had on his contemporaries even at this early stage may therefore be called a personal triumph; it laid the foundations for his later work of spiritual direction among those who exerted influence over others, and also served as a long-term preparation for his founding of a new kind of religious order.

The bishop of Geneva died while Francis was on his way home from Paris. After a long retreat at the castle of Thorens, a time of great grace to which he often refers in his letters,[1] he was consecrated bishop on 8 December 1602, the ceremony taking place, at his own wish in the village church where he had been baptized. He settled down quickly at Annecy where he was known and loved by all. He followed a rule[2] which he had drawn up during his retreat, he lived without show but also without ostentatious poverty, he worked hard, gave as much time as he could to prayer, organized meetings and study or retreat days for his clergy. There was no seminary in his diocese and ordinations numbered about twenty a year; but during the twenty years of his tenure of office the average number rose to forty a year, an increase which is to be attributed almost entirely to his personal influence and organizing capacity. The bishop was available to all, 'like a fountain', as he himself said, 'in the market place'. He spent hours in the confessional, choosing the box nearest to the entrance door, and he himself took over the children's catechism class which was soon attended, not only by every child in the town but by most of the devout adults, including his own mother, Madame de Boisy. He considered preaching one of his main responsibilities and wrote a short treatise on it in the shape of a letter to Monseigneur de Bourges, Madame de Chantal's brother.[3] This admirable letter has not dated; it is concise, systematic and informative; it is also most revealing of the principles which guided Francis as a spiritual writer, that is, as one whose chosen instrument was the word, whether spoken or written. 'Form, says the Philosopher, gives a thing being and life. Say wonder-

[1] Letter 114.
[2] A. XXII, p. 111.
[3] A. XII, p. 299-325, too long to be included in this selection. Cf. Letter 7, p. 70.

ful things but say them badly and it amounts to nothing; say little and say it well, and it amounts to a great deal. How then ought we to talk when we are preaching? Beware of a lot of "quamquams" and the long periods of pedants, their gestures, expressions, movements, because this is what ruins preaching. Our speech should be unconstrained, noble, generous, straightforward, strong, devout, grave and deliberate. But how are we to achieve this? Quite simply by speaking with feeling and devotion, candidly and trustfully, by really being in love with the doctrine we are teaching and trying to get people to accept. The great art is to be art-less. The kindling power of our words must not come from outward demonstration but from within, not from the mouth but straight from the heart. Try as hard as you like but in the end only the language of the heart can reach another heart, while the sound of the tongue does not get past your listener's ear.'

It was by the hidden power of this kind of preaching that Francis reached the heart that was to be most closely linked with his for the rest of his life. In 1604 he was invited to preach the Lenten sermons at Dijon where he stayed with the young archbishop to whom the letter was addressed. His sister had come up from the country to hear the sermons. Jane Frances Frémyot de Chantal[1] was a young widow with four small children and a very difficult father-in-law in whose house she lived in humiliating circumstances. Her husband had been killed by one of his friends in a tragic hunting accident; after his death Jane Frances had given herself up to a life of austere piety under the direction of a confessor whose counsels inspired fear and anxiety rather than peace of mind. She turned to Francis for help, and following upon another meeting with her later that same year he agreed to undertake her direction. He directed her to sanctity.

In the vividly written contemporary life of Jane Frances by her secretary, Mother Chaugy,[2] we have some record of their

---

[1] See Index of Correspondents, p. 301.

[2] *Mémoires sur la Vie et les Vertus de Sainte Jeanne-Françoise Frémyot de Chantal*, par la Mère Françoise-Madeleine de Chaugy, Secrétaire de la Sainte et quatrième Supérieure du Monastère d'Annecy. *Vie et Oeuvres de Sainte Chantal*, Paris, 1893. Vol. I.

annual meetings during the next six years before she came to
settle at Annecy and found the first convent of their new order;
but the real story of their relationship is told in Francis's letters
to her. It was in trying to meet the spiritual need of a personality equal in calibre to his own and whom he loved that Francis
found himself as a director, and because of the circumstances,
as a letter-writer. During those early years he could still spare
time to write letters peacefully. He wrote with care, entering at
length into all difficulties, questions and scruples, generously
pouring out all his gifts of heart and mind. Letters were highly
prized in those days when people had few books and lived in
the country remote from all opportunities for spiritual guidance
or instruction. Madame de Chantal's friends at Dijon who had
also placed themselves under Francis's direction, the Présidente
Brûlart and her sister, the Abbess des Puis d'Orbe, had their
share of letters at this time. From the beginning he can be seen
in action with people of very different character and requirements.

Madame Brûlart was the type of young married woman
who, having seen the spiritual light, at once felt she wanted to
abandon house and home and a somewhat insensitive husband
to enter the peace and solitude of Carmel. Her sister was a
timid, perpetually discouraged and ailing nun whose desires
were excellent but who lacked the grit necessary for really
generous self-giving and for the difficult task of reforming her
abbey. Madame de Chantal's brother had got his preferment
much too young and he needed practical help, advice and
spiritual guidance. Her father, a former president of the parliament of Dijon and an extremely able lawyer, was getting on
in years and wanted to learn how to face old age and death.[1] At
home in Annecy Francis's young cousin, Madame de Charmoisy, coming from Paris and often returning to court, wanted
to know how to combine a really devout inner life with the
role she had to play in society and in the world.

Francis, who was himself as yet under forty, faced these
varied spiritual claims upon him with calm equanimity, coun-

[1] Letter 5.

23

selling prudently, advising without a trace of patronage, restraining or encouraging with equal wisdom and love. He referred his readers to books like the *Imitation of Christ*, the *Spiritual Combat* and the writings of Theresa of Avila who had not long been beatified, but he could not point to anything which had been written specifically for devout lay people and their problems. His letters had in some sort to supply this deficiency. Together with essays on various spiritual topics which he called 'Mémoire' or 'Exercice'[1] and which circulated among those he directed, the letters formed the basis of his first and most immediately successful work, the *Introduction to the Devout Life*. It was first published in 1608, carefully revised and then reprinted as often as forty times and translated into English, Italian, Latin, Spanish and German, all within his lifetime. Francis implied in his preface, and it has often been repeated, that the *Introduction* was based on the letters written to one particular person, later assumed to be Madame de Charmoisy; but quite apart from the fact that no letters to her have been preserved, it can be taken that the Philothea who is addressed throughout this book is really the type of all those who wanted to be devout this side of the cloister. This is a frame of mind which has not gone out of fashion and which accounts for the fact that the book is still a spiritual best-seller. Anyone who is familiar with this work and then turns to the letters cannot fail to identify the particular correspondents that Francis had more especially in mind at any given point of the *Introduction*, though much of it may also apply to anyone setting out resolutely on the way of devotion.

What was completely new in this book, apart from its whole conception, was the easy and unpontifical tone in which the bishop of Geneva explained the most serious subjects to Philothea. A complete programme of sanctity which in fact made the greatest possible demands on her was unfolded with conversational suppleness and in easily assimilated stages developing logically one out of the other. After an initial dedication to the devout life she was taught how to pray and make the best

[1] A. XXIV, *Opuscules*.

use of the sacraments. Then the practice of virtues proper to her state was explained to her and she was put on her guard against the temptations which beset her kind of life. Finally she was exhorted and encouraged to renew her resolutions to love God, and then to go cheerfully on her way. The careful arrangement and inner balance of the subject matter is reflected in the symmetry of the outer form, a series of brief chapters divided into five books. Whereas in the *Introduction* system prevails, though well disguised by informality, in the letters on which it is based there is the added immediacy which comes of realizing that a known and individual correspondent is being addressed in just the particular tone and terms which the situation requires. In later years when Francis was busier and more exhausted he would often simply refer his correspondents to the *Introduction* in the course of his letter, though he was always ready to explain personal variations where they were needed. Each Philothea and Philotheus remained an individual to him to the end. Indeed, it is astonishing that he did not repeat himself more often, considering how little, on the face of it, spiritual needs vary; but it is just this extra effort of love guided by imaginative insight of a very high order that distinguishes the letters of an artist who was also a saint.

In an indirect way he conjures up the portrait of all his correspondents. After his death Madame de Chantal destroyed all the letters she had written to him and which he had carefully kept and even annotated. The loss of one half of what would have made a unique spiritual correspondence may be considered tragic, but it does not need a very great effort of the imagination to reconstruct the nature and general tenor of her letters from Francis's own. She was ardent, generous and strong, inclined, at the beginning, to rush to extremes, exacting in the demands she made on herself though not on other people, untiring in her love and charity towards those in need, absolutely forthright and fearless in her dealings. She came of a family of distinguished lawyers and though she had little formal education and her spelling was highly erratic, she was a woman of great intelligence, able to express herself concisely and analyse in clear

terms a thing as intangible as a spiritual state of mind. Francis
himself commended her for this ability. She had charm, wit and
was a shrewd judge of character, qualities which need not cause
surprise in Madame de Sévigné's grandmother. Madame de
Chantal's son to whom Francis addressed one of his most
famous letters,[1] was the father of Marie de Rabutin-Chantal
who became perhaps the most famous of all letter-writers.

Madame de Chantal responded whole-heartedly to Francis's
direction which changed her inner life completely, freed it, not
indeed from great trials which always remained, but from all
excess, scruples and anxiety, leaving the way clear for the work
of God's grace in her. She had dedicated her state of widowhood to God and wanted to leave the world as soon as her responsibilities to her children would allow it. In the same way as
Francis had formulated a new type of spirituality of Christian
humanism for those who remained in the world, so he created a
new kind of religious congregation for Madame de Chantal and
others of her kind who had a vocation for the religious life. On
6 June 1610 he founded the first convent of the Visitation of
Holy Mary at Annecy with Madame de Chantal, Marie-Jacqueline de Favre, Charlotte Bréchard and one lay-sister, Jacqueline
Coste,[2] a remarkable peasant woman whom he had met earlier
on in the course of his mission work in Geneva. The congregation was contemplative, open to widows as well as to the usual
kind of younger postulant but received people who might have
been refused by a more austere order for reasons of health. The
nuns led a simple, hidden life of prayer, not marked by any extremes of penance and austerity, following what Francis called
'the way of simplicity'. Until the second foundation was made
at Lyons in 1615 the nuns did not take solemn vows, were not
enclosed and used to go out to visit the sick. Whereas the
Visitation then became entirely contemplative, the idea of
nursing the sick, at that time unheard of for nuns who were
thought of as strictly enclosed, was taken over by Francis's
friend, St. Vincent de Paul, when he founded the Sisters of
Charity. Francis had intended the visiting which was strictly

[1] Letter 58.   [2] Letter 49.

limited in time and scope to be a help towards a healthy and balanced contemplative life and subordinate to it; for the main stress of the congregation was always on this. He yielded on this point to the conservatism of the archbishop of Lyons who considered that the presence of unenclosed nuns in his town would lead to scandal and all kinds of difficulties.

Francis was now faced with the task of directing a new institute, a contemplative community, and for the help of those who had left the world to lead a more perfect life of prayer he wrote his *Treatise on the Love of God*. Although the book only appeared in 1616 the plan of the *Treatise* had been made and work begun on it before the *Introduction* was actually published in 1608. There was no break or sudden transition in Francis's writing activity, but the book reflects a considerable change and development in those for whom he was writing and probably also in himself. As he witnessed the mystical life growing in the Visitandines and saw it as it were concretely and objectively outside himself, the things that were going on in his own soul gradually grew ripe for formulation. Francis saw the mystical life as the active love of God unfolding in the soul. He therefore set himself to study—in the scriptures, in the Fathers, in St. Thomas, in the 'very learned ignorance', as he called it, of St. Theresa of Avila, in other writers of his own time, but above all in his own soul and in those whom he directed at Annecy—the relationship of love between man and God. This led him to examine Christian morals systematically in the light of love increasing in the soul, and to describe the practical effects of growing love on prayer, on human relationships, on daily life. The 'mountain-tree' of this unique personality was firmly rooted in its native earth; and in the same way Francis, the theologian, set the structure of his mystical theology firmly upon the basis of ascetical theology, thus producing a synthesis of great originality. Inspired intuition is held in balance by sound, logical thought, resulting in a kind of *Summa* of divine love. Not that he claimed to have said anything new. All he did, perhaps all that great discoverers in the realm of the spiritual life ever do, was to combine old truths in a new way.

The book was written for Théotime this time, for any soul that is already devout and wants to advance in the love of God. Although the personal form of address is not lacking, one has the impression that the basic literary pattern is no longer that of the letter but that of the more discursive colloquy, the exchange of ideas which took place in the Visitation parlour or in the convent orchard overlooking the lake and the mountains. And here Francis was no longer only the guide and teacher, but the learner together with other learners. Many of the ideas in the treatise do still find their place in letters and were originally formulated there, but on the whole there is a change of atmosphere in the letters from about 1610 onwards. Regular correspondence with Madame de Chantal had ceased though there was a constant interchange of notes between the bishop's palace and the convent, and there were letters of greater length when she went away to make foundations or when either was ill. Théotime gets fewer letters than Philothea did, and he is asked instead to pick up his copy of the *Treatise* and to read a chapter of it if his affection for his spiritual father sometimes makes him long to have a letter which seems to be slow in coming.[1] But of course other Philotheas come to take the place of the earlier ones and they are treated with equal love and respect for their uniqueness as personalities; only there is greater simplicity, a more insistent emphasis on the one thing needful in which he himself was immersed.

Not that there was ever a clear-cut distinction between the ascetical and the mystical in Francis, for indeed throughout his life the two run side by side and merge into one another, though one kind of emphasis may appear more prominent at various stages and ages. It is one of the characteristic features of Francis de Sales' spiritual correspondence as a whole that no sharp dividing line exists at any time between one 'stage' and another. It is only that a different atmosphere is sensed, a slight shifting of emphasis, often within one and the same letter. It would in any case be mistaken to look for theories of the mystical as such in letters which were dictated by changing

[1] A. XVII, p. 276, letter of 15 August 1616 to the Duc de Bellegarde.

personal and practical requirements. The counterpart to the *Introduction* on a different level is rather to be found in the *Spiritual Conferences*. These have been preserved in transcriptions made by the Visitandines of talks given in answer to specific questions and on special occasions. It remains true that everything Francis said or wrote during these last few years of his life bears the imprint of his own constantly deepening love of God. There is an ever greater simplicity, an intensity of purpose which is reflected in the very rhythm of the sentences he writes as his life draws to a close.

There were still years of toil and suffering to come but his heart remains as it were enclosed at the Visitation, leading the hidden life of prayer which he longed for increasingly as the years went on.[1] The affairs of his diocese remained excessively burdensome and intricate, his relations with his sovereign, a suspicious and unreasonable man, were always difficult. Within his own lifetime Francis supervised, through Madame de Chantal, the foundation of thirteen other Visitation convents in various parts of France. He suffered from continual ill-health, from calumny, from an ever increasing load of business and correspondence. For business letters he employed a secretary, but right to the end every letter of direction—and there were times when he wrote fifty or more letters a day of one kind or another—was written in his own hand, in his upright, beautifully formed italic characters, legible and vital right up to the very last letter of all. In the spring of 1617, and again in the following year, he made new contacts at Grenoble when he preached the Lenten sermons there. Each Philothea of these later days received letters which entered into her problems, little and great, with the same inexhaustible patience as of old, but it was now also possible for the director to harness some of the new-found ardour to furthering the spread of the Visitation. This was an excellent practical object which drew off usefully a good deal of spiritual energy from the first immediate object of its projection, Francis himself.

No one can read his letters without being deeply struck by

[1] Letter 123.

the untiring generosity with which he received the affection he inspired and with which he returned it as soon as he saw that anyone sincerely wanted to serve God through the help of his direction. It lay in the nature of things that these people were mostly women, for as he himself said in a letter to Madame de Chantal from Grenoble that same year: 'It is the ladies who excel in devotion in this town, for here like everywhere else men leave the cares of the household and the practice of piety to their women-folk.'[1] But the letters to the Duc de Bellegarde, one of the greatest statesmen of his time, are only an instance among many others that Francis's affections went out equally to all. As soon as any person, whatever the difficulties of his or her temperament, is judged to be in real earnest in the desire to lead a devout life, Francis adopts a new child into the ever-growing household of his heart. A man is forthwith addressed and really becomes *mon très cher fils*, a woman *ma très chère fille*, while the bishop himself asks to be called without ceremony by the name he held dearest: *mon père*. As one can see in the autographs the words *ma très chère* are written, as time goes on, in one connected movement of the pen and become a single concept; no one could be his child without being very dear to him. Nor is this an empty formula; he means it and he repeats the personal form of address often throughout the letter to the beloved son or daughter vividly present to his mind. He was not afraid of love or of allowing himself to be used as a channel for the love of God.

In November 1618 he went to Paris in the suite of Cardinal Maurice of Savoy who was charged with negotiating the marriage between Christine of France and the Prince of Piedmont. Madame de Chantal also went there to see to the newly founded Visitation convent. He spent practically a whole year in the capital, a time of incessant labour, attending at court, preaching almost daily, receiving visitors and counselling all who called upon his help. His most remarkable friendship at this time was no doubt that with Vincent de Paul to whom he entrusted the direction of the Visitation and of Madame de Chantal after his

[1] A. XVII, p. 356.

death, and who became one of the witnesses at the first process of canonization in 1628. 'His ardent fervour,' said Vincent, 'shone through his public preaching as well as his ordinary conversation. When I thought about his words afterwards I admired them so deeply that I felt sure he was the best living portrait of the Son of God on earth. I remember thinking again and again: How good you must be, my dear God, since Monsieur de Genève who is but your creature is so wonderfully good and kind!' This was the sort of impression he made on people and none seemed able to resist his spell. His letters from Paris reveal a man entirely carried by God's love and united to Him, a man who was making a last great effort in the face of exhaustion to meet an infinite number of demands. From the point of view of his correspondence his most important contact was that with Angélique Arnauld, the young Abbess of Port Royal who placed herself under his direction and enlisted his help in the reform of her convent. She was an extraordinarily gifted woman but tempestuous and self-willed; this is only too evident by implication in the letters which Francis wrote to her. He made a supreme effort of charity to save her from herself, for he loved and admired her and predicted great things for her if only she could learn to let God have His way. He cannot have been wrong in thinking her the kind of person who had it in her to rise to great heights, but the opposite tendency was also there to balance this and he was well aware of it. Had Francis lived and had she been able to enter the Visitation as she wished, she might never have been deceived by Jansenism.

The cardinal's suite followed the court to Tours and spent some time there. Francis arrived home towards the end of the year 1620, having once more refused all honours and benefices, even the succession to the see of Paris. He went about his work in Annecy with as much zeal as ever, though with increasing difficulty and with an ever greater longing to retire, to write at leisure, to fix his mind wholly on God. The next autumn, one crisp September day, he went up into the mountains to bless a sanctuary, a hermitage where the holy founder of the Abbey of Talloires had ended his days in solitude. After the ceremony, as Francis stood looking out over the landscape he loved, the fields and valleys of the foothills, the snow-capped mountains beyond the lake, he told the abbot how he longed to leave the heat and burden of the day to another, to live in a solitude of this kind, 'serving God with his rosary and his pen'. At the beginning of that year his brother John had been appointed his coadjutor. He had some help from him but he also had the task of training a successor, a man of uncertain temper to whom he always showed unalterable good humour.

In the autumn of 1622 Francis joined the court of Savoy for a meeting with the court of France at Avignon and later at Lyons, where Louis XIII conferred with the Prince of Piedmont and Christine. Francis knew when he left Annecy that he would not return. At Lyons he refused all offers of sumptuous lodgings and chose to stay in the gardener's cottage in the grounds of the Visitation convent a little way out of the town. All the hours he could spare from official duties were spent with the nuns and it was there he saw Madame de Chantal for the last time. She had been away from Annecy in Paris and making foundations elsewhere; she had not seen him for three years. She had hoped that they would talk as of old of spiritual matters, of her own state of soul and of his; but he saw fit to confine their long conversation entirely to practical administrative affairs concerning the Visitation. As soon as all business was settled he asked her to leave at once for a visit to the convent at Belley which needed her presence. No personal word passed between them, though for the whole of the month that Francis spent at Lyons his cottage was open to all the great and little people who cared to consult him. His last letter,[1] written on Christmas Eve, was an appeal for a poor man who was out of work. To the end the pattern of his life remained the same, one of complete self-abnegation and of perfect self-giving. On 27 December he had a seizure and he died the next day on the feast of the Holy Innocents, at the age of fifty-five. According to his own wish he was buried in the church of the first Visitation convent in Annecy which also became the resting place of

[1] Letter 125.

Jane Frances de Chantal when she died twenty-four years later in 1646.

'In his writings he showed a safe and plain way to Christian perfection.'[1] Although this was said of St. Francis's works in general it can be applied in a special way to his letters in which he showed individual people their own particular road to the good life. To attempt to draw a clearly defined and systematized doctrine from the letters on their own would mean introducing a semblance of system where none was ever intended. St. Francis laid down the main lines of his teaching in his other works, a plan for the devout life in the world and a study of the contemplative life of the soul. The letters show these ideas in action, varied as they apply to diverse personal needs. The distinguishing feature of St. Francis's direction as it is revealed in his letters was precisely that it was not systematized but wholly personal. He applied no ready-made set of principles, no rigid set of rules to the living personality which confronted him; nor does he provide any penny-in-the-slot type of answer to difficulties. He was a casuist in the very best sense of that word. Every single one of the hundreds of letters of direction he wrote was addressed to an individual man or woman in a particular set of circumstances and of a particular temperament which he understood with penetrating insight. This is where he begins, not from any set of preconceived ideas imposed from without. He judges his correspondent's psychological and spiritual situation intuitively from within, but also by acute and clear-sighted observation, harbouring no illusions about human nature but always judging justly, with love and compassion. There are few human quandaries on which he does not at some time comment in his correspondence and one might perhaps try to categorize the counsels he gave. In a brief introduction, however, it is more to the point to try and give a general idea of the atmosphere in which St. Francis's direction moved and then allow the letters to speak for themselves.

Now this atmosphere can best be described as one of inspired

[1] Second nocturn of the breviary lesson for the feast of St. Francis de Sales.

common sense. 'Mon esprit,' he wrote, 'est extrêmement ami de la simplicité.'[1] It was the simplicity of love by which he was himself possessed and which he tried to pass on to those who put themselves under his direction. He taught them to go cheerfully about their ordinary everyday tasks, to avoid haste and over-eagerness, never to try and force things, to be uncomplicated and unafraid, putting their whole trust in God and not in themselves. They were to use all available means—their state of life, the difficulties of their temperament, everything great and small that happened to them—to one supreme end: the love of God. To further this end they were to use the ordinary channels of grace—the sacraments, prayer, the practice of virtues, avoiding all exaggeration, all extremes, and disciplining themselves to a middle way. A picture in an emblem book on St. Francis[2] shows a small sailing ship being steered safely across stormy waters between two towering rocks. It illustrates the spirit of his direction with the motto: *medium tenuere beati*, 'blessed are they who keep to the middle way.'

To people in the world he proposes the true humanist ideal of inconspicuous but very real piety which was to attract and not repel all who came into contact with it. To people in religion a similar ideal of unostentatious and hidden sacrifice is proposed. But the guiding star by which the ship is safely steered between extremes is love, for God is love and the soul strives towards Him so as to reach final union with Him. Another emblem[3] in this book shows a formally laid-out garden with a giant sunflower turning towards the source of life and heat: *te quocumque sequar*, 'may I follow whithersoever you lead'. The picture illustrates St. Francis's perfect conformity to the spirit of love and the will of God. His direction consisted in an initial effort to help the soul set itself in a well-weeded plot of ground, teaching it to turn towards its true sun in prayer, then standing aside to leave the rest to God. His instructions on prayer are

[1] Letter 114, p. 276.
[2] *La Vie Symbolique du bienheureux François de Sales, comprise sous le voile de 52 Emblèmes*, par A. Gambart. Paris 1664. There is a copy in the British Museum.
[3] See illustration facing p. 210.

EMBLEME XXVI.

Son esprit de conduite & de direction.

Parmy tous les perils que l'on voit en ce lieu,
Les plus heureux sont ceux qui tiennent le milieu.

*Emblem to illustrate the spirit of St. Francis
de Sales's direction (see page 34)*

flexible in the extreme and varied according to individual needs, though at the outset he always advised systematic meditation to anyone capable of it. Offering every task to God, lifting up one's heart in short, ejaculatory prayers throughout the day, being faithful to regular, daily periods of prayer will establish the soul in God and He will see to the rest. St. Francis was guarded in his letters in his approach to the higher realms of prayer, even with Madame de Chantal for the first few years, careful to clear away all obstacles in God's path and teaching the soul to follow the leading of grace rather than try to rush ahead of its own accord. But when prayer became hard and temptations of every kind beset the soul his counsel was enlightened and authoritative. He spoke from personal experience as well as from his wide learning; but he did more than explain and counsel. He comforted people with the greatest tenderness, he kindled their courage and spurred them on to new effort. He could also make them smile, take themselves less seriously and persuade them to cultivate a detached, serene and sensible attitude to all personal difficulties—at any rate until the next letter was due. For the chief thing was that they were not to lose heart but be prepared to begin all over again every day. He was always firm, sincere and outspoken and on rare occasions he could be extremely severe.[1]

The letters of St. Francis reflect his personality more faithfully than any other single work. How is this? He rarely makes any personal statements about himself, he gives no news in the ordinary sense. Although those of his letters which are not primarily letters of direction are full of interest for the historian and the archivist, he has no time for the kind of smalltalk that makes the correspondence of past centuries such fascinating reading. The content of the letters was dictated by the questions and the frame of mind of his correspondent and he kept strictly to the points at issue. Indeed, he had no time to do anything else. The revelation of personality lies in the letterform itself, in the general atmosphere that pervades correspondence, but more especially in his own particular use of this

[1] Letters 121 and 122.

form. It is natural that the content of these letters, their message, should always have received more attention than the secondary and more intangible element of form, and he himself would be the first to object if the content were neglected in favour of the form; yet the man who devoted months of careful labour to revising his works even after they had been printed repeatedly[1] cannot have been indifferent to the way in which he said what he wanted to say.

He writes clearly and with absolute directness; however pressed he is for time he constructs each individual sentence with equal care so that every word of it is poised and balanced within the sentence just as every sentence is poised within the larger unity of the paragraph and then of the whole letter. Not that this clarity of architectural structure is obtrusive; one is merely aware that ideas are being communicated with ease and facility. 'His manner of speaking was so precise and intelligible,' says St. Jane Frances, 'that he made people understand with great ease and readiness the highest and most delicate truths of the spiritual life.'[2] This clarity of statement is there from the beginning and becomes more and more marked as time goes on, as his intellectual grasp of spiritual truth became increasingly concentrated and infused with holiness of spirit. In 1877 Pius IX conferred on St. Francis de Sales the title of Doctor of the Church. This entails a long process of inquiry lasting over a period of years after which the written works of a man 'eminent in doctrine, distinguished in sanctity' may be quoted publicly with full authority as representing the mind of the Church. The letters were included in the scrutiny so that they too bear the hallmark of being the work of a man who was not only a saint but a doctor, that is, one who can teach. The power of teaching spiritual truths by means of the written word implies literary ability as well as holiness.

Although St. Francis's sentences are so carefully constructed,

---

[1] There are over a thousand variants in the first two editions of the *Introduction*, studied by Francis Vincent, *Le Travail du Style chez St. François de Sales*, Paris 1923.
[2] Letter to one of St. Francis's earliest biographers, Dom Jean de Saint François. *Oeuvres de St. Chantal*, Vol. 3, p. 247. Paris 1876.

they make an impression of spontaneity; his style, like that of Montaigne, still had a great deal of the fluidity and flexibility of the sixteenth century without too much of the elaborate balance and interplay of long periods characteristic of Bossuet and the later seventeenth century. He uses stylistic devices in the most natural way possible, with the art, as he postulates in his letter on preaching, that hides art. Meaning is reinforced by the repetition of synonymous adjectives, usually in groups of two or three, a device of rhetorical or legal origin by which force is added to an argument as its climax approaches. He uses antithesis, contrast and symmetrical balance of phrase in order to drive home his point and make it more telling. The use of imagery of a simple, homely kind drawn from everyday life around him, from nature, from husbandry, comes naturally to a man who spent most of his life in the country. These images are more abundant in the earlier letters; the *Introduction* is famous, indeed almost notorious for its luxuriant wealth of similitudes. Later on even these comparisons dear to the preacher in St. Francis seem to fall away; we are left with the brief phrase, the bare word charged with deep feeling and love. During the years when he was writing the *Treatise* and trying to describe states of soul which can only be expressed by analogy, he tends to abandon a multitude of small comparisons for a few basic, timeless and simple ones: the lover and his beloved, master and servant, mother and child. He writes parables. The first version of some of these is to be found in letters to St. Jane Frances, for instance that of the statue that has been placed in a niche and forgotten by its king and master; that of the musician who has gone deaf and can no longer take joy in the melodies he plays for his king.[1] These are no longer similes but metaphors; they affect the reader as does a symbol, conveying meaning and significance that lies beyond the conscious realm and yet has power to move the will and shape conscious attitudes.

In the letters the actual occurrence of parables of this kind is rare, but the *secrette vertu*[2] that invested his words in general is

---

[1] Letters 52 and 78. [2] A. XV, p. 148, letter to M. Antoine des Hayes.

37

apparent in every letter he ever wrote. It is possible to attempt to analyse his style, to describe how his letters were constructed to a similar pattern: a warm greeting to begin with, a few initial words of personal import, questions answered and difficulties explained, an affectionate appeal to his correspondent's reason and will, a final assurance of his love and prayer for them; nevertheless, the secret remains and defies analysis. The explanation does not explain, though it states a true fact: 'His words have that precious quality of penetration which is peculiar to the words of the saints; they are full of the unction of the Holy Spirit,' (Bishop Hedley). But perhaps we can make a last attempt to approach the mystery from another angle.

St. Francis saw his letters as a conversation with someone he loved, as a dialogue; in the true humanist tradition he even introduces actual dialogue into the parables just described and also into the letters, imagining his correspondent's objections and countering them.[1] In this way he actually creates the illusion of the give and take of interchanged words and opinions in the reader who cannot avoid feeling that he is being personally involved in intimate colloquy. The rhythm of these letters, where an occasionally elaborated periodic style may suddenly be succeeded by colloquial idiom, is that of the spoken word with all its ease and informality, its slight hesitations, its rapid and flexible change of emphasis. The voice becomes more and more familar as one reads on. It is a most pleasing voice, distinct, calm and reassuring, never over-emphatic, yet quietly insistent, always courteously mindful of the person who is being addressed. St. Francis's prose, more especially as the years go on, has a marked inner rhythm which seems to reflect the balance and integration of his personality, the harmony of a poised tension between feeling on the one hand and will and intelligence on the other. When these forces are of almost equal power, as they sometimes are in the contemplative or mystical writer, his written words have a quality of soft rhythmical emphasis, capable of great, indeed mysterious effect on the reader. But it is hardly necessary to add that this kind of

Letters 93, 118, 121.

rhythmical emphasis which is the result of an infused attitude and not of deliberate effort, is extraordinarily difficult to convey in translation. 'Sure I am and can assure thee,' says the Benedictine nun who first translated St. Francis's Spiritual Conferences into English,[1] 'that if thou have the spirit of the author or the matter, thou wilt interpret and pardon all friendly, freely and fully, and that if thou find as much profit in the perusal of it, as she did that translated it, thou wilt bless God and pray for her.'

The first collection of the letters of St. Francis de Sales[2] was made by Louis de Sales, the saint's nephew, under the supervision of St. Jane Frances de Chantal and of Michel Favre, his confessor. It contained 519 letters and appeared at Lyons in 1626. A second revised version with a further dozen letters followed two years later. The letters were not in chronological order but arranged according to subject matter and classified in groups according to the state of life of the correspondents: dignitaries of the Church, royal personages, people in the religious, secular or married state. For reasons of discretion the recipients were mostly unnamed and few of the letters were dated.

Among the many originals and copies at their disposal the editors chose only those which they considered of spiritual interest. Letters were shortened and rearranged as was thought fit, expressions of affection were cut, St. Jane Frances herself scoring out with a firm pen in the very autographs whatever seemed to her unfit for the public eye. When, as a result of this pruning, a letter seemed too short, Louis de Sales fitted in one or two suitable paragraphs from elsewhere in the correspondence. A good many of the documents which reached the editors were in any case incomplete as pieces had been cut out and given away as relics. But even this edition had sufficient appeal to be reprinted more than forty times in the course of the

---

[1] *Delicious Entertaynments of the Soule.* Written by the holy and most Reverend Lord Francis de Sales, Bishop and Prince of Geneva. Translated by a Dame of our Ladies of Comfort of the order of S. Bennet in Cambray. Imprinted at Douay by Gheerart Pinson, 1632. There is a copy in the British Museum.

[2] For details of all editions mentioned, see the Bibliography.

seventeenth century until in 1758 the Abbé Corru made the first attempt to present a collection of 831 letters in a more scholarly way, in chronological order and with the name of the recipient. Further important additions to this volume appeared in the course of the nineteenth century, notably in the edition of Migne who returned to the original arrangement of the letters by subject matter. By this time 1,360 letters had been collected. A selection of 367 of these was made by Veuillot and appeared in 1865.

The first complete edition of the saint's works with a critical apparatus was begun in 1892 by the Sisters of the Visitation at Annecy under the editorship of an Englishman, Dom H. B. Mackey O.S.B., who devoted his life to this task. The correspondence, published from 1900 to 1923, fills eleven of the twenty-six volumes; 2,100 letters were collected, checked by autographs as far as was possible and fully annotated with all relevant details. The letters were given as St. Francis wrote them, with careful regard to his own variations of spelling and grammatical forms and in the French of the early classical period in its transitional stage from the sixteenth century. It is estimated that what has survived of the correspondence is only about a tenth of the whole, but even so it may be said that a true picture of St. Francis de Sales as a letter writer has now emerged as a result of this great edition. A final volume which will contain indices and some errata connected with the correspondence and with other works is now in preparation at Annecy.[1]

The first English translation of a substantial number of letters (159) appeared anonymously in 1871, this was followed in 1883 and 1888 by a translation of the 367 letters selected by Veuillot. This was the work of Dom Mackey and formed part

[1] A note in the appendix to J. Calvet's second edition of his *Littérature Religieuse de François de Sales à Fénelon*, 1956, makes the statement, unsupported however, that a number of forgeries by the Swiss forger, Henri-David Favre, have slipped into the Annecy edition of the letters. Those now in charge of the work on this final volume at Annecy have authorized the present translator to say that careful examination has shewn that there is little substance in this statement and that only a few minor alterations will have to be indicated in the errata as a result of the inquiry.

of the *Library of St. Francis de Sales* which he initiated. The same basic pattern of arrangement by subject matter and according to the recipient is maintained in the extracts from the letters published in 1933 by the Sisters of the Visitation of Harrow-on-the-Hill. The extracts are linked together by a commentary and given partly in Dom Mackey's translation and partly in a revised one based on the Annecy text. The first French selection of 114 letters in chronological order, based on the new text but presenting it in modern French, was published by E. Le Couturier in 1952.

The present selection contains complete letters wherever practicable[1] and in the order in which they were written. Any selection is in the last instance a matter of personal preference even though it has been made with a definite end in view. Here the aim has been to give as complete and varied a picture as possible of St. Francis de Sales as a writer of spiritual letters during the twenty or so most important years of his life and to convey some idea of his own development both as a director of souls and as a writer. This should provide a new and more personal background to his other spiritual works which are at present far more widely known in English-speaking countries —the *Introduction to a Devout Life* and the *Treatise on the Love of God.*

[1] Omissions of unimportant or repetitive matter have been indicated thus: . . .

To Soeur de Soulfour, Novice at the Filles-Dieu Convent in Paris

Annecy, 16 January 1603

My very dear and much loved Sister and Daughter
in Jesus Christ,

May God alone be your rest and consolation. I have received both your letters through President Favre, though a little later than you expected and than I should have wished; soon enough, however, to afford me consolation as they proved to me that you feel easier in your mind. Praise be to God eternally.

In reply I should like to say first of all that I do not want you to use phrases of ceremony and excuse when you write to me, for by God's will I bear you all the affection you could wish, nor can I help it. I love your soul steadfastly because this is what I think God wants, and tenderly because I see that it is still feeble and young. So write to me in full confidence and quite freely, asking whatever you think you need for your good. Let this be said once and for all.

I see that there is a contradiction in your letter which has crept in without your being aware of it; for you tell me you are delivered from your anxiety and nevertheless I still see you very anxious to become perfect in a great hurry. I will try and explain now what I mean. . . . It seems to me that you are pursuing perfection with far too much eagerness; this is what makes you afraid to welcome little consolations of devotion. I should like to impress on your mind what is written in the Book of Kings:[1] God is not in the mighty wind, nor in the earthquake, nor yet in these fiery flames but in the soft and gentle stirring of a breeze that we can hardly feel. Let yourself be ruled by God, do

[1] 3 Kings xix, 11, 12. (Douay version)

not think about yourself so much. If you want me to give you an express command, since your Novice Mistress agrees to this, I will gladly do so. My first rule for you is this: as you have made a general and all-inclusive resolution to serve God as best you can, do not waste time examining and minutely analysing how best to do it. This is a pointless activity characteristic of your agile and alert mind which wants to tyrannize over your will and guide it by a fallacious over-subtleness.

You know what God wants in general: that we should serve him by loving him above all things and our neighbour as ourself; and in your particular case, he wants you to keep a rule. That is enough. You must do this in good faith, without trying to be too clever and subtle, doing it all after the fashion of this world where nothing is perfect, doing it in a human and timebound way until the day comes when you may be able to act in a divine and angelic way in the light of eternity. It will not support your general resolution if you are restless, eager and agitated; the desire is right and good but it must be peaceful. I expressly forbid you this sort of over-eagerness, for it lies at the root of every other imperfection. Therefore do not inquire so minutely whether you are being perfect or not, and that for two reasons: firstly, this kind of examination is futile, for even if we were the most perfect people in the world we should neither know nor realize this but always think ourselves imperfect. In our self-scrutiny we should never aim at discovering whether we are imperfect, for this should never be a matter of any doubt. It follows that we should not be astonished to find ourselves imperfect, for we should never see ourselves otherwise in this life; nor should we let this upset us, as it cannot be helped, but rather let it be a cause for humility, for this is the way to correct our faults and gradually improve. This is indeed the whole point of our being left with imperfections, and we cannot be excused if we do not try to mend our ways, nor yet called inexcusable if we do not entirely succeed, imperfections and sins being in a different case.

The other reason is that this self-scrutiny, if it is anxious and perplexed, is just a waste of time; and those who indulge in it are like soldiers who prepare to go into battle by too much skirmishing and sham-fighting among themselves, so that when the time comes for the actual combat they find they are weary and completely spent. One might also compare them to musicians who sing themselves hoarse by too assiduously practising their motet. The mind which wears itself out with continual, fervid self-inspection is exhausted when it should go into action in real earnest. This is my first rule for you.

The second follows from the first: if your eye is simple your whole body will be the same, said our Saviour.[1] Simplify your judgement, do not reflect on yourself so much nor argue inwardly, but go on your way simply and with confidence. As far as you are concerned there is nothing in this world except God and you; all the rest should not touch you except in so far as God may command and as he commands. I beseech you not to look about you so much but to keep your gaze fixed on the relationship between God and you. You will never see anything but goodness in God or neediness in yourself, and you will see his goodness supplying your need, and your poverty the object of his bounty and compassion. So do not look at anything at all except that—I mean of deliberate intent—and glance at all the rest only in passing. Moreover, do not analyse what other people are doing or speculate what will become of them, but look upon them simply, generously, with kindness and affection. Do not demand more perfection from them than you do from yourself and do not be surprised at the various forms that imperfection may take, for imperfection is not more imperfect for being unusual and odd. Be like the bee and gather your honey from every flower and herb alike.

My third rule is that you should be like a little child who while it knows that its mother is holding its sleeve walks boldly and runs all round without being distressed at a little fall or stumble; after all, it is as yet rather unsteady on its legs. In the same way, as long as you realize that God is holding on to you by your will and resolution to serve him, go on boldly and do not be upset by your little set-backs and falls; there is no

[1] Matt. vi, 22.

need to be put out by this provided you throw yourself into his arms from time to time and kiss him with the kiss of charity. Go on joyfully and with your heart as open and widely trustful as possible; and if you cannot always be joyful, at least be brave and confident. Do not shun the company of your sisters even though it may not be to your taste; rather shun your own taste when it does not accord with their ways. Love the holy virtue of mutual forbearance and of fitting in with others, for in this way, says St. Paul, you will fulfil the law of Jesus Christ.[1]

Finally, God has given you a temporal father from whom you can get much spiritual consolation; look on his advice as coming from God for God will give you many blessings through him. He has sent me his translation of Blosius' *Institutions*.[2] I have had it read aloud at table and liked it very much indeed; please do read it and reflect on it, for it is well worth it. For the rest, when you are troubled by doubts about the way of life you have entered upon do not look to me for help in the first instance because I am too far away from you and you would be left without help for too long; there are plenty of spiritual fathers close at hand; appeal to them confidently. I do not say this from any wish not to have your letters, for on the contrary, they give me consolation and I look forward to having them; I mean that I am happy to know all the details of what is going on in you spiritually (and the length of the present letter will prove to you that I am not tired of writing to you). But I do not want you to lose time and be buffetted and harmed by the enemy while you are waiting for help from so far away.

As to my mass, you may be quite certain that you always have a share in it. I offer you on the altar every day with the Son of God and I hope God will look favourably on my offering. Assure Sister Anne Séguier that the same applies to her, and also your novice mistress whose greetings I conveyed to good Monsieur Nouvelet, and who was quite delighted. If only you

[1] Gal. vi, 2.
[2] Probably: *Institution Spirituelle avec l'appendice des livres de Taulère et autres exercices*, par Loys du Bloys. Douai, 1603.

knew what a great variety of different things I have to see to and how I am set about by the difficulties of my office you would have pity on me and pray for me from time to time and God would look favourably on your prayers. I beseech you and also Sister Anne Séguier often to say with the Psalmist: 'I am thine, save me,'[1] and with Mary Magdalene kneeling at his feet: 'Rabboni, O my Master!',[2] and then leave the rest to him. He will work in you, without your aid, and yet by you and for you and out of you the sanctification of his name, to which be honour and glory.

Your affectionate and humble servant in Jesus Christ,

Francis de Sales,

most unworthy Bishop of Geneva.

2

To Mademoiselle de Soulfour

Annecy, April–May 1603

Mademoiselle, my very dear Daughter in Jesus Christ,

I have received your letter in which you try to describe your state of soul to me. I must admit that it makes me very happy to see that you feel sure of my affection which is indeed as great and as constant as you could wish. Blessed be God in all things and everywhere. And now let me get down to a few little comments on your letter.

First of all, you may be absolutely certain that your idea that you ought not to receive comfort from God except through me is just a temptation sent by him who is in the habit of making us concentrate on what is far away so as to deprive us of the use of what is close at hand. People who are physically ill often have a mental craving for the doctor who is at a distance, preferring him to the one who is close by. You must not long for the impossible or try to build on things which are difficult and uncertain of attainment. It is not enough to believe that God

[1] Ps. cxviii, 94.   [2] John xx, 16.

can help us through every kind of instrument; you must believe that he does not want to use people who are far off, and that he does want to use those who are near us. While I was near you I should not have rejected this idea of yours but now it is completely out of place.

Now it seems to me that you have discovered what is really wrong with you when you tell me that you are suffering from a surfeit of desires which have no chance of ever being translated into action. Surely this is a temptation similar to the first, or rather this completes the picture which the first only outlined. A mixture of different kinds of foods, if eaten in quantity, is always a strain on the digestion and proves disastrous if the organs are weak. When the soul has given up concupiscence and has purged itself of evil and worldly affections, at the same time discovering spiritual and holy things, it acts like any starved person, stuffing itself so greedily and with so many desires that the effect is overwhelming. Beg Our Lord and the spiritual fathers near you to give you healing draughts; people who can examine at first hand what is wrong with you will know perfectly well what remedies to apply. All the same I propose to tell you straight out what I think.

If you do not make yourself put some of these desires into effect they will go on multiplying and your mind will be so cluttered up that you will not be able to sort yourself out from them. So you must get down to action. But where are you to start? Try first of all doing tangible and external things which are within your reach and power. For example, it is perfectly legitimate for you to want to serve the sick for love of Our Lord, to do menial household tasks in a spirit of humility; for these are basic desires without which all the rest should be despised and suspected. So encourage yourself as much as you can to have desires of this kind, for you will not lack opportunity to translate them into action. This sort of thing is within your capacity and so you should do it; for if you neglect to do what is within your reach your plans for more remote objects will remain idle dreams. So act faithfully on your desires for lowly and abject works of charity, humility and other virtues, and you will find that this will do you a lot of good. Mary Magdalene had to wash Our Lord's feet first, kiss them and dry them before she could speak to him heart to heart in the secret places of prayer. She had to anoint his body before she could pour out the balm of her contemplation upon his divinity.

It is a good thing to have great desires, but you must introduce order into your desires and realize each in due season and according to your capacity. You prevent the formation of leaves on vines and trees so as to preserve enough moisture and sap for the fruit later on and not waste too much of the vine's natural force in producing foliage. It is a good thing to prevent the formation of too many desires for fear that our soul might waste time on them and neglect real tasks; for the least attempt at practical action is more profitable than great desire for what is beyond our power. God would rather we were faithful in little things which he puts within our reach than ardent for great things which have nothing to do with us. Our Lord compares the soul which desires perfection to a woman who brings forth a child;[1] but surely, if the pregnant woman wanted to produce two or more children at the same time and together she would die of it. Each must wait its turn. If you let each child of your soul, that is to say every desire of yours to serve God in various ways, emerge singly and in turn you will find this a great relief to your soul.

But if after all this you cannot find peace in these remedies, be patient; wait till the sun rises, it will scatter the morning mists. Be of good cheer: this sickness will not be unto death but so that God may be glorified by it.[2] Learn a lesson from people who are bad sailors and feel all the horrors of sea-sickness: after they have gone swaying all round the ship, exploring it to find relief, they finally come to rest by clinging to the mast and hold on to it tightly so as to prevent the dizziness which seizes them. It is true that their relief is short-lived and uncertain; but if you humbly cling to the foot of the Cross you will at least find patience sweeter there than anywhere else, and distress more pleasant.

[1] John xvi, 21.   [2] John xi, 4.

D   49

My reason for saying these things to you is rather to show you that I long for your good than because I think myself capable of helping you at this juncture. And of course you may be quite certain that I am praying for you to the Father of Light; I do it most willing and gladly, in the consoling belief that you will do the same for me. Indeed I need your prayers badly as I have launched out on the most stormy and troubled waters of the sea of the Church.

I do not forget Sister Anne Séguier[1] whom I love tenderly in Jesus Christ. May God be her protector when she leaves the convent. I commend her to you when she gets back home for she will not really be out of the world. I doubt if she will find another monastery in her father's house as you have done in yours; but all the same I hope that God will make her walk in his ways and be perfect. I have confidence in God's mercy that he will turn this to her good.

I will end this letter by entreating you to be faithful to the resolution made in the course of your letter: 'I declare before God and before you that I only want him and his service. Amen.' This is meet and right, as God, for his part, only wants the gift of yourself from you. I am unchangingly and most willingly, Mademoiselle my very dear daughter in Jesus Christ, your most affectionate servant in him,

Francis, Bishop of Geneva.

3

To the Baronne de Chantal

26 April 1604[2]

I think that God gave me to you; every hour makes me more sure of it. I can say no more; commend me to your guardian angel.

---

[1] All that is known of her is that she returned to her convent and died there in 1641 aged 56.

[2] This note was written during the first halt St. Francis made on his homeward journey after preaching the Lenten sermons at Dijon where he first met Madame de Chantal.

4

To the Baronne de Chantal

Annecy, 3 May 1604

Madam,

I should like you to feel more and more reassured and this is why I am observing as faithfully as possible my promise of writing to you as often as I can. The greater the external distance between us the closer do I feel our inward link and union to be. I shall never cease to pray God graciously to perfect his holy work in you, that is to say, to further your excellent desire and design to lead a perfect Christian life, a desire which you should love and foster tenderly in your heart as given to you by the Holy Ghost and as a spark of his divine fire.

I once saw a tree in Rome which had been planted by St. Dominic; people go to see it and they love it for love of the saint who planted it. In the same way, now that I have seen the tree of your desire for holiness which Our Lord has planted in your soul I love it tenderly and take even more pleasure in looking at it than when we were together. I exhort you to do the same and to say with me: 'O beautiful tree of God's planting, divine and heavenly seed, may God watch over your growing and make you bear fruit in due season, protecting you from the wind which makes the fruit fall where evil beasts can devour it.' This desire of yours, dear Madam, should be like the orange trees on the sea coast at Genoa, covered almost the whole year round with fruit, flowers and leaves growing all at the same time; for your desires should always be bearing fruit as you put some of them into effect every day, and at the same time you should never cease longing for some new occasion of progress. These longings are the flowering branches on the tree of your purpose in life; the leaves are your frequent realization of your weakness and keep your good works and your good desires in a healthy state. All this may be called one of the pillars of your tabernacle.

The other is your love for your widowhood, a love which is holy and desirable for as many reasons as there are stars in the sky and without which widowhood is false and not honourable. St. Paul commands us to honour widows who are widows indeed; but women who do not honour their widowhood are only widows outwardly while their heart is still in the married state. 'Blessing I will bless the widow,'[1] does not apply to them, nor yet the promise that God will be the judge, protector and defender of widows.[2] Praise God who has given you this dear and holy love; allow it to increase every day and the comfort you find in it will grow in like measure since the whole structure of your happiness rests on these two pillars. Examine them at least once a month to see whether they are both quite firm and stable, making use of some devout meditation and consideration similar to the one of which I am enclosing a copy and which has proved helpful to other souls in my care. All the same, do not tie yourself down to this particular meditation, for this is not my reason for sending it; I only want to indicate to you the general direction which your monthly examination and testing is to take if it is to be helpful. If, however, you really prefer this particular set of words it will not prove useless. But note that I say: if you really prefer it, for my chief desire for you is that you should always feel unfettered in your spirit, enjoying a holy liberty in the means you use to reach perfection. As long as you keep the twin pillars of your tabernacle in good condition and make them ever more firm and stable it matters little how it is done.

Beware of scruples and rest in what I said to you by word of mouth, for I said it in Our Lord. Keep yourself constantly in the presence of God in the way you know. Be on your guard against eager haste and restlessness for nothing is a greater hindrance on our way to God. Hide your heart gently in Our Lord's wounds, without making any vehement effort; have great confidence that in his mercy and goodness he will not forsake you, yet cling closely to his holy cross. Next to love of Our Lord I commend to you love of his holy bride, the

[1] Ps. cxxxi, 15,   [2] Ps. lxvii, 6.

52

Church, that gentle dove which alone is able to rear true fledglings for her bridegroom. Praise God a hundred times a day for
making you a daughter of the Church, following the example
of Mother Theresa[1] who found great comfort in repeating this
often at the hour of her death. Fix your eyes on the bridegroom
and the bride and say: 'O how beautiful is your bride, how
divine the bridegroom who is yours!' Have great compassion
and feeling for all the pastors and preachers of the Church, consider how they are scattered over the whole face of the earth
and how there is no corner of the world without at least a few
of them. Pray God for them so that they may fruitfully save
souls while saving themselves; and this is where I beseech you
never to forget me since God has given me such a strong will
not to forget you either.

I am sending you something I have written concerning the
perfect life for all Christians.[2] I did not write it for you but for
a number of others; all the same you will see how to make it
serve your own purposes. I beg you to write to me as often as
you can and with the fullest confidence, for in my great longing
for your good and your progress I shall be unhappy if I do not
know how things stand with you. Commend me to Our Lord
for I need it above all men in the world. I beg him to fill you
abundantly with his holy love, and also all who are dear to you.

I ever remain, and beg you to look upon me as

Your most sincere and devoted servant in Jesus Christ,
Francis, Bishop of Geneva.

5

To Président Bénigne Frémyot[3]

Sir,   Sales, 7 October 1604
   ... I know that your life has been long and most honourable,
distinguished by absolute faithfulness to the Holy Catholic

---

[1] St. Theresa of Avila.   [2] A. XXVI, p. 185 and 188.
[3] Madame de Chantal's father (see Index of Correspondents). St. Francis gave
him a copy of Cardinal Paleotti's book *De Bono Senectutis* with the following

Church; but all the same it has been spent in the world, in the management of worldly affairs. It is a strange thing, but one confirmed by experience and by various authors, that when a horse, however fine and strong, follows in the trail and tracks of a wolf, it becomes torpid and stumbles. It is not possible for us who live in the world to avoid being soiled with its dust, even though we may only be in contact with it by the soles of our feet in passing. Our fathers of old, Abraham and his children, used to offer their guests water to wash their feet; I think, Sir, that the first thing to do is to cleanse the affections of our soul so as to look forward to our dear Lord's hospitality in paradise.

It seems to me that it is always a matter of great reproach to mortals that they should die without having thought about death; but it is doubly wrong for those whom Our Lord has favoured with the blessing of old age. Those who get their armour ready before the alarm sounds are always better prepared than people who rush round collecting their breastplate, thigh pieces and helmet when the alert has actually been given. We must bid the world a calm and deliberate farewell and withdraw our affections from created things little by little.

Trees uprooted by the wind are not fit for transplanting because their roots are left behind in the soil; but if they are to be moved to another plot of ground their roots must be deftly and gradually disengaged one by one. And because we are to be transplanted from this miserable earth to the land of the living we must loosen our affections one by one from this world. I am not saying that we should roughly sever all the ties we have formed (for indeed that would cost very great effort); but we must disentangle ourselves from them and loosen their hold upon us. When people have to leave a place unexpectedly they may be excused if they have not said good-bye to their friends and set off ill equipped; but not so those who have been able to foresee the probable time of their departure. We must be ready,

inscription: 'Franciscus, Episcopus Gebennensis, felicissimam senectutem at bonum optimum senectutis amplissimo D. Benigno Fremyoto exoptans, ei hunc librum, observantiae ac amoris pignus mittit.' This book is preserved in the public library at Dijon.

not as if to set out before we are due to leave but so as to await the time of our leave-taking more peacefully.

To this end, I believe, Sir, that it would bring you unbelievably great comfort to set aside a space of time every day, and putting yourself in the presence of God and of your guardian angel, to turn over in your mind what you need to do so as to have a happy death. How would you arrange your affairs if the end were to be soon? I know that such thoughts will not be new to you; but you should let them pass through your mind in a new way, in the presence of God, with calm attention, seeking to engage your affections rather than to enlighten your intellect.

For the benefit of old people St. Jerome often told the story of Abishag, the Shunammite, who slept in David's bosom but only so as to give him warmth.[1] Young people often frequent the study of philosophy and wisdom but in order to recreate their minds rather than to move their affections; but in the arms of old people wisdom should only serve to provide the true warmth of devotion. I have seen and had the privilege of enjoying your fine library: for your spiritual instruction on this point I suggest that you should read De Bono Mortis by St. Ambrose, De Interiori Domo by St. Bernard, and several scattered homilies of St. Chrysostom.

Your St. Bernard says[2] that the soul which wants to reach God should begin by kissing the feet of the crucifix, purge its affections and firmly resolve to withdraw gradually from the world and its vanities. Then the new element which enters the soul after its affections are purged and changed makes it kiss Our Lord's hands; and finally, as the soul unites itself to this supreme goodness by a burning love, it kisses his mouth. This is how we gradually proceed to a right and happy death.

It is said that Alexander the Great, sailing on the high seas, was the first man to discover Felix Arabia by the scent of the aromatic trees there; he alone found it because he alone was seeking it. People who are sailing on the broad ocean of

[1] 3 Kings i, 1-4.
[2] Serm. lxxxvii, De diversis.

worldly affairs and yet striving to reach the land of eternity have a certain presentiment of heaven which cheers and encourages them in a marvellous way; but they should keep on the look-out in the prow of the ship and have their nose turned in the right direction.

We owe ourselves to God, to our country, our relations, our friends. God comes first, then our home; but our heavenly home takes precedence over our home on earth. Then our relations; 'but who is more closely related to us than we are to ourselves?' asks our Christian Seneca.[1] Finally, our friends; but are you not your own closest friend? I notice that St. Paul said to his dear Timothy: *'Attende tibi et gregi,'* that is, see to yourself first, then to your flock.[2]

That is quite enough, Sir, if not too much, for this year which is fast running out and in two months' time will prove to us the vanity of its existence like all the other years which have gone before. You commanded me to write you a letter of this kind year by year; now I have finished my task for the present year, in the course of which I entreat you to withdraw from the world as much as you can, uprooting your affections in so far as you are able, and transplanting them to heaven. And I implore you by your own humility to forgive me for taking you quite simply at your word in writing to you at such length and so freely. I am fully aware that you are very well able to face the situation which you are in and this ought either to have silenced me or made me measure my words with exact moderation. Here is water, Sir; even if it comes out of the jawbone of an ass, Samson will not refuse to drink.

I beg God to fill your years to overflowing with his blessings, and I remain with all filial affection, Sir,

Your most humble and obedient servant,
Francis, Bishop of Geneva.

[1] St. Bernard.   [2] Acts xx, 28.

6

To the Présidente Brûlart

Sales, 13 October 1604

Madam,

I was very happy to have and read your letter; I should so much like my letters to give you equal joy and more especially to provide you with some sort of solution for the anxieties which have arisen in your mind since we last saw one another. May God inspire my pen. . . .

You ask how you should set about acquiring devotion and peace of mind. A very comprehensive question, my dear sister, but I will try and see what I can do for you, as you have every right to ask me. Now listen carefully please. The virtue of devotion is a general inclination and readiness to do what we know to be pleasing to God; it is that opening out of the heart to God of which David said: 'I have run in the way of thy commandments, when thou didst enlarge my heart.'[1] Ordinarily good people walk in God's ways, but the devout run, and the really devout run swiftly. I will give you a few rules to keep if you want to be really devout.

The first thing is to obey God's general commandments which apply to all faithful Christians; failing this, as everyone knows, there can be no sort of devotion. Over and above the general commandments you should carefully observe the particular commandments which concern your state of life; anyone who neglects to do this, even if he were to raise the dead to life, is in a state of sin and will be damned if he dies in this frame of mind. Bishops, for instance, are commanded to visit their flock, to teach, correct and console: if I were to spend the whole week praying and all my life fasting while yet neglecting my duty towards my people, then I should be lost. A married person may work miracles and yet refuse the marriage debt to her partner, or neglect the children; in that case she is being

[1] Ps. cviii, 32.

worse than unfaithful, says St. Paul;[1] and this applies in other similar cases. These two kinds of commandments faithfully observed should then form the basis for all devotion; and yet the virtue of devotion does not consist in merely observing them but in doing so promptly and willingly. Now there are several things to be considered if you want to acquire this promptness in the service of God.

Firstly, it is God's will we are fulfilling, and this is precisely why we should hasten to do it, for we are in this world for no other purpose. Alas! Every day we ask for his will to be done, and when it comes to doing it, we find it so hard! We offer ourselves to God so often, saying over and over again: Lord, I am yours, I give you my heart; and when it actually comes to the point we are so cowardly! How can we go on saying that we belong to him if we are not prepared to make our will fit in with his?

Next we should consider what God's commandments are like: gracious, gentle and sweet. This goes not only for his general commandments but more especially for those connected with our state of life. What is it, then, that makes them hard for you? Nothing, surely, except your own self-will which wants to dominate you at all costs and which rejects the very thing it might well want to do if it were not a matter of commandment. From amongst a great number of delicious kinds of fruit Eve chose the forbidden one, and if she had been free to eat it she would very probably not have wanted it. The fact is, we want to serve God, but according to our own will, not his. Saul was told to destroy everything he found in Amalek: he destroyed all except those things he considered precious enough to be offered as a sacrifice, but God said that he would not have sacrifice against obedience. God commands me to serve souls and I want to give myself up to contemplation: the contemplative life is good, but not if it interferes with obedience. It is not for us to choose according to our own will; we must find out what God wants, and if God intends us to serve him in one thing we must not want to serve him in another. God wants

[1] I Tim. v, 8.

Saul to serve him as a king and a captain, and Saul wants to serve him as a priest. The latter is unquestionably the more perfect office; all the same, God will not have this, he wants to be obeyed.

Another good instance: God gave the children of Israel manna in the desert, a most delicious food; and what happens? They do not want it but set their heart on the garlic and onions of Egypt. Our miserable nature always wants to have things its own way and not God's way. As we come to have less self-will we shall find it easier to obey God's will.

Thirdly, you must consider that every state of life is in some way irksome, bitter and unpleasant; and what is more, except for those who are wholly resigned to God's will, people are all inclined to want to change places with others. Bishops would rather not be bishops, married people would rather be single, and single people would like to get married. How can we account for this general restlessness except by admitting a certain innate rebellion against constraint of any kind, and a certain perverse disposition which makes us feel that everyone else is better off than we are? But it is all no good; whatever we do we shall never find rest unless we are wholly resigned. No place is comfortable to those who are sick of a fever: they spend a quarter of an hour in one bed and then they want to change over to another. There is nothing wrong with the bed but the trouble is that their own fever torments them wherever they find themselves. A person who is not suffering from the fever of his own self-will puts up with everything; provided that he is serving God he does not care in what capacity God uses him, and as long as he is doing God's divine will he has no personal preference.

But that is not all. Not only should we want to do God's will, but do it cheerfully, if we are going to be devout. If I were not a bishop, may be that knowing what I do know, I should not want to be one. But seeing that I am already a bishop, I am not only obliged to do what this hard calling requires of me; over and above that I must do it joyfully, finding pleasure and happiness in it. This is what St. Paul says: each of you is to remain in the condition in which he was called before God.[1] We have each got to carry our own cross, not anybody else's; and this means renouncing yourself, that is, your own will, according to Our Lord's desire. I should like this or that, I should do much better in some other place—ideas like that are a temptation. Our Lord knows quite well what he is about; let us do what he wants and stay where he has put us.

And now, my dear daughter (allow me to speak to you from my heart, for that is how I feel towards you), you would like me to give you a few practical points for your guidance. Besides what I have told you to think about,

1. Make a meditation every day, either in the morning or before dinner, or else an hour or two before supper; let your subject be the life and death of Our Lord. Your meditation should not last longer than a good half hour, certainly no more, and you should end by thinking about Our Lord's obedience to God his Father; for you will find that all he did was done to fulfil his Father's will. Then firmly make up your mind to love God's will.

2. Before you actually begin on any trying task connected with the duties of your particular life, remember how cheerfully the saints did greater and harder things: some suffered martyrdom, others dishonour in the eyes of the world. Francis and so many religious of our own age kissed people afflicted with leprosy and running sores, not once but a thousand times; some lived in desert places, others on galley ships with the soldiers; and all was done to please God. And what do we do to compare with such hardship?

3. Consider often that all we do derives its true value from our conformity with God's will; if I am eating or drinking and doing it because God wants me to do it, I am more pleasing to God than if I were to endure death without the intention of doing God's will.

4. Often ask God in the course of the day to make you love the duties of your vocation, and say, as St. Paul did when he was converted: 'Lord, what wilt thou have me do?'[2] Do you

[1] Cf. 1 Cor. vii, 24.   [2] Acts ix, 6.

want me to serve you by doing the humblest task in your
house? Oh, I shall be only too happy to do it, for as long as
I'm serving you I don't care in what way. And coming to the
special thing that is bothering you, you say: is this what you
want me to do? Dear Lord, this is much too good for me and I
don't deserve it; I'll do it gladly. And in this way you will
practise great humility. O dear Lord, what great treasure you
will be storing up for yourself! Greater than you can possibly
imagine.

5. I should like you to consider how many saints, both men
and women, have lived in the married state like you, and that
they all accepted this vocation readily and gladly, both in the
new dispensation and the old: Sarah, Rebecca, St. Anne, St.
Elizabeth, St. Monica, St. Paula and a host of others. Let that
encourage you and ask them to pray for you. We must love all
that God loves, and he loves our vocation; so let us love it too
and not waste our energy hankering after a different sort of life,
but get on with our own job. No cross is too hard to bear. Be
Martha as well as Mary, and be both gladly, faithfully doing
what you are called to do, withdrawing often into your heart,
saying as you kneel at Our Lord's feet: My Lord, I am all
yours, whether I'm busy working or not; and you are all mine,
my bridegroom, and you take first place in my heart, and all I
do is done for love of you, every single thing.

I am sending a 'Method of prayer' to Madame des Puis
d'Orbe[1] which she will show you. I should like you to make a
copy of it and use it. I think that if you make half an hour's
mental prayer every morning you should content yourself with
hearing one mass a day and doing half an hour's spiritual
reading, for instance Granada or some other good author. In
the evening make an examination of conscience and make
aspirations all day long. Read and reread *The Spiritual Combat*,[2]
I particularly recommend it to you. On Sundays and feast days
you can hear vespers (without any sense of obligation) and a
sermon, as well as mass. Do not forget to go to confession

[1] Her sister, Abbess des Puis d'Orbe. Cf. Letter 7, p. 75.
[2] By Lorenzo Scupoli.

once a week or whenever you have anything really weighing on your conscience. As for holy communion, if your husband disapproves, do not for the present go more often than we arranged; keep to that and make spiritual communions, God will give you credit for your heart's desire to receive him.

Remember what I have so often told you: do honour to our devotion by making it very lovable to everyone who knows you, especially your own family; live in such a way that everybody speaks well of your piety. How fortunate you are to have such a reasonable and tolerant husband! You ought to be very grateful to God and thank him. When anything crosses your will, resign yourself whole-heartedly to Our Lord and take comfort in the thought that he only gives his favours to people who are good, or trying to be good.

And now let me assure you that I am all yours. God is my witness that I never forget you and your family in my feeble prayers; you are deeply written in my heart. May God be your heart and your life!

Francis, Bishop of Geneva.

7

To the Baronne de Chantal

Sales, 14 October 1604

VIVE JÉSUS

Madam,

May God give me as much power as I have will to make myself understood in this letter. I feel sure that you will be helped by at least some of my answers to your difficulties, especially in your doubts—insinuated to you by the enemy—about having chosen me as your director. I will see what I can do to explain briefly what I consider relevant to your needs in this matter.

First of all, your choice shows every sign of a good and legitimate election; I entreat you to have no further doubt. You were carried along and almost forced to do it by a strong and consoling impulse; I thought carefully before agreeing to it; neither you nor I relied on ourselves in this matter but applied the judgement of your confessor, a good, learned and prudent man; we gave your initial excitement time to calm down, supposing your conscience had been mistaken; we prayed, not for one or two days but for several months. Taken together, these are beyond all doubt infallible signs that we acted according to God's will.

Had these impulses of yours been prompted by the evil spirit or by purely human motives they would have been very different. For these are terrible and vehement but vacillating. The first thing which they whisper to their victims is not to listen to any advice, or if they do listen, then the advice should come from people of little or no experience. They urge and speed you on, wanting you to strike the bargain quickly before terms have been stated, satisfied with a brief prayer which is little more than pretence when it comes to deciding really important questions.

There is nothing like this in our action. Neither you nor I made the final decision in the matter; it was made by a third person who could only have had God's ends in view. The fact that I demurred at first, which was only the result of the deliberation I was bound to apply to it, should put your mind entirely at rest; for believe me, it was not from any lack of inclination to serve you spiritually (this was great beyond words), but because in a matter of such moment I did not want to follow either your desire or my inclination but God and his providence. I beg you to take your stand there and not to go on arguing with the enemy on this subject; tell him boldly that it was God who wanted it and who brought it about. It was God who launched you on your first period of spiritual direction, profitable to you at that time; it is God who has led you to this decision and he will make this direction fruitful and useful even though the instrument is unworthy.

For the second point, my very dear sister, let me repeat what I have already said, that from the beginning of your consulting with me on your interior life God gave me great love of your soul. When you spoke to me more openly I felt my love for your soul grow in a wonderful way and this made me write that God had given me to you.[1] I could not, I think, have added to my affection for you in any way, especially when I was praying for you. But now, my dear daughter, a new quality has been added to which I do not seem to be able to give a name; I can only describe it by its effect which is a great interior sweetness that I feel in wishing you perfect love of God and all other spiritual blessings. I am not in any way adding to the truth, and what I say is said in the presence of the God of my heart and of yours. Every affection differs in some particular way from every other. My affection for you has a special quality which consoles me infinitely, and if all were said, is of great profit to me. Take this as a matter of absolute fact and have no more doubt about it. I did not want to speak as openly as this but one word leads to another; besides, I feel you will know how to take it.

Another thing to consider, my daughter, is this: the holy Church of God, imitating her Spouse, does not teach us to pray only for ourselves but always for ourselves and our fellow-Christians, in the plural: 'Give us' and 'grant us' and many similar terms of this kind. When using this general form of speech I had never before thought more particularly of any one person. Since I went to Dijon several people who asked for my prayers come to my mind when I say this word 'we', yourself almost invariably first among them; and when you are not first, which is rare, you are last, so that I have time to dwell on the thought of you. Can I say more than that? But please do not pass this on to anyone else; for I am saying just a little too much, though in all truth and purity. Well, now you have quite enough matter to help you battle against all those suggestions, or at least to give you courage to laugh at their author and spit in his face. I will tell you the rest one day, either in this world or the next.

For the third point you ask me what to do about the evil spirit's temptations against the faith and the Church. I take it that is what you mean. I will tell you what God guides me to

[1] Letter 3.

64

say. In this case you must act as one does in temptations of the flesh: do not make any attempt to argue. Do as the children of Israel did with the bones of the pascal lamb which they did not even break but simply threw into the fire. You must not reply at all or even show that you can hear what the enemy is saying to you; let him hammer on the door as much as he likes, you must not as much as say: 'Who goes there?' That's all very well, you will say to me, but he upsets me and the noise he makes is such that we can't hear one another speak indoors. Never mind; be patient. You will have to use sign-language: cast yourself down at God's feet and stay there. He will understand by this humble posture that you mean to be his and that you want his help, although you have no words to tell him this. But the chief thing is to keep the door well locked and not to open it, however little, to spy who is there or to shoo away this disturber of the peace. In the end he will get tired of shouting and will leave you alone. And about time too, you will tell me!

Please have by you a book called *On Tribulation* written by P. Ribadeneira in Spanish and translated into French;[1] Father Rector will tell you where it was published. Read it carefully. And now courage! Things will improve all in good time. Nothing is lost as long as the enemy does not get in. Meanwhile it is a very good sign that he is hammering and raging at the door because it proves that he is not getting what he is after. Had he got it he would not go on shouting; he would walk in and be quite still. Remember that so as to avoid scruples.

And now I want to suggest another remedy. Temptations against the faith aim directly at the understanding, striving to draw it into argument, to occupy and absorb it. Do you know what to do while the enemy is wasting his energy trying to scale the intellect? Make a sally through the gates of the will and charge him roundly; when the temptation against faith presents itself in order to draw you into argument, saying: 'How can this be? And if this applies, how does that fit in?' you arrange things in such a way that instead of arguing with the

[1] Pierre Ribadenaira, S. J., *Traicté de la Tribulation*, nouvellement mis en François. Douay, 1599; Paris, 1600.

enemy by parleying, your will and your feelings round on him boldly while you cry out with heart and voice: 'Traitor! Wretch! You left the Church of the angels and you are trying to get me to leave the Church of the saints! You are disloyal, faithless, perfidious! You gave the first woman the apple of perdition and now you want me to taste it too! Get thee behind me, Satan; it is written, thou shalt not tempt the Lord, thy God.[1] No, I will not argue, I will not dispute with you. Eve thought she could argue with you and she was lost. May Jesus reign supreme, I believe in him; may the Church triumph, I cleave to it!' And use other similar words of loving ardour. Speak to Jesus Christ and to the Holy Ghost in words which will be given to you; also speak to the Church, saying: 'O mother of the children of God! I will never separate myself from you; I want to die and live in your keeping.'

Am I making myself quite clear? I mean that you must fight back with your heart and will and not with reasoning, with passions and not with considerations of the mind. True that at this time of temptation your poor will is quite dry, but so much the better; its blows will be all the more terrible to the enemy, who seeing that far from hindering your progress, he is making you exercise many virtues, especially that of faith, will leave you in peace at long last.

Finally, it would be good sometimes to take fifty or sixty strokes of the discipline, or else thirty, as you feel. It is amazing how effective this recipe has proved for someone I know. I suppose the reason is that outward feeling distracts from interior difficulty and affliction, and calls out God's mercy; and also that the evil spirit, seeing his partisan and confederate, the flesh, being beaten, gets frightened and takes himself off. But this remedy must be used in moderation and according to the profit you derive from it after the experience of a few days. When all is said and done, these temptations are only afflictions like any others and you must take comfort from the words of the scriptures: 'Blessed is the man that endureth temptation: for when he has been proved he shall receive the

[1] Matt. iv, 10, 7.

66

crown of life.'[1] I must tell you that I have known few people make progress without this particular trial and you must be patient; for after the storm God will send peace. Concentrate on the first and second suggestion I made. . . .

If you happen to omit or forget anything that I tell you to do, have no scruples about it, for here is the general rule of our obedience written in capital letters:

LOVE AND NOT FORCE SHOULD INSPIRE ALL YOU DO;
LOVE OBEDIENCE MORE THAN YOU FEAR DISOBEDIENCE

I want you to have a spirit of liberty, not the kind that excludes obedience, for that is the liberty of the flesh, but the kind that excludes constraint and scruples or over-eagerness. If you really love your obedience and submission, I want you to look on any right and charitable call made on you to leave your exercises as another form of obedience, and I want you to make up by love for what you happen to omit.

I want you to have a French translation of all the prayers you say; not that I want you to say them in French, but in Latin, for they will give you more devotion; but I do want you to understand their meaning properly, also of the litanies of the name of Jesus, of our Lady as well as the other prayers. But do all this without anxiety and in a spirit of gentleness and love.

Your meditations are to centre on the life and death of Our Lord. I approve of your using the *Exercises* of Tauler,[2] the *Meditations* of St. Bonaventure and those of Capiglia; for the gospels are after all the life of Our Lord. But you must set about it as I told you in my written instructions. Meditation on the four ends of man will be useful to you as long as you always end up with an act of confidence in God, never thinking of death and hell on the one hand without seeing the cross on the other, so that having aroused your fear you may return to confidence. Your meditation should last three quarters of an hour at the most. I like spiritual canticles but sung as though you meant them.

[1] Jas. i, 12.
[2] *Méditations sur les Évangiles et festes des Saincts*. Paris 1601.

As for brother ass, I approve of fasting on Fridays and of a frugal supper on Saturdays. I agree that he should be brought to heel all the week, not so much by cutting down the quantity of food (provided there is moderation) as by cutting down choice. You may make much of him sometimes by giving him oats, as St. Francis did, to make him go faster: in other words, the discipline, which has a marvellous power of quickening the spirit by stinging the flesh; but only twice a week. Do not go to communion less often, unless your confessor instructs you otherwise. It is a special consolation for me on feast days to know that we are going to communion together.

For the next point, it is indeed true that I cherish your son Celse-Bénigne and your other children with very special love. As God has put into your heart the desire to see them wholly dedicated to his service you must bring them up with this end always in view, gently encouraging them in thoughts of this kind. Have a copy of the *Confessions* of St. Augustine and read it carefully from the eighth book onwards: then you will get to know St. Monica when she was a widow and looking after her son, Augustine, and you will find much to console you in your own task. As for Celse-Bénigne, generous motives must be implanted in him and his little soul filled with noble and valiant ideas of God's service, while notions of purely worldly glory must be cried down; but this should be done little by little. As he grows up we shall, with God's help, think of what particular course to take. Meanwhile do see that not only he but also his sisters sleep on their own, as far as possible, or else with people whom you can trust as completely as you would yourself. I cannot tell you how important this advice is; experience commends it to me every day.

If Françoise wants to be a nun of her own accord, well and good; otherwise I do not approve of her will being influenced in advance by resolutions, but only, as in the case of the other girls, by gentle encouragement. We must act on the minds of others as far as possible as the angels do, graciously and without coercion. I approve, however, that you should send her as a boarder to the convent of Puis d'Orbe where I hope that a spirit of devotion will really flourish again soon. I should like you to co-operate towards this end. But see that you root out vanity of soul from all the girls; it seems to be innate in the sex. I know that you have St. Jerome's *Epistles* in French; look up the one he writes about Pacatula and the others about the education of girls;[1] you will find them diverting and also helpful. All in all, you must use moderation; my ideas are summed up in the words 'gentle encouragement'.

I see that you have a debt of two thousand crowns; repay this as soon as you possibly can, and be as careful as you can never to withhold from others anything that belongs to them. Give alms in a small way but with great humility. I like the idea of your visiting the sick, old people, particularly women, and young people, those who are really young. I like to think of you visiting the poor, especially women, with great humility and meekness.

I approve of your dividing your time between your father and your father-in-law and your working towards the good of their souls in the manner of the angels, as I described it. If your stay in Dijon is a little longer than the other, it does not matter; it is also your first duty. Try to make yourself more agreeable and more humble every day towards both your fathers, and work towards their salvation in a spirit of gentleness. It will probably suit you better to spend the winter at Dijon.

I am writing to your father,[2] and because he asked me to write something for the good of his soul I did it in all simplicity, perhaps too much so. My advice centres on two points: firstly, that he should review his life as a whole so as to make a general confession, without which no man of honour should die. Secondly, that he should try to divest himself gradually of worldly ties, and I have told him how to set about this. I put forward these matters quite clearly and gently, I think, and suggested that he should not make a sudden break with worldly affairs but do it gradually by unknotting and loosening ties

---

[1] Ep. cxxviii, ad Gaudent; Epp. xxii, ad Eustoch.; cvii, ad Laetam; cxxx, ad Demetriad.
[2] Letter 5.

here and there. He will probably show you the letter; help him to understand it and put it into effect. You owe him the great charity of leading him to a happy end and no considerations of respect should prevent you from working towards this with humble ardour; for he is your nearest relation and God has put you under an obligation to love him. And the first thing you should love in him is his soul, and in his soul, conscience, and in his conscience, purity, and in this purity, his eternal salvation. And the same goes for your father-in-law. Perhaps your father who does not know me well may take my liberty amiss; but make me known to him, and I trust he will love me chiefly on account of the very liberty I have taken.

I am writing a letter of five sheets to Monsieur de Bourges[1] in which I explain to him how to preach; I have also told him freely what I think about various duties in an archbishop's life. I have no fear that he will take offence at this. Well now, what more could you wish? Your father, brother, children—they are all infinitely dear to me.

Now for the next point, about the spirit of liberty. I will try and explain what this is. No upright man is the slave of actions which involve mortal sins, and he is emancipated from them: this kind of liberty of spirit is necessary for salvation and this is not what I mean. What I mean is the liberty of children who know that they are loved. And what is that? The complete detachment of a Christian heart following God's known will. You will soon see what I mean if God gives me the grace to explain the marks, signs, effects and occasions of this liberty.

The first thing we ask of God is that his name may be hallowed, that his kingdom may come and his will be done on earth as it is in heaven. What else can this be but the spirit of liberty? For as long as God's name is hallowed, his Majesty reigning in our heart, his will being done, the soul does not mind about anything else. The first sign: the heart enjoying this liberty is not at all attached to consolations and accepts afflic-

---

[1] Madame de Chantal's brother, the young archbishop of Bourges. Cf. Introduction, p. 21.

tion with all the meekness possible to the flesh. I am not saying
that the soul does not love consolation and long for it, but
without clinging to it. Second sign: a man who has this spirit
does not set his heart on spiritual exercises, and if illness or
some other emergency prevents them he is in no way upset.
Again, I am not saying that he does not love them, but that he
is not attached to them. Thirdly, he does not lose his joy, because no loss or lack can sadden one whose heart is perfectly
free. I am not saying that it is impossible for him to lose his joy,
but it will not be for long.

The effects of this liberty are great sweetness of mind, great
gentleness and a ready kindness in everything which does not
entail sin; it is that supple and gentle attitude which is ready to
do anything virtuous and charitable. For example: try inter-
rupting the meditation of someone who has got attached to
this exercise. You will see him taken aback, upset and irritated.
A person who has real liberty of spirit will leave his prayer with
an unruffled face and a heart well disposed towards the importunate friend who has disturbed him. For it is all the same to
him whether he is serving God by meditating or by bearing
with his neighbour; both are the will of God, but helping his
neighbour seems to be necessary at that special moment. The
occasions which call for this liberty are to be found whenever
anything happens against our inclinations; a person not
attached to his inclinations does not get impatient when he
cannot have his way.

There are two opposite vices which beset this liberty: instability and constraint, lack of discipline and slavishness.
Instability or lack of discipline is a certain excess of liberty
which makes one want to change one's devotional exercises or
state of life without adequate reason and without knowing
whether it is God's will. The least pretext is enough to make
one change an exercise, a plan, a rule; a mere trifle causes one
to give up a rule or good habits, and in this way the heart
grows dissipated and distracted; it is like an orchard unfenced
on all sides so that the fruit is not for the owner but for any
chance passer-by.

Constraint or slavishness is a certain lack of liberty as a result of which the mind is overwhelmed with irritation or anger when it cannot carry out its plans, even though something better may offer. For example: I plan to do my meditation every morning; if I lack stability and discipline, the very least thing will make me put it off till evening—a dog that disturbed me and kept me from going to sleep, a letter I have to write although it is not at all urgent. If, on the contrary, I am moved by a spirit of constraint and slavishness I shall refuse to leave my meditation even though a sick person greatly needs my help, or even if I have to see to the dispatch of a very important letter which cannot well be postponed; and so on.

It remains for me to give you two or three examples of this liberty which will make you understand what I cannot quite explain. But first of all here are two rules to be observed if you are not to come to grief in this respect. No one should leave his exercises and go against the ordinary rules concerning the virtues unless he sees it to be the will of God. Now the will of God shows itself in two ways: necessity and charity. This Lent I want to preach in a certain little town in my diocese. If, however, I fall ill or break my leg, it is no good worrying about not being able to preach, or even regretting it, for it is a sure thing that God wants me to serve him by suffering and not by preaching. But if I am not ill and an opportunity offers for me to go to another place, and if in this place some people will turn Huguenot unless I go, that is a sufficient indication of God's will to make me change my plan without any fuss. The second rule is that when charity requires us to use our liberty it should be done without giving scandal and without injustice. For example: I may know that I should be more useful somewhere far away from my diocese: I cannot use my liberty in this matter for I should give scandal and commit an injustice: I am under an obligation to stay where I am. Thus it is a false use of liberty for married women to go away from their husbands without a legitimate reason, putting forward the pretext of devotion and charity. So this liberty should never interfere with one's calling; on the contrary, it tends to make everybody content and happy in their particular walk of life, for people must realize that they are put there by God's will.

Now take the case of Cardinal Borromeo who is going to be canonized in a few days.[1] He was one of the most precise, unbending and austere men imaginable; he lived on bread and water, he was so strict that after he became archbishop he only entered his brothers' house twice in twenty-four years, and that was when they were ill; he only went into his own garden twice. Nevertheless, this strict man, who often accepted invitations from his Swiss neighbours in the hope of winning them back to the truth, made no difficulty about drinking a couple of healths or toasts with them at every meal, over and above what he needed to still his thirst. Here you have a trait of holy liberty in the most austere man of our times. A lax person would have overdone it, one of slavish mind would have feared to commit mortal sin, a true spirit of liberty does it out of love.

Bishop Spiridion of old once took in a famished pilgrim during the season of Lent. There was nothing to eat in his place except salt meat, so he had some cooked and served to the pilgrim. Of course he did not want to take it in spite of his hunger; Spiridion did not need it but out of charity he ate some first so as to remove the pilgrim's scruple by his example. Here you have the loving freedom of a holy man. Father Ignatius Loyola who is also about to be canonized[2] ate meat on Wednesday in Holy Week because the doctor ordered it and thought it expedient for some little trouble he had. A man of slavish mind would have contested the point for a good three days.[3]

But I want to show you a sun that shone more brightly than

---

[1] St. Charles Borromeo, 1538–84, Cardinal Archbishop of Milan. Not canonized till 1 November 1610.

[2] St. Ignatius Loyola, 1491–1556, canonized on 12 March, 1622.

[3] Cf. too, letter of 1 November, 1604: 'I want you to have a look at Chapter 41 of the "Way of Perfection" by blessed Mother Theresa; for it will help you to understand what I have so often told you, that you should not split hairs in exercising virtues, but practise them roundly, frankly and naïvely, in the good old-fashioned French way, acting with freedom, in good faith, *grosso modo.* I am really afraid of the spirit of constraint and melancholy. No, my dear daughter; I want you to follow Our Lord with a great and bold heart, though humbly, gently and in a disciplined way. . . .' A. XIII, p. 392ᶜ.

all these, a soul that was truly free and detached, cleaving only to the will of God. I have often wondered who is the most mortified of the saints I know, and after some reflection I have come to the conclusion that it was St. John the Baptist. He went into the desert when he was five years old and knew that our Saviour and his came on earth in a place quite close by, one or two days' journey perhaps. How his heart, touched with love of his Saviour from the time he was in his mother's womb, must have longed to enjoy his presence! Yet he spends twenty-five years in the desert without coming to see Our Lord even once; and leaving the desert he stays to catechize without visiting him but waiting till Our Lord comes to seek him out. Then when he has baptized him he does not follow him but stays behind to do his appointed task. How truly mortified was his spirit! To be so near his Saviour and not see him, to have him so close and not enjoy his presence! Is this not a completely detached spirit, detached even from God himself so as to do his will and serve him, to leave God for God, and not to love God in order to love him better? The example of this great saint overwhelms me with its grandeur.

I forgot to mention that the will of God is known not only by the claims of necessity and charity but also by obedience, so that if you receive a command you should believe that this is the will of God. Am I not writing too much? But my mind runs on more quickly than I wish, carried away by my ardent desire to serve you.

For the next point, remember the feast day of blessed King Louis, the day on which you took the crown of your kingdom from your own heart so as to put it at the feet of Jesus, the King; the day on which you renewed your youth like the eagle's, plunging into the sea of penance; the day which heralded the eternal day for your soul. Remember that I said 'Amen' to your great resolution of belonging to God in body, heart and soul; I said it on behalf of the whole Church, our Mother; and at the same time the Blessed Virgin with all the angels made heaven resound with a great 'Amen' and 'Alleluja'. Remember that all the past is as nothing and that you must say with David every day: 'Even now have I begun'[1] to love my God as I should. Do a great deal for God and do nothing without love; refer everything to this love; eat and drink with this in mind.

Be devoted to St. Louis and admire his great constancy. He became King when he was twelve years old, had nine children, was continually waging war either against rebels or enemies of the faith, was king for over forty years. And at the end of it all, when he was dead, his confessor, a holy man, swore that he had never fallen into mortal sin, and he had confessed him all his life. He made two journeys overseas. In the course of both of them he lost his army and on his last journey he died of the plague after he had spent much time visiting, helping, serving those who were plague-stricken in his army. He bandaged their sores and cured them, and then died joyfully and with fortitude, a verse from David on his lips.[2] I give you this saint for your special patron throughout the year; the following year, please God, I will give you another, after you have profited much in this saint's school.

Finally, believe two things with regard to me: first, that God wants you to make use of me, so do not hesitate; and secondly, that in the things which regard your salvation God will give me light to serve you; and as to the will to serve you, he has already given me that in such great measure that it could not be greater. I have received the note with your vows and am keeping it carefully, looking upon it as a fit instrument of our union which is wholly rooted in God and which will last to all eternity by the mercy of God who is the author of it. . . .

My mother is very devoted to you. I was happy to hear that you so gladly call Madame des Puis d'Orbe[3] 'sister'; she is a great soul if she is loyally helped, and God will use her for the glory of his name. Help her and visit her by letter; God will reward you. It really looks as though I shall never get to the end of this letter, the only point of which is to try and reply to

[1] Ps. lxxvi, 11.
[2] Ps. v, 8: 'I will enter into your house, O Lord.'
[3] Cf. Letter 6, p. 61.

yours. And yet I really must finish it now, asking for the great help of your prayers; and how I need them! I never pray without including you in my prayers, and never salute my angels without saluting yours. Do the same for me and let Celse-Bénigne do it too; I always pray for you and your little company. Do believe me, I never forget them in my mass, nor yet their dead father, your husband.

May God be your heart, your mind, your soul, my very dear sister; and I am in his merciful love,

Your very devoted servant,

Francis, Bishop of Geneva.

Pray sometimes for the conversion of my unhappy Geneva.

8

To the Baronne de Chantal

Annecy, 21 November 1604

Madam, my very dear Sister,

May our glorious and most holy mistress and queen, the Virgin Mary, whose Presentation we celebrate today, present our hearts to her Son, and may she give us her own heart. Your messenger reached me when I was in the greatest possible difficulty on the tempestuous sea of this diocese, and I can hardly tell you how greatly I was consoled by your letters. I am only wondering whether, hard pressed as I am, I can find enough time to let you have an answer as soon as I should wish, and of the kind you are expecting. I will say what I can in haste and haphazardly, and if anything further occurs to me afterwards, I will send you word again soon by someone I know who is going to Dijon and back. . . .

I want to talk about your cross and I am wondering whether God has allowed me to understand it and to see the whole extent of it, with its four arms. I very much hope and pray that he has, so that I shall be able to say something really helpful. It is a certain incapacity or loss of power, you say, of your faculties or

76

a part of your understanding which prevents it from enjoying the thought of what is good; and what grieves you most is that when you come to make a resolution, you do not feel that your reaction is as strong as usual but that you are brought up against a certain barrier which stops you short; and this is the starting-point of your painful temptations against the faith. This is well put, my dear daughter; you express yourself well. You add that nevertheless by the grace of God your will only wants to cleave simply and firmly to the Church, and that you would willingly die for the faith.

Oh blessed be God, my dear daughter, this sickness is not unto death, but so that God may be glorified thereby.[1] Two nations are in your womb, as Rebecca was told; one is struggling against the other in your spirit, but in the end the younger shall defeat the elder.[2] Self-love never dies until we ourselves die; it has thousands of ways of entrenching itself in our soul, but we cannot cast it out; it is the first-born of our soul, for it is natural, or at least co-natural to us; self-love is attended by a legion of armed horsemen to help it—emotions, activities, passions; it is skilful and knows a thousand subtle twists and turns. To balance this you have the love of God on the other side, which is conceived and born later; and that too has its emotions, inclinations, passions, activities. These two children in the same womb struggle with one another like Esau and Jacob; that is why Rebecca cried out: Would it not be better for me to die than to bear children with so much pain? The result of these convulsions is a certain inner disgust, so that you cannot relish food, however good. But what does it matter whether you relish your food or not, as long as you do not stop eating? If I had to lose one of my senses I should choose taste as being even less necessary than the sense of smell, I think. Believe me, you are only deprived of taste, not of sight. You can see but without satisfaction; you munch your bread and eat it, but as though it were just tow, without taste or relish. It seems to you that your resolutions have no force behind them because they are neither gay nor joyful; but you are wrong, for the apostle Paul very

[1] John xi, 4. [2] Cf. Gen. xxv, 23.

often had only that kind. Poor Leah is a little bleary-eyed and ugly, but your spirit must make do with her before you can have the beautiful Rachel.[1] Be of good cheer, her children will be beautiful, her works agreeable to God. But I must get on.

You do not feel firm, constant or resolute. There is something in me, you say, that has never been satisfied, but I don't know what it is. I wish I knew what it is so that I could tell you, my dear daughter; perhaps some day when we have plenty of time to talk, I shall find out. Meanwhile, I wonder whether the blockage is caused by too many desires thronging in your mind? I have suffered from this illness. A bird chained to its perch is not conscious of its captivity and does not feel the pull of its chain until it wants to fly; in the same way an unfledged nestling only finds out that it cannot fly when it makes the actual attempt. And the remedy for this, my dear daughter, is not to struggle, not to make eager attempts to fly as your wings have not yet grown and you lack power for too great an effort. Be patient until you get the wings of a dove, and then you can fly. I am very much afraid that you are a little too ardent and headlong, that you pursue too many desires rather too eagerly. You see the beauty of light, the sweetness of resolutions; you feel as though you were very, very nearly there, and seeing goodness so close at hand makes you thirst and long for it inordinately; your longing increases your eagerness, you rush forward to reach the object of your desire—but in vain; for your master keeps you chained to your perch, or else your wings are not yet grown. And meanwhile this constant flutter of your heart exhausts your strength all the time. Of course you must try to fly but do it gently and without struggling and without getting flustered.

Examine yourself carefully on this point; perhaps you are straining too much in your desire to taste that sovereign sweetness which firmness, constancy and resolution bring to the soul. You are firm; what is firmness but having the will to die rather than to sin against faith or give it up? But you do not feel you are firm, for if you did, it would give you untold joy. Come

[1] Cf. Gen. xxix, 16–18.

now, stop fluttering and being in a hurry; you will feel all the better for it and your wings will grow all the faster. This straining eagerness then is a fault of yours; and this is the undefinable thing that is not satisfied in you, a certain lack of resignation. You do resign yourself, but it is with a BUT; for you want this and that, and you struggle to get it. A simple desire is not contrary to resignation, but a panting heart, fluttering wings, an agitated will, and many restless movements—all these undoubtedly add up to lack of resignation. Courage, my dear sister; if our will belongs to God, we ourselves are surely his. You have all that is necessary, but without feeling it; that is no great loss. Do you know what you ought to do? As your wings have not yet grown try to find pleasure in not flying.

You make me think of Moses. When this holy man had arrived on Mount Pisgah he saw the whole of the promised land before his eyes, the land which he had longed and hoped for for forty years in the hardship of the desert, while his people murmured and rebelled. He saw the land of promise but did not set foot in it, and died even as he beheld it. He had your glass of water at his lips and could not drink. How deeply his soul must have sighed within him! He died a more blessed death there than many did in the promised land, since God himself honoured him in his burial. Well now, if you too had to die without drinking of the well of the Samaritan woman, what would it matter, as long as your soul is admitted to drink for ever at the source and fountain of life? Do not go chasing eagerly after vain longings, and I would even go as far as to say, do not be eager in avoiding eagerness. Keep quietly on along your way, for it is a good way.

I must tell you, my very dear sister, that I am writing to you with much interruption, and if you find the letter confused it is hardly surprising, because I am continually distracted, but without letting it worry me, thank God. Would you like to be able to tell whether I am right in saying that your fault is lack of complete resignation? You are quite willing to have a cross, but you want to choose what sort it is to be; you want an ordinary cross, a bodily cross, or some other. And what is that, my beloved daughter? Ah no, I want your cross and mine to be no other than Jesus Christ's cross, both as regards its choice and the way it is laid upon us. God knows very well what he is about and why; it is all for our good, you may be sure. God gave David the choice of the rod with which he should be scourged; and it seems to me (blessed be God) that I would rather not have chosen, but have left it all to his Divine Majesty. The more wholly a cross comes from God, the more we ought to love it.

Come, my sister, my daughter, my soul (and this is not going too far, as well you know), tell me, is God not better than man? And is not man as nothing compared with God? And yet here is a man, or rather one who is absolutely nothing in himself, the most miserable of creatures, who sets no less store by your confidence in him, even though you no longer rejoice in it and feel it, than if it were giving you all the pleasure in the world. And so will not God too look with favour on your good will, even though it has no feeling behind it? I have become, said David, like a wineskin dried in the smoke of the fire,[1] so that one cannot tell how it could possibly serve any useful purpose. Let us put up with any amount of dryness and aridity, provided we love God.

But after all, you are not yet in the land where there is no daylight, for at times you see the light and God visits you. Is he not good? What do you think? It seems to me that your grief makes you take greater joy in him. Still, I approve of your showing your grief to our gentle Saviour, but do it lovingly and without excitement, so that you may at least find him in your soul, as you say; for he likes us to tell him how he is grieving us, and does not mind our complaining about him, as long as we do it lovingly and humbly, talking openly to him, as little children do when their beloved mother has punished them. Meanwhile you must suffer a little longer in meekness and patience. I don't think there is any harm in saying to Our Lord: 'Come into our soul'; no, there seems to be nothing wrong with that.

[1] Ps. cxviii, 83.

God wants me to serve him by suffering aridity, anguish, temptations, like Job, like St. Paul, and not by preaching. Serve God as he wants you to serve him; some day you will find him doing all you want, and more than you can possibly want. The books that you should read for half an hour are Granada, Gerson,[1] *The Life of Jesus Christ*, put into French from the Latin of Ludolph the Carthusian, Mother Theresa, the *Treatise on Affliction*[2] which I told you about in my last letter. Come, shall we not all be together in heaven one day, blessing God for all eternity? This is what I hope for and take joy in. . . .

I have not observed any order in replying to you; but the porter hurried me so that it was impossible to do otherwise. I am expecting a great storm any minute, as I told you at the beginning but I am writing quite calmly; it is directed chiefly against me, but I take joy in it; and trusting in the providence of God, I hope that it will be for his greater glory and my own peace, and much else besides. I am not certain that it will happen, but it is threatening. Why should I be telling you this? Indeed, because I cannot help it; my heart has to open out to yours in this way; and as I find consolation and hope of happiness during this time of suspense, why should I not tell you about it? But this is for you alone, please.

I am praying much for our Celse-Bénigne and for the little company of girls; and I ask them to pray for me. Keep remembering to pray for my town of Geneva so that God may convert it. Also, remember to behave with great respect and reverence in all that concerns the Reverend Father Director—(you know whom I mean)[3]—and when you meet his disciples and spiritual children, let them see nothing but real meekness and humility in you. In case you are reproached in any way, behave meekly, humbly, patiently and say nothing that is not absolutely humble. This is essential.

May God be your heart, your mind, your rest for ever, and I am, Madam, your very devoted servant in Our Lord,

F.

---

[1] *The Imitation of Christ*, attributed to Gerson.
[2] By F. Ribadaneira, S. J.　　　　[3] Her former director at Dijon.

Feast of the Presentation of Our Lady, 21 November 1604.

I am adding a note this morning, feast of St. Cecilia. The proverb drawn from St. Bernard: hell is full of good intentions or desires, is not to worry you. Good intentions are of two kinds: one kind says: I should like to do this, but I cannot be bothered and I will not do it; the other kind says: I want to do this, but I have less strength than goodwill, that is what is stopping me. The first fills hell, the second, paradise. The first only begins to wish and desire but does not go on to will; such wishes have not enough courage, they are only half formed and abortive which is why they fill hell. But the second leads to whole and well-formed desires, and that is why Daniel was called the man of desires.[1] May Our Lord give you the constant help of his Holy Spirit, my beloved sister and daughter.

9

To the Baronne de Chantal

Annecy, 18 February 1605

. . . I praise God for the constancy with which you are bearing your tribulations. Nevertheless I still seem to see some lingering anxiety and restlessness which stand in the way of the full effect your patience might have on you. 'In your patience,' says the Son of God, 'you shall possess your souls.'[2] The effect of patience is to give you full possession of your soul, and self-possession increases in proportion to your growth in patience. The less anxious and restless we are, the more perfect our patience. May God therefore deliver you from these two troubles and very soon afterwards you will be delivered from your trial.

But take heart, I entreat you, my very dear sister; you have only suffered the hardship of the road for three years, and you want rest! But remember two things: one, that the children of Israel wandered in the desert for forty years before they reached

---

[1] Dan. ix, 23.   [2] Luke xxi, 19.

the land they had been promised; and yet this journey could easily have been done in seven weeks. Nor were they allowed to inquire why God made them go such a long way round and led them by such rough roads; and all those who murmured, died before the goal was reached. And secondly, remember that Moses, God's greatest friend among the whole host, died on the borders of the land of rest, seeing it before his eyes and not being able to have enjoyment of it.

May we, please God, look less at the condition of the road along which we are toiling, and keep our eyes fixed on him who leads us and on the blessed land which is our goal. Why should we worry whether we are passing through the desert or through meadows, provided that God is with us and that we are going to paradise? Do believe me, you should ignore your misery as far as you can, and even if you feel it you should not dwell on it; for the sight of it will frighten you more than the feeling itself will hurt you. That is why one blindfolds a person who is going to have an operation. I think you dwell rather too much on the thought of your misery.

And now for what you say, that it is a great trial to have the will and not the power to act: I do not mean to say that we must will only what we can actually do, but I do want to say that it is a great matter before God to be able to will. Go further, I beg you, and fix your mind on that great dereliction which our master suffered on the Mount of Olives. See how this dear Son, having asked his Father for consolation, and realizing that his Father did not want to give it, dismisses the thought, stops striving and seeking for it; as if he had never asked for it, he valiantly and bravely carries out the work of our redemption. When you have asked your Father to console you, if it does not please him to do it, stop thinking about it, and summon up your courage to work out your salvation on the cross, as if you were never to be taken down from it, and as if you were never again to see the sky of your life bright and serene. You must resign yourself to seeing God and speaking to him amid the thunder and the whirling winds; you must see him in the bush with its fire and thorns, and in order to do this, must indeed take off your shoes[1] and altogether deny your will and desire. But the divine goodness does not expect you to follow this call without giving you the strength to do it; and it is for him to perfect his work. The process may be rather long, but then the matter needs it; but be patient.

In short, for God's glory yield to his will completely, and never suppose that you could be serving him better in any other way; the best way to serve him is to fall in with his will for us. He wants you to serve him without joy, without feeling, with repugnance and revulsion of spirit. Such service gives you no satisfaction but it pleases him; it is not according to your liking, but according to his. Imagine that you are never going to be delivered of your anguish: what would you do? You would say to God: I am yours; if my miseries are agreeable to you give me more and let them last longer. I have confidence in Our Lord that this is what you would say; then you would stop thinking about the matter, at least you would stop struggling. Well, do this now, and make friends with your trial, as though the two of you were always to live together. You will see that when you have stopped taking thought for your deliverance, God will think of it, and when you stop worrying, God will come swiftly to your help. Enough now on this point till God gives me an opportunity of explaining it to you at leisure, so that we can found our life securely on it. That will be when God lets us meet again. . . .

I do not want to reply to your last letter in detail except for certain points which seem urgent to me. You say you cannot believe, my very dear daughter, that temptations against the faith and the Church come from God. But whoever told you that they did? He can send darkness, helplessness, can keep you tied to your perch, can lead you into dereliction and strip you of all strength, can upset your spiritual digestion and make your inner mouth taste bitter so that the sweetest wine in the world turns to gall; but suggestions of blasphemy, infidelity, unbelief—oh no, these can never come from our merciful God: he is too pure to conceive such ideas.

[1] Cf. Exod. iii, 2-5.

Shall I tell you what part God plays in this? He allows the
evil maker of lies to come and offer us these forgeries for sale,
so that by despising them we may prove our affection for
divine things. And are we to get anxious about it and change
our attitude? O no, never, never! It is the devil who is roaming
all round our soul, spreading confusion and prying to see
whether he cannot find some door open somewhere. That is
what he did to Job, to St. Anthony, St. Catherine of Siena and
an infinite number of good souls that I know, and to my own
soul which is good for nothing and which I do not know. Well
now, my dear daughter, are we to be put out by all this? Let
him kick his heels outside, and keep all the doors and windows
tightly shut: he will get tired of it in the end, and if he does not,
God will make him raise the siege. Remember what I think I
told you once before: it is a good sign that he should be making
so much noise and raising such a tempest in this matter of your
will, for it is a sign that he has not got in.

Take courage, my dear soul. I say these words with great
feeling and in Jesus Christ: my dear soul, courage, I say. As
long as we can say resolutely even though without feeling: May
Jesus reign, we need not fear. And do not say that you feel you
are saying this in a cowardly way, without force and courage,
but, as it were, doing yourself violence. This is it; this is the
holy violence which takes heaven by storm. You see, my
daughter, my soul, this is a sign that all is taken and the enemy
has seized everything in our fortress except for the inner
stronghold which is impregnable, immovable, and which cannot be taken except by its own will. It is, in fact, our free will
which dwells before God, bare and alone in the highest and
most spiritual part of the soul, depending on no one except on
God and on itself; and when all the other faculties of the soul
are defeated and delivered over to the enemy, the will alone
remains in full possession of itself and does not consent.

And now do you understand why souls are afflicted, seeing
that the enemy occupies all the other faculties and carries on his
great noise and tumult in them? One can hardly hear what is
being said and done in the region of the higher will, which in-

deed has a clearer and more penetrating voice than the inferior will; but this other voice is so rough and huge that it drowns the first. Finally, note this: as long as you dislike the temptation, there is nothing to fear; for why should you dislike it unless it is because you do not want it?

In a word, these troublesome temptations come from the devil's malice; but the distress and suffering which they make us feel come from God's mercy, who makes holy tribulation spring from this malice in spite of his enemy, and by this means refines the gold that he wants to put in his treasury. So what I say is this: your temptations come from the devil and from hell, but your distress and affliction come from God and paradise; the mothers come from Babylon but the daughters from Jerusalem. Despise the temptations, embrace the tribulations. . . .

Please have no fear that you might be giving me trouble; for I assure you that I find it deeply consoling to render you service. So go on writing to me, often and without careful arrangement, and do it as simply and openly as you can; it will always give me great joy.

Now I am going away in an hour's time to the little town where I am due to preach, God having wanted to use my services both in suffering illness and in preaching: may he be for ever blessed. The storm which I told you about has not yet broken and nothing has happened to me so far; but the clouds are still heavy, dark and threatening above my head.

You cannot have too much confidence in me, who am perfectly and irrevocably yours in Jesus Christ, whose dearest graces and blessings I wish you over and over again a thousand times a day. Let us live and die in him and for him. Amen.

Your most sincere and most devoted servant in Our Lord,
Francis, Bishop of Geneva.

10

To the Présidente Brûlart

La Roche, March 1605

Madam,

I was extremely happy about your letter of 20 January, because it seems to me that in spite of all the afflictions you describe to me, you have advanced in the spiritual life and profited by your trials. My answer will be shorter than I should like it to be, because I am rather busier than I thought. All the same I shall say enough for you to be going on with till I can write you a really long letter.

You tell me that you are upset because you do not reveal yourself openly enough to me, as it seems. And I tell you that although I do not know what you are doing while I am at a distance because I am not a prophet, it seems to me all the same, that considering how brief our contact was, no one could know you better than I do, both your inclinations and motives. I am convinced that there are few secret places of your heart which are not accessible to me; and when you open the doors of your heart even a very little way, I feel I can look right in and see all there is to see. This is of great advantage to you because you want to use me for your salvation.

You complain that a number of imperfections and faults slip into your life in spite of your longing for perfection and for pure love of God. It is impossible for us to escape from self entirely. While we are here below we have to go on bearing ourselves until God bears us to heaven, and while we are bearing ourselves we are not bearing anything that's any good. So we must be patient and not imagine that we can cure ourselves in a day of all the bad habits we have contracted by being careless about our spiritual health. God did, of course, cure some people suddenly, without leaving them any mark of their former diseases, as for instance in the case of Mary Magdalene whom he transformed from a sink of iniquity into a pure fountain of perfection; nor was she ever troubled from that moment onwards. But on the other hand, the same God left many of his dearest disciples marked with their evil inclinations for some time after their conversion, and this was for their greater good: witness blessed St. Peter who after his first vocation stumbled several times, and on one occasion fell outright and grievously when he denied Our Lord.

Solomon said[1] that a serving maid who suddenly becomes the lady of the house is a very insolent sort of creature. There is a great risk that the soul which has served its own passions and affections for a long time might turn proud and vain if it mastered them immediately. We must acquire this mastery little by little and inch by inch, for the saints themselves spent many decades conquering themselves. I entreat you to be patient with everyone but first of all with yourself.

You say that you do nothing at all in prayer. But what do you want to do when you pray except precisely what you are doing, which is to present and to represent to God your nothingness and your poverty? The most effective appeal which beggars can make to us is to show us their sores and their neediness. But then again, sometimes you don't even do that, you tell me, but you kneel there like something inanimate or a statue. Well, this is no mean achievement either. In the palaces of princes and kings there are statues whose sole purpose is to delight the prince when he happens to see them: be satisfied with playing this part in God's presence. He will give the statue life when he thinks fit.

Trees only bear fruit because of the presence of the sun, some sooner and some later, some every year and others every three years, nor is their harvest always equal. We are very fortunate to be able to remain in the presence of God; let us be content that his presence will make us bear fruit sooner or later, or every day, or sometimes, according to his good pleasure, to which we should wholly resign ourselves.

What a marvellous thing you said when you wrote to me: as

[1] Prov. xxx, 21, 23.

long as I am serving God I don't care what kind of sauce he puts me in. But be careful to chew this over and over again in your mind; let it melt in your mouth and do not swallow it whole. Mother Theresa whom you love so much and in whom I too rejoice, says somewhere[1] that we often say certain words by habit and, as it were, only half aware of their meaning; we think they come from the depths of our soul, but we may discover later on when it comes to the test that this is far from being the case. Well, you tell me it is all the same to you whatever the sauce. Come now, you know very well into what sauce he has put you, into what state of life and condition; and tell me, is it all the same to you? And you also know that he wants you to pay that debt day by day, and you write and tell me about it, and surely this is not all the same to you. Dear Lord, how subtly self-love slips into our feelings, even if they look and seem so very devout!

The great secret is this: find out what God wants, and when you know, try to do his will gaily or at least bravely; and over and above that we must love God's will and the obligation it lays upon us, even if we have to herd swine all our lives and do the most abject things in the world; for it must be all the same to us, whatever the sauce God choses for us. This is the centre of perfection at which we must all aim, and whoever gets closest to it will win the prize.

But don't lose heart, I entreat you; gradually train your will to follow God's will wherever it leads; see that your will is strongly roused as soon as your conscience tells you: God wants this; and little by little these feelings of repugnance which go so deep in you will grow less intense and soon disappear altogether. But the chief thing is that you should struggle not to show outwardly the repugnance you feel inwardly, or at least to tone down the display of feeling. When people are put out or annoyed, some only show their irritation by saying: good Lord, what's all this? And then there are others who speak more heatedly, their words showing a certain pride and spite as well as annoyance. What I mean is that you should gradually

[1] *Way of Perfection*, ch. 38.

89

lessen these exhibitions of feeling, moderating them gradually day by day.

As to your desire to see your family making great progress in God's service and in Christian perfection, I praise it infinitely, and since you ask me, I shall add my feeble prayers to your supplications to God in this matter. But to tell you the truth, Madam, and to speak quite openly: I am always afraid that these desires which are not of the essence of our own salvation and perfection, may have some trace of self-love and self-will in them. For example, we may indulge so much in these not really essential desires as not to leave enough room in our hearts for longings which are more justly indicated and more useful, as for instance our longing to be humble, resigned and meek of heart. And also I am afraid we might pursue these desires so ardently that they make us anxious and over-eager; and finally, we might not submit them so perfectly to God's will as we should.

This is what I fear in desires of this kind, and that is why I beg you to be very careful not to run such risks but to pursue your aims in this matter gently and kindly, that is to say, without being a nuisance to those whom you would like to influence towards perfection, and without even letting them guess your intention; for believe me, that would do more harm than good. So you must work by your example and by what you say, quite gently sowing the good seed which might later on come up; and without making it obvious that you want to instruct them or win them over, you must gradually fill their hearts with holy ideas and considerations. And so you will do much more real good than in any other way, especially if you pray about it.

II

To the Baronne de Chantal

Annecy, 21 July 1605
You expressed so much pleasure about the little letters I sent

to you while you were on your journey that from now onwards
I want to let you have more messages of this kind and not miss
any chance of writing, either briefly or at length. But what am
I going to tell you, my dear daughter? Tomorrow, the feast of
Mary Magdalene, I shall be preaching at the Poor Clares' convent; but to you I will say that one day Mary Magdalene was
speaking to Our Lord, and considering herself separated from
him, she wept and called for him, and was so eager, that seeing
him, she failed to see him. And so courage, let us not be over-
eager and restless; our sweet Jesus is with us, we are not
separated from him, at least I firmly hope so. 'Woman, why
weepest thou?'[1] No, you must no longer be a woman, you
must have a man's heart; and provided our soul has a firm will
to live and die in the service of God, let us not be dismayed by
the darkness, our helplessness or our feeling of being shut out
by some barrier. And speaking of barriers: Magdalene wanted
to embrace Our Lord, and her gentle master put up, as it were,
a barrier: No, he said, 'Do not touch me; for I am not yet
ascended to my Father.'[2] On high there will be no more
barriers, here we must put up with them. It must be enough for
us that God is our God and that our heart is his dwelling place.

Shall I tell you a thought that came to me in that morning
hour you want me to reserve for my poor soul? The point I was
meditating was this petition in the Lord's prayer: *sanctificetur
nomen tuum*, 'hallowed be thy name'. I said to myself, oh who
will give me the happiness of one day seeing the name of Jesus
written in the innermost heart of her who really has it branded
on her body?[3] O how I longed to have the steel of our Saviour's
lance in one hand and your heart in the other! I am sure I
should not have hesitated to do this work. You see, my dear
daughter, how my mind lets itself go? I also remembered the
great houses in Paris on the front of which is written the name
of the prince to whom they belong, and I rejoiced in the
thought that the mansion of your heart belongs to Jesus
Christ. May he live there eternally.

[1] John xx, 15.   [2] Ibid, 17.
[3] She had written the Holy Name over her heart with a red-hot point of steel.

Pray much for me who am so deeply and incomparably yours.

F.

All who belong to you here are well, but no one knows that I am writing to you. I am full of hope in God's goodness that we shall belong to him utterly; I am joyful and full of courage: is God not all ours? Amen. May Jesus reign.

12

To the Baronne de Chantal

Annecy, 1 August 1605

No indeed, in God's name, my very dear daughter, no! I am not going to be in the least distressed, I am not going to be afraid or in doubt about your helplessness or your difficulties. I am not so vulnerable now; the pains of labour are over as far as I am concerned. What can I fear for you at this stage? No, I feel sure in an indefinable way that all is well with your soul.

As Rachel was unable to have children, she gave Bala to her husband as a second in marriage (at that time men were allowed to have several wives so as to multiply the people of God). Bala bore her children on Rachel's knees; then Rachel took them as her own, so that Bala, her second, had no more responsibility for them, at least, no prime responsibility. O my daughter, I think that I have born you once and for all on the knees of the beautiful Rachel, our very dear and sacred Abbess;[1] she has taken you to herself; as for me, I no longer have the chief responsibility for you. Stay there on her knees, or rather humbly prostrate at her feet. That is the first reason why I am not afraid.

The other reason is that there is nothing to be afraid of. When our sweet Jesus died there was darkness over all the land. I think that Mary Magdalene who was with your Lady Abbess, was deeply grieved because she could no longer see her dear

[1] The Blessed Virgin.

Saviour clearly and distinctly; she could only see him indis-
tinctly on the cross, she got up from her knees, fixed her eyes
ardently on him, but she only saw a certain pale and confused
whiteness where he was; yet all the time she was as close to
him as before. Let this be done to you, everything is going very
well. As much darkness as you like, but all the time we are
close to the light; as much helplessness as you please, but we
are at the feet of the Almighty. May Jesus reign! May we never
be separated from him, either in darkness or in light!

Do you know what occurs to me when you ask me for
remedies? I do not remember that Our Lord asked us to heal
the head of the daughter of Sion but only her heart. No, he
certainly never said: Speak to the head of Jerusalem, but what
he did say was: 'Speak ye to the heart of Jerusalem.'[1] Your
heart is in a healthy state since your resolutions hold good. May
there be peace in your heart, my daughter, yours is the lot of
God's children. 'Blessed are the clean of heart: for they shall
see God';[2] he does not say that they are seeing God now, but
that they shall see him.

But here is a little hint of a remedy. Run within the barriers
because they have been put up; it will not stop you from carrying off the ring, and with even greater certainty.[3] Do not force
yourself, do not make yourself miserable: after the rain it will
be fine. Do not keep such an anxious and watchful eye on
yourself. Naturally, when you get news of some scandal you
feel very bad about it. It is not really surprising that a poor little
widow should feel feeble and wretched. But what do you expect? Do you expect her to be far-sighted, strong, constant and
self-sufficient? Accept gladly the fact that your state of mind
matches your condition and that you are a widow, lowly and
abject in every way, except that you do not offend God. Not
long ago I saw a widow in a procession of the Blessed Sacrament, and while the others were carrying large candles of white
wax she was only carrying a tiny tallow candle which she had

[1] Isa. xl, 2.   [2] Matt. v, 8.
[3] Reference to a game, called tilting at the ring. The players run within an
enclosure to carry off a ring which is hung on a post.

probably made herself; and to make things worse the wind put it out. This neither brought her closer to the Blessed Sacrament, nor kept her at a greater distance; she got to the church as soon as everybody else.

I repeat, do not be anxious: you are not the only one to bear this cross. But does this mean that I am now going to tell you how things are going with me, since you ask me to? It is in fact true; all day yesterday and the whole night, I have been carrying a cross similar to yours, not in my head but in my heart; but now it has been taken from me by the confession I have just made. All day yesterday my will was really so helpless that a feather could have crushed it. Well now, even if you were to have a very special cross all to yourself, what of it? The cross would be worth more on that account, and should be dearer to you. My dear St. Peter did not want his cross to be like his Master's, so he had it put upside down; he had his head on the earth and his heart in heaven when he died.

Make use of the little light you have[1] said Our Lord, until the sun rises. The door has not been opened yet, but through the lattices[2] you can see the forecourt and the outside of Solomon's temple: stay where you are. It is not unfitting for widows to be somewhat in the background; there are a whole number of good people who are waiting their turn just as you are, it is reasonable that they should be preferred. And in the meanwhile, have you not got your little tasks to get on with while you are waiting? Am I being rather hard, dear daughter? At least I am truthful. Let us get on to something else; I have little leisure, for it is the feast day of our great St. Peter.

I told you you could see the Huguenots; now I say: yes, see them, but only rarely, and be brief and reserved with them, nevertheless gentle and very humble and simple. Your good patron's[3] son was writing one day to the devout Maxima, his spiritual daughter, and he said something of this kind: be simple and gracious as a dove when you are speaking to heretics, having compassion on their misfortune; be prudent as a

[1] John xii, 35.   [2] Cf. Cant. II, 9.
[3] St. Monica, model of Christian widows.

94

serpent to slip away from their company quickly at chance meetings or on other occasions and after occasional visits. That is what I say to you.

Yes, daughter, I approve of your noting the interior movements which led to imperfections and faults, provided this does not make you anxious. As to your thoughts, you are not asked to account for those which just pass through your head, but only those which like bees, leave their poison and sting when they have wounded you.

I am going to tell you something about myself, very briefly. I wish that you could see me as I am interiorly, provided that my imperfections did not scandalize you. Since you left I have not ceased meeting with set-backs, great and small; but neither my heart nor my spirits have been in any way upset, thank God. Never have I had more inner sweetness and happiness, until last night when my heart was covered over with clouds; and now that I am back from holy mass, all is serene and bright. I have done, in part, what you wanted me to do, that is to say I have been putting aside some time for the relaxation of body and mind. I will do better every day, if God helps me; at least I have the will for it.

I will not try and say how full my heart is for you, but I will say that it is full beyond compare; and this affection is whiter than snow, purer than the sun: that is why I have given it free rein since you left me, letting it have its way. O how impossible to tell, my Lord and God, how consoling it will be to love one another in heaven in this full sea of charity, when even these little brooklets of love give us so much!

Four days ago I received into the Church a young nobleman of twenty and heard his confession. He was as honest as the day and as valiant as a sword. O Saviour of my soul, what joy to hear him accusing himself in such a holy way of his sins; and to see in this God's special providence for him, guarding and shielding him by interior movements of the heart and springs of action which are so hidden from the human eye, so high, so admirable! I was quite beside myself; how I kissed him to wish him peace!

I hear from two sides that there are plans for raising me higher in the eyes of the world; one was the note which I read to you in the gallery of your castle of Sales, the other came from Rome. I answer before God: no, do not be in any doubt, daughter, I shall not as much as bat an eyelid to gain the whole world; it costs me no effort to despise it; if it is not for the greater glory of God no sort of response will stir in me. But all this is between father and daughter; I beg you not to let it go any further. And apropos of the word 'daughter', in future I do not want any other title of honour in your letters except that of 'father': it is more definite, more lovable, more holy, more glorious for me.

How happy I should be to render your uncle some service one day, for I cherish him very much. I send my sincere greetings to your father-in-law and offer him my services. 'I wish your little ones, whom I look upon as mine in Our Lord, a thousand graces'; these are the words of Monica's son writing to Italica, his spiritual daughter. I beg Our Lord to make you grow in his love.

God be with you, my very dear daughter; this great God to whom we are vowed and consecrated, and who has dedicated me for ever and without any reserve to your soul which I cherish as my own and look upon as all mine in our Saviour, who in giving us his soul, joins us inseparably in him. May Jesus reign!

Francis, Bishop of Geneva.

13

To the Baronne de Chantal

Annecy, 28 August 1605

. . . Your temptations have returned, and although you do not enter into argument with them, they besiege you. You do not answer them, and that is right; but you think about them too much, you fear them too much, you are too apprehensive:

else they would not do you any harm. You are too vulnerable to the assault of temptations. You love faith and you do not want to have a single thought contrary to the faith, and as soon as one crops up you are upset and scared. You cling too jealously to the purity of your faith, and you feel that any little thing can spoil it. No, no, dear daughter, let the wind blow freely, and don't mistake the rustling of leaves for the clash of armour.

Not long ago I was near some beehives and a few bees came and settled on my face. I wanted to raise my hand and brush them off. No, said a peasant to me, don't be afraid, and whatever you do don't touch them, they will attack you. I trusted his word and not a single one stung me. Believe me, don't be afraid of temptations, and whatever you do don't touch them, they will not do you any damage; go on, right past them, and don't linger over them.

I have just returned from the confines of my diocese on the Swiss border where I have succeeded in establishing thirty-three parishes in which eleven years ago there were only protestant ministers. I spent three years there all alone preaching the Catholic faith. And God made this journey one of unalloyed consolation for me; for whereas before I only found a hundred Catholics, I now did not find as many as a hundred Huguenots. It is true that the journey caused me much hardship and was fraught with awkward situations; and because it concerned temporal matters and the provision of churches, I met with much opposition; but God gave a very good issue by his grace, and some small measure of spiritual fruit. I say this because my heart cannot hide anything from yours and does not consider itself separate or other from yours, but as it were, one.

Today is the feast of St. Augustine and you can imagine that I prayed to his Master for you and also to God's servant and his mother. How greatly my soul loves yours! Go on putting your trust in my soul and loving it. It is God's will, dear daughter, I am quite certain; and he will use this love for his glory. May he be our heart, daughter, and I am in him, and by his will, all yours. Live joyfully and be generous; that is what God whom

G

97

we love and to whom we are dedicated wants us to be. It is he who gave me to you; may he be for ever blessed and praised.

I had just got to the end of this letter which is so badly put together, when two more of yours were brought to me, one of 16 August, the other of the 20th, together in one packet. I see nothing there except what I have already answered. You are too frightened of temptations; that is the only thing that is wrong. Make up your mind that all the temptations of hell could not possibly stain a soul that does not love them; so just let them have their course. The apostle Paul suffered terrible temptations but God did not want to remove them, and all for love. Come now, dear daughter, be brave; let this heart of yours never leave Jesus to whom it belongs, and let this hateful beast bark and raise his false alarm at the gates as loud and as long as he likes.

Live with your sweet Jesus and your holy Abbess, my dear daughter, among dark shadows, nails, thorns, spears and dereliction; and together with your Mistress[1] live long in tears without getting anything in return; in the end God will raise you up and fill you with rejoicing and will make you see the desire of your heart. I hope so; and if he does not, still we shall not give up serving him, and he will not cease to be our God; for the affection we owe him is deathless and imperishable.

30 August 1605

14

To the Baronne de Chantal

Annecy, 14 September 1605

Do not be in the least distressed on my account because of all you write to me; for you see, where your affairs are concerned I am in the same case as Abraham was of old. He was lying asleep in a place of horror amidst darksome shadows: he felt great terror, but only for a short time, for suddenly he saw

[1] St. Monica.

a fiery light and heard God's voice promising him his blessings.[1]
My spirit certainly lives in the midst of your darkness and
temptations, for it keeps very close to yours; your account of
your difficulties touches me with compassion, but I can see
clearly that all will be well in the end because God, our Beloved,
teaches us a great deal in his school where you have learnt
greater awareness and alertness. Just keep on writing to me
quite frankly about your difficulties and also about the good
things that come your way; and do not be in the least distressed,
for my heart is equal to all that.

Courage, my dear daughter. Let us keep on and on making
our way through these dark valleys; let us live with the cross in
our arms, humble and patient. What does it matter whether
God's voice comes to us amongst thorns or amongst flowers?
Indeed, I do not remember that he has ever spoken where there
are flowers, but his voice has often been heard in deserts and
thorny bushes. So go on your way, my dear daughter, and forge
ahead while the weather is bad and the night dark. But above
all write to me very sincerely; this is the great commandment—
you must be absolutely frank with me, for everything else depends on that. And shut your eyes to every consideration you
might have for my peace of mind, which, believe me, I shall
never lose on your account while I see your heart firmly set on
serving our God; and never, never, please God, shall I see you
in any other frame of mind than this. Therefore do not be in
any sort of distress.

Be brave, my dear daughter; we shall win through with God's
help; and believe me, this is better sort of weather for a journey
than if the sun were glaring down on us. The other day I was
watching the bees and how they stayed quietly in the shelter of
their hives because the air was misty; they came out from time
to time to see how things were going, and yet they did not
seem in any hurry to come out, but were busy eating their fill
of honey. Be of good cheer! We have no control over any
spiritual light or consolation except what depends on our will,
and that is protected and sheltered by our holy resolutions.

[1] Cf. Gen. xv, 12, 17, 18.

While the great seal of God's chancery is upon your heart there is nothing to fear.

I will tell you a word or two about myself. A few days ago I was rather ill; a day's rest put me right again. I am in good heart, thank God, and I hope to improve according to your desire. With what great consolation I read your words to me, that you wished my heart perfection almost more than your own: you are a true spiritual daughter! But however freely you let your imagination run on, it will never get as far ahead as my will in wishing you the love of God.

The bearer is just about to leave and I am going to preach to our Penitents of the Holy Cross. All I can do is just to give you my blessing, which I give you in the name of Jesus Christ crucified; may his cross be our glory and our consolation, my dear daughter. May it be greatly exalted among us and planted on our head as it was on that of the first Adam.[1] May it fill our heart and our soul, as it filled the soul of St. Paul, who knew nothing else. Courage, dear daughter, God is on our side. Amen. I am for ever all yours, and God knows this, for he willed it and wrought it with his sovereign hand and in a very special way.

Francis, Bishop of Geneva.

Feast of the Exaltation of the Holy Cross, 1605.

15

To a Nun

Annecy, September–October 1605

I see that your soul has sincere confidence in mine and an ardent longing for devotion, and this makes me feel fatherly love for you. Now believe me, my dear daughter, we shall make good progress; for this dear and gentle Saviour of our souls does not give us burning desires to serve him without showing

[1] Cf. *Défense de l'Estendart de la Sainte Croix*, A. II, p. 62, where the proofs for this tradition are outlined.

us the ways and means to do it. I am sure that he is only post-poning the hour of putting your holy desire[1] into effect, so as to prepare you all the better; for you see, my very dear daughter, our Redeemer's loving heart metes out and adjusts all the events of this world to profit the souls of those who want to serve his divine love unconditionally. So this happy, longed-for hour will come on the day which God in his sovereign providence has ordained in the secret of his mercy; and then with untold secret consolations you will lay open your heart to his divine Goodness, and he will make water flow from the rocks, your serpent will be turned into a staff, and all the thorns of your heart into as many sweet-scented roses, whose sweetness will give great joy to your soul and to mine. For it is true, dear daughter, that our faults which are thorns as long as they re-main hidden in our hearts are turned into roses and sweetness when they come out by voluntary accusation; for as our malice draws them into our hearts so the Holy Spirit's mercy casts them out.

As you are strong enough to get up an hour before Matins for mental prayer, I approve very much of this. How blissful to be kneeling there completely alone with God, without anyone knowing what is passing between God and your heart except God himself and your heart in adoration.[2] I approve of your meditating on the life and passion of Our Lord.

In the evening between Vespers and supper you will retire for a quarter of an hour or a short half hour, either in the church or in your room; and so as to rekindle the morning's fire, either by resuming the matter already meditated or by taking Christ crucified as your subject, you will make fervent

---

[1] Her general confession.
[2] 'And as my heart urges me to tell you everything consoling that comes my way I want to say that these past three days I have taken incomparable joy in thinking what a great honour it is for the heart of man to be able to commune alone with God, its Creator, immense, infinite, of sovereign power. For only the heart knows, in the first instance, what is being said, and then those to whom God may choose to reveal it. Is this not a wonderful secret? This surely, is what the Doctors mean when they tell us to pray as though there were only God in the whole world; for this undoubtedly concentrates the powers of the soul and allows them to be applied to much greater effect.' Letter to Madame de Chantal, 16 August 1607, A. XIII, p. 311.

and loving aspirations to your Beloved, at the same time renewing your good resolutions of always belonging to him.

Be of good courage, God is undoubtedly calling you to great love and high perfection. He for his part will be faithful in helping you; be faithful on yours in following and seconding him. And as for me, dear daughter, you can be very certain that all my affection is dedicated to your good and to the service of your dear soul; may God bless it for ever with great blessings.

I am then in him all yours,

Francis, Bishop of Geneva.

16

To Madame de Rye, Nun at the Abbey of Baume-les-Dames

Annecy, 10 October 1605

Madam,

As I am, and have every reason to be a man little given to ceremony, I shall tell you quite simply that God has given me so much inclination to wish you his graces and blessings, so much confidence in your virtue, that I could never cease imploring his Divine Majesty to bring his holy love to complete perfection in you; and I am sure that you, in your turn, will be good enough to remember me sometimes, laden as I am with a great burden and having much need of the help of your prayers. To this end I will write to you quite often, not that you may feel obliged to answer as frequently (this would perhaps be putting you to too great trouble), but with the object of recalling myself to your gracious remembrance and of proving to you, as far as I am able, how highly I cherish it.

And now will you please allow me, Madam, to rejoice with you in the affection you brought to bear on the few little words I was able to say to you for the good of your soul. Yes, Madam, you are on the right road: always listen humbly and attentively to what is said to you in God's name, however slight the matter, however insignificant the speaker. I entreat you to go on drawing profit in this way from all you are told. Go on kindling the spirit of joy and sweetness in your heart, and believe firmly that this is the true spirit of devotion; and if you are sometimes attacked by a contrary spirit of sadness and bitterness, make a real effort to lift up your heart to God, committing all to him; then at once seek relaxation by doing something quite different. You might, for instance, try to find some holy conversation with people who have the power to cheer you. Go out for a walk, read one of the books you like best, and as the Apostle advises,[1] sing some holy song. Indeed, this is a thing you should often do, because not only does singing divert you but it renders God service. If you do what I suggest you will gradually learn to ward off all spiritual melancholy and sadness.

I beg God to grant you the continual help of his most Holy Spirit so that you can serve and love him as your heart desires. And meanwhile, I shall remain all the days of my life, Madam,

Your most humble and very affectionate servant,

Francis, Bishop of Geneva.

17

To the Baronne de Chantal

Annecy, 13 October 1605

Having till now been held back by a mass of urgent business, my dear daughter, I am about to leave for this visitation which I call blessed and where I see crosses waiting for me at every turn of the road. My flesh shrinks at the thought but my heart adores it. Yes, I hail you, little crosses and great, spiritual or temporal, exterior or interior; I salute you and kiss you, unworthy as I am of the honour of being in your shadow.

Why am I telling you this? It is because, my so very dear daughter, I adore your crosses with the same affection, and look

[1] Eph. v, 19.

upon them as mine, and I want you (at least, I beg you) to love mine in the same way. I have had a good many crosses since the Pardons[1] here, but they were short and light. Strengthen the weakness of my shoulders, O God, and only weigh them down with a small load, so as to make me realize clearly what a poor soldier I should be if I were to see the armies face to face.

How your letters consoled me, my dear daughter! They are full of good desires, courage and resolution. O how well things are going! And let the enemy threaten and rattle the doors all around us; for God is in our midst, in our heart, and he will always stay there if it is his good pleasure. So stay with us, Lord, because it is towards evening.[2]

I will say no more to you, nothing about your great project of leaving all things and yourself for God, nor about your going forth from your own country and from your parents' house. No, I do not wish to talk about it; may God be pleased to enlighten us and show us his good pleasure, for at the peril of all that is in us we will follow him wherever he leads. O how good it is to be with him, wherever it may be!

I am thinking about the soul of my very good and very holy thief. Our Lord had told him that his soul would be with him in paradise that day; and no sooner was it separated from his body than he at once led it down to hell. Yes, for the soul was to be with our Saviour, and our Saviour had gone down into hell: so the soul went with him. What do you suppose it felt like when it got down there and saw this abyss before its inward eye? I think it must have said with Job: Who will grant me this, O my God, that thou mayst preserve and protect me in hell?[3] And with David: No, I will fear no evil, for, O Lord, thou art with me.[4] No, my dear daughter, while our resolutions hold good, I will not be anxious on your account. Even if we die, and if everything goes wrong, I shall not mind as long as one resolve is firm. Night is as day to us, when God is in our heart, and the day is as the night when he is not there. . . .

---

[1] The pilgrimage which took place every seven years from 6–8 September to Notre-Dame de Liesse at Annecy.
[2] Luke, xxiv, 29.   [3] Cf. Job xiv, 13.   [4] Cf. Ps. xxii, 4.

As I am pressed for time I must end this letter. I pray that Our Lord may make you more and more his; that he may guard your resolutions, defend your widowhood, direct your obedience; that he may be yours and all yours. I pray our holy Abbess, our dear Lady and Queen, ever to be gracious to us and to make us die and live in her Son. I am incomparably yours, my dear daughter, I am all yours, in the merciful love of the Son and of his Mother,

Francis, Bishop of Geneva.

18

To the Baronne de Chantal

Annecy, 5 December 1605

My very dear daughter,

Since I returned from the visitation of my diocese I have had a slight relapse of catarrhal fever; the only remedy the doctor prescribed was rest, and I obeyed him. You know, dear daughter, that rest is a remedy which I too like to prescribe, and that I always forbid precipitation. And so, while I was resting physically I have been thinking about the spiritual rest which our hearts should have in God's will wherever it may lead us; but I cannot possibly discuss this subject properly unless I have a real spell of leisure.

Let us live, dear daughter, in this valley of tears as long as God pleases, completely resigned to his holy, sovereign will. Oh, how grateful we should be to his goodness which has made us long to live and die in his love and renew our desire with so many resolutions! There is no doubt about it, dear daughter, we desire this and have made up our minds to it; let us hope that our great Saviour who gives us the will to do it will also give us the grace to accomplish it.[1]

The other day I was considering what authors tell us about halcyons, small birds that lay their eggs out at sea. It appears

[1] Cf. Phil. ii, 13.

that they make completely round nests and so tightly compact that the water can in no way penetrate them; right at the top there is just a small hole by which they can breathe and draw in air. In this nest they put their little ones, so that when the sea takes them by surprise, they can swim safely and float on the waves without being either water-logged or submerged; and the air which is taken in by the little hole serves as a counterweight and balances these small spheres and tiny boats in such a way that they never overturn. O dear daughter, how I wish that our hearts could be like that, very compact, snugly lined all round, so that when the world's anxieties and tempests beat against them, they cannot force an entry. There is, moreover, no opening except towards heaven, so that we may only breathe towards our Saviour and draw him in as we draw in air. And for whom or for what is this nest to be made, my dear daughter? For our little fledglings, for our love of God, for our divine and heavenly affections.

But while the halcyons are building their nests and while their little ones are yet frail to withstand the power of the tossing waves, see how God takes care of them and has pity on them, so that the sea does not carry them away and swallow them up. For his holy love's sake, his sovereign goodness will safeguard the nest of our hearts against the assaults of the world, protecting us from attack. Oh, how I love these birds which are surrounded by water and live by the air, which hide in the ocean and only see the sky! They swim like fish and sing like birds; and what I find most delightful is that they cast their anchor in an upward, not in a downward direction. O my sister, my daughter, may our sweet Jesus make us such, that surrounded by the world and by the flesh, we may live only by the spirit; that in the midst of the vanities of this earth we may always have heaven in view; that living with men, we may praise him with the angels, and that the anchorage of our hopes may always be on high and in paradise.

O dear daughter, my soul had to cast this thought on paper, at the same time casting its longings at the foot of the cross, so that in all and above all holy divine love may be our great love.

But when, oh when will it consume us? And when will it consume our life so as to make us die to ourselves and be born again in our Saviour? To him alone be for ever honour, glory and benediction!

My dear daughter, what am I trying to say? I mean what is the point of it all? Dear daughter, since our life's unchanging purpose and resolution tends unceasingly towards the love of God, words concerning it are never out of place for us.

Good-bye, dear daughter; yes, I call you my true daughter in him whose holy love constrains me and, as it were, consecrates me to be, to live, to die and to rise again for ever yours and all yours. May Jesus reign! May Jesus and our Lady reign! Amen.

Francis, Bishop of Geneva.

The Eve of glorious St. Nicholas.

19

To the Présidente Brûlart

Chambéry, February–March 1606

Madam, my very dear sister,

I see that you are still languishing with the desire for greater perfection. I praise this kind of languor for it does not make you languorous, as I know very well; on the contrary, it animates you and spurs you on to conquest.

You live, so you tell me, subject to thousands of imperfections. Very true, my good sister; but don't you try to make them die in you hour by hour? While we are weighed down with so heavy and corruptible a body, there is always and undoubtedly an indefinable something lacking in us. Have I never told you that we must be patient with everyone and primarily ourselves? For we are more troublesome to ourselves than anyone else, because we can distinguish between the old and the new Adam in us, the interior and the exterior man.

You say that you always have a book in your hand while you

are meditating, otherwise you get nothing done. Well, and what of it? What difference does it make whether you do it with a book in your hand and at various times? When I told you you should only spend half an hour meditating, that was at the beginning, when I was afraid of forcing your imagination; but now there is no danger in spending an hour at it.

There is no danger in doing all sorts of good and necessary tasks and in working on the day when one has been to communion. In the primitive church when everyone went to communion every day, do you think that they sat there with their arms folded for the rest of the day? And St. Paul, who generally said mass, went on earning his living by the work of his hands.

There are only two things to avoid on the day of communion: sin and pleasures of the senses which one seeks of one's own accord, for as to those which are due or demanded, or are necessary, or are the result of honourable condescension on our part, they are in no way forbidden on that day; on the contrary, they are a matter of counsel, provided a gentle and holy modesty is observed. No, I should not wish to abstain from going to an honourable feast or an honourable assembly on that day, if I were asked, although I would not go out of my way to seek it. Another instance is that of married people who on that day can and indeed should pay their debt, though not demand it without some risk of impropriety; this would not however be mortal sin. I have given you this instance on purpose.

You ask me whether people who want to live with some degree of perfection ought to see so much of the world and society. Perfection, my dear lady, does not consist in not seeing the world, but in not relishing and savouring it. Everything conveyed to us by sight is to some extent dangerous, for seeing a thing puts us in peril of loving it; but if we have really made up our mind, what we see does us no harm. In a word, my sister, a perfect life is the perfection of charity, for the life of our soul is charity. Our first Christians belonged to the world in body but not in heart and were none the less perfect.

My dear sister, I should not wish there to be any make-believe in us, not real make-believe. Straightforwardness and simplicity are the virtues proper to us. But I am put out, you say, by the wrong impression people have of me; I am worthless, and people think the opposite; and you ask me for a prescription. Here it is, my dear daughter, as the saints taught it to me: if the world despises us, let us rejoice, for the world is right and we know very well that we are contemptible; if it esteems us, let us despise its esteem and its judgement, for it is blind. Do not inquire much into what the world thinks, do not let it bother you in any way, despise its scale of values and its contempt and let it say what it likes, good or evil.

So I do not approve of your committing faults so that people should have a bad opinion of you; a fault is still a fault and leads one's neighbour to commit a fault. On the contrary, I should like us to keep our eyes fixed on our Saviour and do what we have to do without looking to see what the world thinks and what sort of face it is making. One can avoid giving a good impression of oneself but not go out of one's way to give a bad one, especially by doing wrong things with that end in view. In a word, despise the world's opinion of you and do not let it upset you in any way. It is a good thing to say that you are not what the world thinks you when it thinks well of you, for the world is a charlatan, and always exaggerates both good and evil.

But what is this you say? You are envious of the others whom I like better than you? And the worst of it is you say you really know this to be a fact. How do you know this, my dear sister? In what way do I prefer the others? No, believe me, you are dear, very dear to me; and I know very well that you do not like the others more than me, although you really should. But I will speak freely to you: our two sisters who live in the country[1] have more need of assistance than you who are in town where you have plenty of religious exercises, counsel and all that you need, while they have no one to help them.

[1] Her sister, the Abbess du Puis-d'Orbe, and Madame de Chantal.

20

To the Baronne de Chantal

Annecy, April 1606

... It is impossible not to use imagination and understanding in prayer; the point is that we should only use the imagination in order to move the will, and when that has been set in motion we should rely on it more than on imagination and understanding. This good Mother[1] says that there is no need to use the imagination to picture the sacred humanity of our Saviour. No, perhaps not for those who have already gone a long way up the mountain of perfection; but I think it is expedient for the rest of us who are still in the valleys, although we long to mount higher, to use all our resources including the imagination. All the same I did note for you somewhere that this use of the imagination should be very simple, and as it were, a needle into which we thread our soul's affections and resolutions. This is the great highway, my dear daughter, which we must not leave for yet awhile until the light grows a little stronger and we can see the paths more clearly. It is very true that these inner pictures of the imagination should not be complicated with much detail but remain simple. Let us stay a little longer, my dear daughter, in these lowly valleys, let us go on kissing our Saviour's feet for yet a little while longer: when he thinks fit he will call us to kiss his holy mouth. Do not depart from our method until we see one another again.

But when will that be, you will say to me? My dear daughter, if you think that you can get so much help from my presence, draw as much fruit and spiritual provision as you describe to me in your letter, and if you long for it very much, I shall not be so hard as to put you off till next year, but willingly go back to our original plan; the only trouble this will give me is the thought of your hard journey; otherwise I am pleased and de-

---

[1] Mère Marie de la Trinité, formerly Mlle d'Hannivel, the only French nun among the Spanish Carmelites who had recently settled in Dijon.

lighted. The difficulty is that I am only free during the octaves of Whitsun and of Corpus Christi. Choose one or the other and you will find me very ready, and with God's help, very happy to serve you.

And now, my dear daughter, in unimportant matters, or when I cannot well discern the point at issue, do not take my words too rigorously; for the last thing I want is for my pronouncements to tie you down; I want you to be free to do what you yourself think best. If then you think that your journey will be very profitable, I agree that you should come, but come absolutely freely and without any scruples. Only you must let me know which of the two weeks you choose because I should like my mother to be here when you come; and believe me that both she and I will be much consoled by your visit, at the expense of the trouble it will give you.

May God be with us for ever and may he live eternally in our hearts. Good-bye, my very dear daughter; I am he whom God has made so uniquely yours.

F.

21

To the Baronne de Chantal

Annecy, 8 June 1606

So we shall see one another again next year, please God, my very dear daughter; but without fail and always at about Whitsun or Corpus Christi, and we need not wait to make any other assignation provided we arrange things beforehand. And how shall we go about it? We will resign ourselves entirely and without reserve to Our Lord's holy will, renouncing into his hands all our consolations, whether spiritual or temporal. We shall commit the death and life of all who belong to us purely and simply to his providence, allowing him to arrange according to his good pleasure which is to outlive the other; for we are certain, provided his sovereign goodness is with us and in us and for us, that this is all we need.

You want me to ask that I should outlive you? O come now, may God do as he pleases, and let it be sooner or later: this is really not a point I could except if I made an act of resignation. But you go on to say that you are not yet detached in this matter. Dear God, what is this you are telling me, my very dear daughter? Is it possible that I, who have no greater desire than to see you enjoy an entire and perfect liberty of heart, as of the children of God, should serve as a tie for you? But I understand what you really mean, my dear daughter, and you do not mean that; you mean that my survival might be for the glory of God, and that is why you are attached to it. Therefore it is to God's glory that you are attached, not to his creatures. I am sure this is what you mean and I praise his Divine Majesty for it.

But do you know what I should like to promise you? To be more careful about my health in future, although I have always taken more care of it than I really deserve; and thank God, I feel it is very good now as I have cut out late nights altogether and the writing I used to do at that time; also I am eating more sensibly. But believe me, your wishes play quite a big part in this resolution; for I have great feelings of affection for your contentment and consolation, though at the same time my heart remains quite free and open, this affection settling silently and softly upon it, like a fall of dew. And if you want me to tell you the whole truth, this affection was not so calm when God first sent it to me (for of course it comes from him) as it is now; for now it is infinitely strong, and it seems to me, ever increasing in strength, though evenly and without vehemence. I have said too much on a subject on which I did not want to say anything at all.

And now I want to tell you about your time-table. Go to bed at nine o'clock if possible, or ten if it cannot be avoided; get up at five, for you need seven or eight hours' sleep. Morning meditation at six o'clock, to last half or three quarters of an hour; at five o'clock in the afternoon a short recollection of about a quarter of an hour, and reading for a quarter of an hour, either before or after your recollection; at night, a short quarter of an hour for your examination of conscience and night prayers; during the day, many holy aspirations to God.

I have been thinking about what you wrote and told me: Monsieur N. advised you not to use your imagination or your understanding or long prayers, and that Mère Marie de la Trinité had said the same thing to you about the use of the imagination. If you used it vehemently and dwelt on it very emphatically, then you no doubt needed that correction; but if you imagined something briefly and simply, only to make your spirit attentive and lead its powers towards meditation, I do not think you need as yet give it up altogether. You must neither linger over it nor yet despise it completely. Neither must you go into excessive detail, as for instance thinking about the colour of our Lady's hair, the form of her face and so on; but simply in rough outline, seeing her sigh after her Son, and situations of that kind, and that briefly.

I say the same thing about not using the understanding. If without forcing it, your will keeps pace with your affections, there is no need to linger over considerations; but because this does not generally happen to the rest of us who are imperfect, we have to resort to considerations for yet a little while.

From all this I gather that you should abstain from long periods of prayer (for I do not call a half or three quarters hours' prayer long), from the use of your imagination in a forced, particularized and long-drawn-out manner; your use of it should be simple and very brief, only serving as a mere bridge from distraction to recollection. And all the same, apply your understanding to your prayer, for it serves to move the affections, the affections move us to resolutions, resolutions to practice, and practice leads us to accomplish the will of God into which our soul should melt and be dissolved. This is what I think of the matter. If I told you anything contrary to this, or if you understood it differently, you must of course revise your practice.

I approve of your abstinences on Fridays, but without a vow or too much constraint. I approve even more that you should work with your hands, as for instance spinning and so on, at times when you have nothing more important to keep you busy, and that your handiwork should be destined either for the altar or for the poor; but not that you should do it so rigorously that if you happened to make something for yourself or your own people, you should tie yourself to giving the poor the value of it; for the most important thing is that a holy liberty and freedom should reign in us and that we should have no other law or constraint except that of love; and if love tells us to do some work for our own people, we may not punish it as though it had done something bad and force it to make amends as you suggest. For whatever love invites us to do, be it for the poor or for the rich, it does all things well and is equally agreeable to our Saviour. I think that if you really understand my meaning you will see that what I say is true, and that I am fighting for a good cause in defending a holy and charitable liberty; you know that I honour it to an extraordinarily high degree, as long as it is genuine, and far removed from dissolute licence which is only a mask of liberty.

And then I really laughed, and a good, hearty laugh it was too, when I read that you planned to give me some serge for my use and then expected me to give whatever it was worth to the poor; all the same, I don't mean to make fun of this suggestion because I see that it wells up from a good and clear desire although the waters of the resulting brook are slightly troubled. O may God make me such that everything serving for my use may be restored to his service, and that my life may be so much his, that everything serving to maintain it, may be said to serve his Divine Majesty.

I laughed, my dear daughter, but my laughter was mixed with a vivid realization of the difference that exists between what I am and what some people think I am. But let it be! May your intention stand you in good account before God! I am happy to accept a length of cloth from you; but who is going to price it correctly for me? For if I were going to give the poor the price which I put on it, I assure you I should not have that sum at my disposal. Never will a garment have kept me so warm as this; for its warmth will go straight to my heart, and I shall not think it is purple, but rather crimson and scarlet, because, so it seems to me, it will be dyed the colour of charity.[1] Well and good then, for this once; for let me tell you that I do not have clothes made every year but only when I need them; and for the other years we shall find some way of using your work according to your wish.

But that is not yet all. This plan of yours gave rise to a great many gay thoughts on my part; but I will only tell you about one of them which came to me on the octave day of Corpus Christi when I was carrying the Blessed Sacrament at the last procession. It seemed to me that I was preparing a lot of work for you to spin, and on a good distaff. You see, I was adoring him whom I was carrying, and my heart knew that he was the true Lamb of God who takes away the sins of the world. O holy and divine Lamb, I said, how poor and needy I was without you! Alas, I have no other clothing but your wool to cover my misery before the face of your Father. And here is what Isaias said about this thought, that Our Lord in his passion was as a lamb before his shearer and did not open his mouth.[2] And what is that divine fleece if not the merit, if not the example, if not the mystery of the cross? It seems to me therefore that the cross is the beautiful distaff of the bride in the Canticle, of that devout Shulamite; the wool of the innocent Lamb, his merit, his example, his mystery, is richly wrought there.

Put this distaff reverently at your left side and go on spinning all the time with considerations, aspirations and good exercises, in holy imitation. Spin, I say, and draw forth all this delicate white wool from the spindle of your heart: the cloth that you will make of it will cover you and save you from confusion on the day of your death; it will keep you warm in winter, and as the Wise Man says, you will not fear the cold of the snows. And this is perhaps what this same Wise Man had in mind when he praised the virtuous woman, saying that, 'She hath put out her hand to strong things: and her fingers have taken hold of the spindle.'[3] For what are these 'strong things' connected with the

[1] The purple soutane made from cloth woven by the Baronne de Chantal is still preserved at the Visitation at Annecy.
[2] Cf. Isaias liii, 7.   [3] Prov. xxxi, 19 and 21.

spindle, if not the mysteries of the Passion spun by means of our imitation? And then I wished you thousands and thousands of blessings, and prayed that on the great day of judgement we might all find ourselves clothed, some as bishops, some as widows, some as married people, some as Capuchins, some as Jesuits, some as vineyard workers, but all clothed in a garment of that same red and white wool, for these are the colours of the Bridegroom.

That was what was in my heart, my dear daughter, while I had in my hands the Lamb itself of whose wool I am speaking. But it is a fact that the thought of you practically always comes to me during these divine exercises, without however, in any way running counter to them or diverting them, thanks be to God's goodness. Am I doing right, my dear daughter, in telling you my thoughts? At least I think that I am not doing any wrong and that you will take them for what they are.

All the desires you feel to see yourself removed from all worldly recreations can, as you say, only be good because they do not disturb you. But be patient, we shall talk about them next year if God keeps us here on earth. That will be time enough, and I have not wished to fall in with your desires for you to leave your home country and to join a noviciate of women who aspire to religion: all that, my dear daughter, is much too important to be dealt with on paper; and there is plenty of time. Meanwhile you will wield your distaff, not with those great loaded spindles, for your fingers would not know how to handle them, but only in accordance with your small capacity. Humility, patience, abjection, gentleness of heart, resignation, simplicity, charity to the poor who are sick, putting up with those who are difficult, and imitating Christ in ways such as these can well be wound on your little spindle. You will find yourself in the company of St. Monica, St. Paula, St. Elizabeth, St. Liduvina and a good many others who are all at the feet of your glorious Abbess who was herself able to wield any sort of spindle but preferred these smaller ones; I think she did this so as to give us an example.

Well, I have spoken enough for this time about the wool of

our immaculate Lamb; but are we not to eat of his divine flesh a little more often? O how sweet and wholesome it is! I think that if it can conveniently be managed it will be good to receive communion once on a week-day, on Thursdays, as well as Sundays, unless there happens to be some feast on another week-day. But this is to be done without any fuss, without upsetting your usual way of life or neglecting to spin one or other of your distaffs. . . .

I shall be leaving here in ten days' time to go on with my visitation, and I shall be spending five whole months among our mountains where our good people are looking forward to our visit with much affection. I shall look after myself as much as possible, first of all for love of myself whom I love only too much, and then for love of you, because you wish it and because you will have a share in anything good that is to be done, as you share in all that happens in my diocese in so far as my position empowers me to communicate it.

My brother, the Canon,[1] wanted to write to you, but I don't know if he will. The poor lad is not well and drags himself about more on will-power than by real strength. He will be able to recuperate for a while at his mother's house while I am leaping from one rocky mountain to the next. . . .

Good-bye, my dear daughter, may we always belong to God without reserve, without intermission. May he live and reign for ever in our hearts. Amen.

F.

May Jesus reign, my dear daughter, may Jesus reign for ever! Amen.

22

To the Baronne de Chantal

July–August 1606

How your letters console me, my good daughter, and how

[1] Jean-François de Sales (see Index of Correspondents, p. 305).

vividly they show me your heart whole and entire, and your confidence in me, a trust so pure that I cannot help believing it to be the work of God's own hand.

During the past few days I have seen terrifying mountains covered with great glaciers,[1] and the people who live in the valleys round here told me that a cowherd going out to look for one of his animals fell into a deep crevasse where he froze to death. Dear God, I said, and was the ice not able to cool this shepherd's ardour when he went in search of his beast? And why am I then so cowardly in going to look for my sheep? You may be sure that this saddened my heart and that my frozen heart was all melted. I saw wonderful things in these parts: the valleys were all full of houses, and the mountains were all ice, right to the foothills. Little widows, little village women, like lowly valleys, are so fertile in goodness, and bishops, who hold such a high rank in God's Church, are so frozen and cold! Oh, is there no sun strong enough to melt the ice that chills me?

When I was there I was brought an account of the life and death of a saintly village woman belonging to my diocese who had died in June. What was I to think of it? One day I will send you an extract of it, for I assure you there is some indefinable quality of excellence about this little story of a housewife, who in her goodness was a great friend of mine and had often commended me to God.

I have just been speaking to Our Lord about you in the most holy mass, my very dear daughter, and really I did not dare to ask him outright that you should be delivered from your trial; for if it is his pleasure to burn the offering which is to be presented to him, it is not for me to wish he should not do it; but I implored him and I continue to implore him by that extreme dereliction which made him sweat blood and cry out on the cross: My God, my God, why hast thou forsaken me?[2] that he may always hold you with his holy hand as he has done up till now, although you do not know where he is holding you, or at least you do not feel it. Indeed, you would do well simply to

[1] His visitation had taken him to the Mont Blanc district.
[2] Matt. xxvii, 46.

look at our crucified Lord, and to tell him of your love and utter resignation, however dry, arid and unfeeling it is, without dwelling on what is wrong with you and examining it, not even in order to tell me about it.

For after all we belong wholly to God, without reserve, without division, without any sort of exception, and without any other claim than the honour of belonging to him. If we had the smallest trace of affection in our hearts which did not belong to him or come from him, we should uproot it very swiftly. So let us live in peace and say with the great lover of the cross: From henceforth let no man be troublesome to me: for I bear the marks of my Jesus in my heart.[1] Yes, my very dear daughter, if we knew of the smallest nook or cranny of our heart not marked with the cross we should not suffer it for a moment. What is the point of worrying? My soul, hope in God; art thou still downcast? Wilt thou never be at peace?[2] For God is my God, and my heart is a heart that belongs all to him.

And so, my very dear daughter, pray for him who unceasingly wishes you all blessings, and the blessing of all blessings, which is his holy and perfect love.

23

To the Baronne de Chantal

Cluses, 6 August 1606

May God help me, my very dear daughter, to reply usefully to your letter of July 9th. I desire this infinitely but I foresee that I shall not have leisure to arrange my thoughts; it will be as much as I can do to express them at all.

You are right, my daughter, speak to me frankly, as to me, that is to say as to a soul which God by his sovereign authority has made all yours. You are beginning to put your hand to the task, you tell me. O dear God, how greatly this consoles me! Keep on doing this, putting your hand to the task, spinning a

[1] Cf. Galat. vi, 17.   [2] Cf. Ps. xli, 6.

little every day, whether by daylight, in interior joy and brightness, or at night, by the lamplight of helplessness and dryness
of spirit. The Wise Man praises the valiant woman for this:
'Her fingers,' he says, 'have taken hold of the spindle.'[1] How I
should like to talk to you about these words! Your distaff is the
store of all your desires: spin just a little every day, draw out
the thread of your plans until you put them into effect, and you
will certainly do well. But beware of over-eager haste, else
your thread will get into a knotted tangle and you will not be
able to work your spindle. Let us keep going all the time; however slowly we get on, we shall still make plenty of way.

Your spiritual helplessness is doing you a lot of harm, you
say, because it prevents you from entering into yourself and
getting close to God. But you are quite wrong. God leaves you
in this state for his glory and your own great profit; he wants
your poverty to be the throne of his mercy, and your helplessness the seat of his omnipotence. Did not God put the divine
strength he gave Samson into his hair, the frailest part of his
frame? Let me hear no more words of this kind from a daughter
who wants to serve God according to his divine pleasure and
not according to her own taste and delight. 'Although he
should kill me,' says Job,[2] 'I will trust in him.' No, my daughter,
this helplessness does not stop you from entering into yourself;
but it certainly stops you from self-complacency.

We are always wanting this and that, and although we have
our sweet Jesus resting on our heart we are not satisfied; and
yet this is all we can possibly need and desire. One thing alone
is necessary—to be near him. Now tell me, my dear daughter,
you know, don't you, that at the birth of Our Lord the
shepherds heard the angelic and divine songs of heavenly be-
ings; this is what the scriptures tell us. But nowhere does it say
that Our Lady and St. Joseph, who were closest to the child,
heard the angels' voices or saw the marvellous radiance; on the
contrary, instead of hearing the angels sing they heard the child
crying, and by the wretched light of some poor lantern they
saw the eyes of this divine boy full of tears and saw him chilled

[1] Prov. xxxi, 19.   [2] Job xiii, 13.

by the cold. Now tell me frankly, would you not rather have
been in the dark stable which was full of the baby's crying,
rather than with the shepherds, ravished with joy and gladness
by sweet heavenly music and the beauty of this marvellous
light?

Yes, indeed, says St. Peter, it is good for us to be here,[1] when
he saw the Transfiguration (and the Church is celebrating this
feast today, 6 August); but your Abbess is not there; she is there
later on Mount Calvary where she sees nothing but death,
nails, thorns, helplessness, extraordinary darkness, utter desolation and dereliction. I have said enough, my daughter, and
more than I intended on this subject which has already come up
so often between us: but not again, I entreat you. Love God
crucified in the darkness, stay near him and say: It is good for
me to be here; let us make here three tabernacles, one to Our
Lord, the other to Our Lady and the last to Saint John. Just
three crosses, and then stand by the Son's or by his mother's,
or his disciple's: you will be welcome there with the other
daughters of your order[2] who are all there with you.

Love your abjection. But what does that mean, you ask, to
love your abjection? For my understanding is darkened and
powerless for any good. Well, my daughter, it is no more than
just that. If you stay humble, still, gentle and confident in this
state of darkness and helplessness, if you don't get impatient, if
you take things calmly, if you don't let yourself be upset by all
this, but embrace this cross and stay in this darkness willingly
(I will not say happily, but I do say whole-heartedly and
firmly), then you will be loving your abjection. For what else is
it than being obscure and helpless? Love yourself in this state
for love of him who wants you to be like this, and you will be
loving your own abjection.

The Latin word for abjection implies humility, and humility
implies abjection; so that when Our Lady said: 'Because he has
regarded the humility of his handmaid,'[3] she means: 'because he
has looked graciously on my abjection and lowliness'. Nevertheless there is a difference between the virtue of humility and

---

[1] Matt. xvii, 4.   [2] The 'order' of Christian widows.   [3] Luke i, 48.

abjection, because humility is the recognition of one's own abjection. Now the high point of humility is not merely recognizing one's abjection but loving it; and this is what I have encouraged you to do.

In order to make myself clearer let me explain that there are two sorts of troubles which beset us, abject and honourable. Many put up with honourable ills, few with the abject. For example: consider a Capuchin friar all in rags and feeling the cold; everyone honours his torn habit and pities him because he is cold. But take a poor workman, a poor student, a poor widow in the same case; people jeer at them and their poverty is abject. A religious will patiently suffers a rebuke from his superior, everyone will call that mortification and obedience; a gentleman who accepts the same sort of rebuke for the love of God is called a coward; so that is an abject virtue, a despised form of suffering. Here is a man who has an ulcer on his arm, another has one on his face; the former hides it and only has to bear his affliction; the latter cannot hide it, and together with the affliction he suffers scorn and abjection. Now I say that we must love not only the affliction but also the abjection.

Moreover, there are abject virtues and honourable virtues. Among lay people patience, meekness, mortification, simplicity, are generally speaking abject virtues; almsgiving, courtesey and prudence honourable ones. There are actions which are equal in virtue, some being abject and others honourable. Giving alms and forgiving injuries are works of charity: the first is honourable, the second is abject in the eyes of the world.

I am taken ill amongst people who find this a nuisance: here we have abjection added to affliction. Young women of the world, seeing me dressed as a real widow should be dressed, say that I am putting on pious airs, and when they see me laugh, though modestly, they say that I still want to be sought after; they will not believe that I no longer want honour and rank which are not mine, and that I really love my vocation without repining: all these things are little examples of abjection; to love this sort of thing is to love one's own abjection. . . .

Nevertheless, my daughter, mark this, that even while we

love the abjection which comes of some evil, we must not stop trying to remedy the evil. I shall do what I can not to have a bad sore on my face; but if it comes, I shall love the abjection it brings. And this rule is even more important in a matter of sin. I have done wrong in this way or in that: I am grieved about it, although I willingly embrace the abjection that ensues; and if the two were separable, I should carefully keep the abjection and remove the evil and the sin. And we must not forget charity which sometimes requires us to remove the abjection for our neighbour's edification; but in that case we must only hide it from his eyes, and not from our own heart which is thereby edified. 'I have chosen,' says the prophet, 'to be abject in the house of my God, rather than to dwell in the tabernacles of sinners.'[1]

Finally, my daughter, you want to know which are the best sort of abjections. I answer such we have not chosen or which are least welcome, or, rather, those for which we have little inclination; but, to put it plainly, I mean those connected with our vocation and profession. As for example, this married woman would chose anything rather than abjection connected with the married state; that nun would obey anyone rather than her superior; and I myself would rather be rebuked by a superior in religion than by my father-in-law at home. I answer that the particular abjection laid upon each of us is the most profitable; choice takes away the better part of our merit. Who will grant us grace really to love our abjection, my dear daughter? Only he who so loved his own abjection that he was willing to die so as to preserve it. I have said enough.

Finding yourself absorbed in the hope and idea of entering religion, you are afraid of having offended against obedience. No, I did not tell you not to hope for it and think of it, but only not to linger over such thoughts and indulge in them; because quite certainly nothing so much hinders us from reaching perfection in our own vocation as longing for another. Instead of tilling the field in which we find ourselves, we send our plough and oxen elsewhere, into our neighbour's field, where of course

[1] Ps. lxxxiii, 11.

we cannot reap any harvest this year. And all this is a waste of time, and when our thoughts and hopes face in another direction it is impossible for us to set our heart steadily on the virtues required in the place in which we find ourselves. No, my daughter, Jacob never really loved Leah while he was longing for Rachel; cherish this maxim, for it is very true. But you see, I am not saying that you are not to think and hope, only that you are not to pursue such ideas or let yourself dwell on them too much. We are allowed to look towards the place which we would like to reach, but on condition that we always look straight ahead. Believe me, the Israelites could never sing in Babylon because they were thinking of their own country; and what I think is that we should be able to sing everywhere and anywhere. . . .

Keep yourself wholly resigned in Our Lord's hands, my daughter; give him the remaining years of your life, and beg him to use them for whatever kind of life is most pleasing to him. Do not allow your mind to be preoccupied with a vain promise of tranquillity, delight, merit; but hold up your heart to your spouse, completely empty of all affections other than his chaste love, and beg him to fill it purely and simply with the inclinations, desires and wishes which are in his own heart, so that like a pearl oyster your heart only conceives by the dew of heaven and not by the waters of the world; and you will see that God will help us and that we shall do well, chosing rightly and putting our ideas into effect. . . .

I cannot think of anything else to say to you about your apprehension of your particular trouble, nor of the fear of being impatient in bearing it. Did I not tell you the first time I spoke to you about your soul that you pay too much attention to what tempts or afflicts you; that you should only consider it *grosso modo*; that women, and sometimes men too, reflect too much about their troubles and that this entangles thoughts and fears and desires, which then so constrict the soul that it cannot free itself. I entreat you, my daughter, don't be afraid of God for surely he doesn't want to hurt or harm you; love him very much for he wants to do you a great deal of good. Carry on quite simply in the shelter of our resolutions and reject your reflections about your trouble as a cruel temptation.

What can I say to stop the flux of these thoughts in your heart? Do not strive to heal yourself of them, for such anxious striving would make your heart more sick. Do not struggle to overcome your temptations, for this effort would strengthen them; simply despise them and do not dwell on them. Fix your mind on Jesus crucified. What else are you looking for on earth except God? And him you have. Keep firm in your resolutions; stay in the little boat in which I have launched you; come storm, come tempest, may Jesus reign in you, and indeed you will not perish. He will be asleep, but in his own good time and place he will waken so as to restore your calm.

My dear St. Peter, as the scriptures say, seeing that the storm was raging, was afraid; and as soon as he was afraid, he began to sink and to drown, so he cried out: 'O Lord, save me.' And Our Lord caught hold of his hand and said to him: 'O thou of little faith, why didst thou doubt?'[1] Look at this holy apostle; he walks dry foot on the water, the waves and the winds could not make him sink; but fear of the wind and the waves will make him perish unless his master saves him. Fear is a greater evil than the evil itself. O daughter of little faith, what do you fear? No, do not be afraid; you are walking on the sea, surrounded by wind and water, but you are with Jesus: so what is there to fear? But if terror seizes you, cry out loudly: O Lord, save me. He will stretch forth his hand towards you; clasp it tight and go joyfully on your way.

In short, don't philosophize about your trouble, don't argue with it, just go straight on, quite simply. No, God would not allow you to be lost while you live according to our resolutions so as not to lose him. If the whole world turns topsy-turvy, if all around is darkness and smoke and din, yet God is still with us. But if we know that God lives in the darkness and on Mount Sinai which is full of smoke and surrounded with the roar of thunder and lightning, shall not all be well with us as long as we keep close to him?

[1] Matt. xiv, 31.

So live, live, my dear daughter, live wholly in God, and do not fear death. Jesus in his goodness is all ours; let us be all his. Our most honoured Lady Abbess has given him to us; let us cling to him. Courage! my daughter. I am infinitely yours, and more than yours.

Francis, Bishop of Geneva.

24

To the Présidente Brûlart

End of October 1606

Madam, my Sister,

. . . What a good father and what a very good husband you have got! Alas, they are a little jealous of their authority and dominion over you, and when you do something without their permission and sanction it seems to them that their rights have been in some sense violated. Well, you must allow them this little touch of human nature. They want to be master in their own home, and isn't this right? Of course it is, in things connected with the service you owe them; these good gentlemen are not of the opinion that one must believe what directors and spiritual doctors say about the good of the soul, nor that, saving their rights, you should seek your spiritual welfare along the lines judged right by those appointed to guide souls. But in spite of all that, you should fall in with their wishes as far as you can, put up with their ideas and modify our good plans as much as possible without altogether disregarding them. Your fitting in in this way will please Our Lord. I have told you before: the less we live according to our own taste and the less personal choice there is in our actions, the better and the more solid is our devotion. We must sometimes leave Our Lord in order to please others for love of him.

No, I cannot stop myself from telling you what I think, my dear daughter; I know that you will not take offence at anything said to you in a spirit of sincerity. Perhaps you have given your father and your husband occasion to take exception to your devotion in some way? I don't know; maybe you were too eager and fussy about it, wanting to press and force them into it in some way? If that is the case, this is surely why they are now making a stand. We must, if possible, avoid making our devotion a nuisance.

Now I shall tell you what you had better do. When you can go to communion without troubling your two superiors, do it according to your confessors' advice; when there is any risk of irritating them, be content with a spiritual communion, and believe me that inner mortification and depriving yourself of God will be extremely agreeable to God and will put him high in your heart. Sometimes you have to advance by seeming to retreat. I have often admired the extreme resignation of St. John the Baptist who stayed in the desert for such a long time quite close to Our Lord without making special efforts to see him or going to hear him and follow him. And how is it that after having seen him and baptized him he can let him go without attaching himself to Jesus in his bodily presence as his heart was so close to him? But he knew that he was serving this same Saviour by doing without his real presence. I want to make it clear to you that you will be serving God if, in order to gain the heart of these two superiors that God has set over you, you do without his real communion for a little while. And it will be a very great consolation to me to know that my advice does not make your heart in any way uneasy. Believe me, resigning and abnegating your own will will be of very great profit to you.

You are nevertheless allowed to make use of secret opportunities of going to communion; for provided that you defer to the will of these two superiors and do not court their impatience, I will not give you any other rule for your communions than that given by your confessors; they see the present state of your soul and can judge what is required for your good. The same thing goes for your daughter: let her go on longing for holy communion till Easter because she cannot receive it before without offending her father: God will reward this delay.

From what I can see, you really are practising resignation and indifference now because you cannot serve God according to your own will. I know a lady, one of the greatest souls I have ever met[1] who lived for a long time in such subjection to her husband's ideas that when she was at the height of her devotion and ardour she had to wear low-cut dresses and appear in public trapped out in vanities of all kinds. She could never go to communion (except at Easter) save in secret and without anybody knowing about it; otherwise she would have raised a terrible outcry in her household. And by this road her soul advanced very far, as I know from having often been her confessor. So mortify yourself joyfully, and in proportion as you are prevented from doing the good that you desire, do all the more ardently the good that you do not desire. You do not want that form of resignation, you would like some other form; but do what you do not want to do, for that is of more value. . . .

Keep your heart very wide open to receive all sorts of crosses and resignation and self-denial for the love of him who received so many for you. May his holy name be for ever blessed and his kingdom confirmed for ever and ever. I am in him and by him wholly yours, and more than yours, your brother and servant,

F.

25

To the Baronne de Chantal

Annecy, 20 January 1607

God who sees my heart knows that it is full of fervent wishes for your spiritual advancement, my dear daughter. I really am like those fathers who are never satisfied and can never say enough to their children to make them nobler and greater. But what am I to say to help you to be great, my dear daughter?

[1] Madame Acarie (1566–1618)' who after the death of her husband in 1613 became a Carmelite lay-sister. She was largely responsible for the introduction into France of St. Theresa's reformed Carmel. St. Francis met her in Paris in 1602. (Cf. Introduction, p. 20 and Letter 118, to Madame Acarie's daughter).

Be quite little, always, and make yourself smaller in your own eyes every day. Dear God, how very great is the greatness of this littleness! It is the real greatness of widows, but even more of bishops. Please ask for it continually on my behalf, for I need it so much.

May we be for ever attached to the cross and may a hundred thousand arrows pierce us, provided that our heart has first been pierced by the burning shaft of the love of God. May this arrow make us die that holy death which is worth more than a thousand lives. I shall go and beg this of the Archer who bears the quiver, and by the intercession of St. Sebastian whose feast-day we celebrate today. Open your heart wide, my dear daughter, and as long as the love of God is your desire, and your aim is his glory, live with joy and courage. How ardently I long for the Saviour's heart to be king of all our hearts!

I cannot write any more, and I am he whom God wanted to give to you in the way that only he knows. To him be eternal honour and glory. Amen.

Francis, Bishop of Geneva.

26

To the Baronne de Chantal

Annecy, 14 April 1607

O my very dear daughter, here we are at the end of Lent and at the time of the glorious Resurrection. How I long for us to be risen indeed with Our Lord! I am going to beg him for this, as I do every day; for I have never before applied my communions so closely to your soul as I have done this Lent, and with such a special feeling of confidence that God's goodness will be favourable to us. Yes indeed, my dear daughter, we must be full of courage.

It is all to the good that your way of bearing your domestic trials should be interpreted as dissimulation. Do you think I am exempt from attacks of this kind? But there you are, all I do is to laugh at them when I happen to think of them which is not at all often. Dear God, why do I not pay as little regard to other things and malicious suggestions as I do to personal insults and to the bad opinion others have of me? It is true that these insults are neither bitter nor numerous; but all the same, I think that even if there were many more attacks I should not get excited about them, provided the Holy Spirit helped me. Courage, my very dear and well loved daughter, for this is what we need: that the little virtue we have should be misunderstood and should disappear completely in the eyes of the world.

Good-bye, my very dear daughter, may we belong to God in time and in eternity; may we always unite our little crosses to his great cross.

Yesterday (I must just tell you this) I preached a sermon on the Passion before our Poor Clares who had asked me so insistently after the sermon I gave in town. And when I got as far as considering how Our Lord was loaded with the cross and how he embraced it, and how with his cross and in it he had knowledge of all our little crosses, taking them to himself and kissing them so as to sanctify them, I went on to say in greater detail how he kissed our dryness, our contradictions, our bitterness; and I can assure you, my dear daughter, that I was much consoled and could hardly refrain from tears. Why am I telling you this? I do not know, except that I could not stop myself telling you. This little sermon which was the source of a good deal of consolation to me was also attended by twenty-five or thirty devout people from the town apart from those in the monastery; so that I had every chance of giving free rein to my poor little thoughts on so great a subject. May our loving Jesus be for ever the king of our hearts.

I love our little Celse-Bénigne and little Françon.[1] May God be for ever their God, and may the angel who has always guided their mother bless them eternally. For indeed, my daughter, it was a great angel[2] who inspired you with your

[1] Madame de Chantal's children.
[2] 'Et vocabitur nomen ejus magni consilii Angelus', Introit, Missa in die Nativitatis Domini.

good desires; may he give you the power to carry them through and to persevere.

May Jesus reign, he who made me and keeps me for ever all yours.

Francis, Bishop of Geneva.

Saturday in Holy Week, 1607.

27

To the Baronne de Chantal

Annecy, 2 July 1607

I think you must have arrived home by now, my very dear daughter, for it is the octave day of your departure; and now I am going to see you again in this letter and in spirit, and ask you how your journey went. Did you keep well, my dear daughter? Did you not meet our Saviour on your way? For he was waiting for you everywhere. Indeed you did, I have no doubt of it. I often begged this of him, although very badly in my usual pitiable way, more especially at mass and in our night prayers when we said the litany of our dear Lady and mistress; I asked all our priests to pray for you so as to make up for my deficiency.

Yesterday, my dear daughter, I was so consoled at high mass when I heard them singing: 'He that eateth this bread shall live for ever';[1] it was often repeated. And it came into my heart, perhaps my daughter is even now eating this Bread. Thereupon a certain increase in hope for you filled my whole mind with very great sweetness. Yes, my very good daughter, we must hope with great confidence that we shall have eternal life. And what would Our Lord do with his eternal life if he did not give a share of it to poor and weak little souls?

Our good Father Bonivard left yesterday and agrees with me, infinitely approving of the choice I have made for you.[2] As for

[1] John, vi, 59.
[2] On Whit Monday, 4 June of that year, St. Francis had told Madame de Chantal for the first time about his plans for founding a congregation. This is considered the first official act leading to the foundation of the Visitation in 1610.

myself I feel it rooted ever more firmly in my soul; and because we have made up our minds after taking so much thought, praying so earnestly and making sacrifices, do not allow your heart to entertain any other desires; but blessing God for the excellence of other vocations, remain humbly in this, which is more lowly and less worthy, but more suitable to meet your need and more worthy of your littleness. Cling to this resolution quite simply, without looking either right or left.

I am in a hurry and I shall have to end this letter. I am well. I shall try to keep well and to grow in love of the service of our common Master. All you love here are well.

My dear daughter, open your heart wide and often let it rest in the arms of divine Providence. Courage! Courage! Jesus is ours; may our hearts be his for ever. He has made me yours, my dear daughter, and makes me more yours everyday, it seems to me, at least more perceptibly, more sweetly, wholly, in all things and without reserve, uniquely and inviolably yours; but yours in him and by him, to whom be honour and glory for ever and ever, and to his holy Mother. Amen.

F.

28

To the Baronne de Chantai

Thonon, 7 July 1607

How I long for your consolation, my dear daughter! Provided it is his divine Majesty's pleasure; for if he wants you on the cross, I bow to his will. And so do you, my beloved daughter, don't you? But are not God's crosses sweet and full of consolation? Yes, provided you die upon them, as our Saviour did. So let us die on our cross, my dear daughter, if need be.

Do not let us be anxious about the storms and tempests which sometimes rage in our hearts and rob us of our calm. Let us mortify our spirit utterly, and as long as our beloved faith holds firm, even if everything else comes crashing down around us, we shall yet live secure. Provided that God lives in us, what need we care if everything else dies in us. Let us go on steadily, my daughter, we are on the right road. Do not look either right or left; no, this is the best road for us. Do not let us waste time thinking how attractive the other roads look, but let us just salute those who pass along other roads, saying quite simply to them: may God guide us so that we may all meet at home.

Our resolutions grow ever firmer in my heart, you would hardly believe how firm, and how all things seem to conspire together to this end. It is a thought which fills my heart with an extraordinary sweetness, as does also the thought of the love which I bear you; for I love this love incomparably. It is strong, unswerving, boundless and unlimited, but gentle, free, completely pure, completely tranquil; in short, if I am not deceiving myself it is all in God. Why then should I not love it? But what am I saying? All the same I shall not cross out these words; they are too true and hold no danger. God who knows the secret places of my heart knows that there is nothing in this which is not for him and in accordance with him, without whom, if he gives me his grace, I do not want to mean anything to any other person, nor anyone else to mean anything to me; but in him I not only want to keep, but also nurture and increase this unique affection most tenderly. But I must confess that I did not really give my soul leave to open out like this; it escaped me. We must forgive it for this once on condition that it does not say another word on the subject.

You ask me if you spoke too often about your dear late husband. What am I to answer, dear daughter? For I do not remember. But now having thought about it, I should say that there is no danger in talking about him when the occasion arises, for this is only a due witness to your memory of him; but I think it would be better to speak of him without words and sighs pointing to a love which still clings to his bodily presence; and also, instead of saying: 'my poor late husband', I should say: 'my husband on whose soul God may have mercy';

saying these words with a feeling of love undimmed by the passing of time, but set free and purified by a greater love. I think you will see what I mean, for you always do understand my meaning.

Hold your heart firm and raised on high in God by complete trust in his holy providence, for God does not fill your heart with the idea of serving him without at the same time giving you the means to do so. Be very humble, but let it be a gentle humility and not over-eager; for one can be too eager even in trying to be humble.

Good-bye, dear daughter, I am not writing to you at leisure; my pen has moved swiftly so far, I had to go out before mass and again afterwards. Let us belong to God for ever, without end, measure, limit. Pray often for him who could not pray without making you a part of his prayers, nor desire his own salvation more than yours. Watch over your vows and resolutions, keep them safe and sheltered in the depths of your heart. And if this treasure were all that remained to us—and it most certainly will remain—we should be rich enough, with God's help. May he make me ever more firmly and completely yours. Amen. May Jesus reign!

Francis, Bishop of Geneva.

29

To the Baronne de Chantal

Thonon, 10 July 1607

Yesterday I went out on the lake[1] in a very small boat to visit the Archbishop of Vienne,[2] and I was very happy that apart from divine providence I had to depend utterly on a few narrow planks of wood. And I was also very happy to be under obedience to the boatman who made us sit still without moving, as he thought fit: and really I did not stir. But do not take

[1] The Lake of Geneva.
[2] Pierre de Villars (see Index of Correspondents).

these words to imply anything out of the ordinary in the way of courage, my daughter. These are just imaginary little virtues which serve to delight my heart; for when it comes to any real danger I am not so brave. I cannot help writing to you with great openness and simplicity of heart.

May God be with you, very dear daughter, that same God whom I adore, who has made me so uniquely, so intimately yours; may his name be blessed for ever, and the name of his holy Mother. Yesterday I also remembered St. Martha, exposed in a small boat with Mary Magdalen; God was her pilot and cast her upon our shores here in France.

Once more, may God be with you, live full of joy and trust in our dear Jesus. Amen.

30

To the Présidente Brûlart

Viuz-en-Sallaz, 20 July 1607

Madam, my very dear Sister,

I cannot refrain from writing to you at every opportunity that comes my way. Please believe me—do not be over eager; be very careful to serve God with great gentleness, for this is the right way of setting about his service. Do not want to do everything, but only something, and no doubt you will do much. Practise the mortifications which come your way most often for that is how to begin; then we shall go on to others. You should often kiss the crosses which Our Lord has himself put into your arms; do not stop to find out whether they are made of precious and fragrant wood: they are crosses all the more when they are made of vile, worthless, foul-smelling wood. It is strange how this always comes back into my mind and how this is the only song I seem to know. I am sure, my dear sister, that this is the hymn of the Lamb; it is rather sad, but harmonious and beautiful: My Father, may it be done not as I will, but as you will.[1]

[1] Cf. Matt. xxvi, 39.

Mary Magdalen is looking for Our Lord and it is him she holds; she is asking for him, and it is him she asks. She could not see him as she would have wished to see him; that is why she is not content to see him in this form and searches so as to find him in some other guise. She wanted to see him in his robes of glory and not in the lowly clothes of a gardener; but all the same, in the end she knew it was Jesus when he said to her: Mary.

You see, my dear sister and daughter, it is Our Lord in his gardener's clothes that you meet every day in one place and another when quite ordinary occasions of mortification come your way. You would like him to offer you different and more distinguished mortifications. But the ones that look best are not in fact the best. Do you not believe that he is saying: Mary, Mary? to you. No, before you see him in his glory he wants to plant many flowers in your garden; they may be small and humble, but they are the kind that please him; that is why he comes to you clothed in this way. May our hearts be for ever united to his, and our will to his good pleasure. Be of good cheer, let nothing dismay you; let us belong wholly to God, for God is ours. Amen. I am without end and most wholly, Madam, my dear Sister,

Your most humble brother and servant,
Francis, Bishop of Geneva.

31

To the Baronne de Chantal

Viuz-en-Sallaz, 24 July 1607

It was only last Sunday, the feast of Mary Magdalen, that I received both your letters at the same time, that of the 4th and of the 12th of this month. You would not believe how happy I was to have news of you, for this morning when I was praying I was specially moved to recommend you to our Saviour, who seemed most approachable and open to my entreaty at the house of Simon the Leper. But out of respect for our dear Mary Magdalen we did not dare to throw ourselves at his feet; instead we cast outselves down at the feet of his holy Mother, who was also there, if I am not mistaken. And I was very grieved that we had neither as many tears nor such sweet-smelling ointment as this holy penitent; but Our Lady was content with the few little tears we shed upon the hem of her garment, for we did not dare touch her sacred feet. One thing comforted me greatly: after the dinner was over, Our Lord put his dear convert in Our Lady's charge; and from that time onward you see her almost always together with the holy Virgin who made very much of this sinner. This filled me with great courage and I was extremely happy in that thought.

I have not the leisure to answer your letters fully but I will just make a few comments. . . . Long journeys are not good for people of your sex, nor do they edify your neighbour: on the contrary, people gossip about them, putting them down to flightiness and blaming the spiritual director. We are no longer in the times of Paula and Melania.[1] So let us have no more for the present. We shall have plenty to do putting our resolutions into effect; and these seem better to me every day, for I see more and more that they are for God's glory, and I put my hope for their realization entirely in his providence.

I wonder if you know me well? I think you do know certain aspects of me. I am not at all prudent, and it is moreover a virtue which I do not like too much. I can only force myself to love it because it is necessary, indeed very necessary; and knowing this, I go on in good faith under the protection of God's providence. No, indeed, I am not at all simple; but I am extremely fond of simplicity. To tell you the truth, helpless little white doves are much more attractive than serpents; and when we have to join the qualities of one with the other, I for my part would not like to give the dove's simplicity to the serpent, for the serpent would remain a serpent; but I should like to give the serpent's prudence to the dove, for it would still be beautiful.

[1] Celebrated for their pilgrimages to Palestine.

So much then for holy simplicity, the sister of innocence, the daughter of charity. However, the action you describe does not seem to be marked by any great duplicity, at least the inside of it does not seem to be of such bad fabric; for what were you trying to gain for yourself when you said that the count was in the habit of fasting? Offensive duplicity is when you have a good action prompted and, as it were, lined by a bad or vain intention. Well now, will you write and tell me about those duplicities which worry you most, for I think I can help you.

Dear daughter, read Chapter 28 of the *Spiritual Combat*[1] which is my well loved book and which I have carried about in my pocket for all of eighteen years and which I never reread without profit. Hold fast to what I have told you.

As to your old temptations, do not cling too much to the desire to be delivered from them; hide it from yourself that they are attacking you and do not be terrified by their assault. With God's help you will soon be delivered from them, and I shall beg this of him, but you may be sure that I shall entreat him fully resigned to his good pleasure; and my resignation will be gay and gentle. You long for God to give you peace in this matter, you say; and I long for God to give you peace in all things and do not want one of our desires to be contrary to his. And I do not want you to put your will into desiring this peace which is useless and perhaps harmful. But do not harass yourself trying to practise this commandment; for I do not want you to allow these desires or any others whatever to harass you. Don't you see, my dear daughter, that you have these desires too much at heart? As long as the spirit of faith lives in us we are very well off. You see, Our Lord will give us his peace when we resign ourselves to live humbly and quietly in a state of war.

Courage, dear daughter, keep your heart firm; Our Lord will help us and we shall belong to him and love him well. You are right not to trouble about your soul and to leave it in my care;

[1] 'Of Sensible Devotion and of Spiritual Dryness which we sometimes find in prayer" (Chapter 59 in modern editions, cf. translation by Thomas Barns, 1909, p. 275, and note p. 296).

if you go on doing this all will be well. God will be with me for all that concerns your spiritual guidance, and with his grace we shall not go astray. Believe me, my own soul is not dearer to me than yours. I have one and the same desire and the same prayers for both of us, without difference or distinction.

I am yours: Jesus wants it, and I am indeed yours.

Francis, Bishop of Geneva.

32

To a Nun

Annecy, about 20 August 1607

Your sense of spiritual coldness, my very dear daughter, should not in any way dismay you provided you have a real desire for warmth and that you do not let your coldness stop you from going on with all your usual little exercises. Tell me, dear daughter, was not our sweet Jesus born in the heart of the cold season? So why then should he not stay with us even in our coldness of heart? I mean that sort of coldness, which I think you mean, not consisting in any slackening of our good resolutions but simply in a certain weariness and heaviness of spirit making it hard for us to follow the road we have set out on, and from which we never want to stray until we have reached the harbour. Am I not right, dear daughter?

If I can, I will come for your feast day and confirm you. I pray to have some share in the spirit of the saint who gave you his name[1] when you were baptized and who will confirm it in your favour on the very day that the whole Church is celebrating him. On that day I will tell you a few of his sayings which imprinted our Saviour so deeply in the hearts of his disciples.

Meanwhile live wholly in God, and for the love he bore you, bear with your own self in all your misery. Finally, you do not always have to enjoy consolation so as to be a good servant of God or always be in a state of spiritual sweetness, without re-

[1] St. Bernard.

pugnance and aversion for doing good; for if that were so, neither St. Paula, nor St. Angela of Foligno, nor St. Catherine of Siena would have served God well. To be a servant of God means to be charitable towards one's neighbour, have an unshakable determination in the superior part of one's soul to obey the will of God, trusting in God with a very humble humility and simplicity, and to lift oneself up as often as one falls, endure oneself with all one's abjections and quietly put up with others in their imperfections.

For the rest you know I cherish you in my heart, more than you can tell, my very dear daughter. May God be our all for ever. I am, in him, all yours.

33

To the Baronne de Chantal

Sales, 2 November 1607

Is it not reasonable, dear daughter, that God's most holy will should be done, in the things we cherish as in everything else? But I must hasten to tell you that my dear mother accepted this cup[1] with Christian constancy, and her goodness, which I always esteemed highly, has gone much beyond my expectations.

On Sunday morning she sent for my brother, the Canon; and having seen the evening before that he and all my other brothers were very sad, she said to him: 'I have been dreaming all night that my daughter Jeanne is dead; please do tell me, is this true?' My brother was waiting for my arrival to tell her, for I was away on visitation; but seeing this good opportunity of giving her the bitter cup and seeing her in bed, he said: 'It is true, mother,' and that was all, for he was quite unable to say another word. 'May God's will be done,' said my dear mother, and wept freely for some time; and then, calling her maid,

---

[1] Her daughter, Jeanne de Sales, had died in Burgundy while in the charge of Madame de Chantal to whom she had been sent for her education.

Nicole: 'I want to get up,' she said, 'to go and pray in the chapel for my poor child.' And she at once did as she said. Not a word of impatience, not a moment's loss of peace; she blessed God many times and resigned herself to his will. I never saw a more tranquil grief; she shed a great many tears because of the anguish of her heart but there was no rebellion. And yet Jeanne was her dear child. Am I not right to love this mother of mine most dearly?

Yesterday, All Saints' Day, I was confessor to the whole family and with the Blessed Sacrament I sealed my mother's heart against all sadness. Meanwhile she thanks you very much indeed for the care and motherly love that you showed towards this girl, and feels as deeply obliged to you as if God had preserved her life by this means. All my brothers send you the same message; they all showed up very well, especially de Boisy,[1] whom I love all the more for it.

I know that you would like to ask me: What about yourself? How did you take it? Because you want to know what I am doing. Alas, dear daughter, I am human and no more. My heart was more grieved than I could have imagined possible; but the truth is that your grief and my mother's had a large share in this, for I feared for you both. But as to the rest, may Jesus reign! I shall always take the side of divine providence: it does all things well and disposes everything for the best. How happy is this child to have been snatched from the world so that malice cannot pervert her spirit, and to have escaped the mire without being sullied! Strawberries and cherries are picked before even the most delicious kinds of pears and apples; but that is because they are in season at a different time. Let God gather to him whatever he has planted in his garden; he takes nothing out of season.

You can imagine, dear daughter, how dearly I loved this child. I was her father in Our Lord, for I had baptized her with my own hand about fourteen years ago: she was the first being on whom I exercised my priestly office. I was her spiritual father and had high hopes of making something good of her;

---

[1] Jean-François de Sales, his brother's successor as Bishop of Geneva.

and what made her very dear to me (I am telling you the truth) is that she was in your charge. Nevertheless, dear daughter, in my heart of flesh and blood, which feels this death so keenly, I am very much aware of a certain sweet, tranquil and restful repose of my spirit in divine providence, and this makes me happy in the midst of my grief. I have described my feelings to you as best I can.

But you, my dear daughter, what do you mean by saying that you revealed yourself as you really are on this occasion? Tell me, did your compass point all through to its guiding star, to its God? What did your heart do? Did you give any scandal to those who saw you in this extremity? Answer me clearly on this point, my daughter; for you see, I did not think it right that you should offer your own life or the life of one of your own children in exchange for hers. No, dear daughter. We must not only accept God's stroke, but also be willing that he should strike wherever he sees fit; we must leave the choice to God, for it is his right. David offered his life for his son, Absalom, but that was because he was dying as a lost soul; and this is a case in which one can entreat God. But in temporal losses, my daughter, let God strike whatever chord he chooses on our lute, his harmony cannot but be good and right: Lord Jesus, may your will be done upon our father, mother, daughter, in everything and in every way, without any qualification, without an if, without a but, without any exception, without reserves. Of course I do not mean that we should not desire and pray for their preservation; but to say to God: leave this, and take that, dear daughter, that you must not do. And so with the help of his divine goodness we will not do it, will we, my daughter?

I seem to see you before me, my dear daughter, with your vigorous heart which loves and wills powerfully. I like it for that, for what is the use of these half-dead hearts? But we shall have to make a particular practice, once a week, of wanting and loving the will of God more vigorously than anything else in the world; not only in things which are bearable, but in those which are most unbearable. You will find a good deal about it in the little book which I have so often recommended to you, *The Spiritual Combat*.

To tell you the truth, my daughter, this lesson is an exalted one; but then God for whom we learn it is the Most High. You have four children; you have a father, a father-in-law, a brother whom you cherish, and also a spiritual father: all these are very dear to you, and rightly so, for God wishes it. Now if God were to deprive you of all of them, would you not still have enough in having God? Is that not everything, in your opinion? If we had nothing except God, would that not be a great deal? Alas, the Son of Man, my dear Jesus, had hardly as much as that on the cross when he had left everything for love of his Father, and in obedience to him, and was then, as it were, forsaken and left by him; and when the torrent of passions carried away his bark to the waters of desolation, he could hardly see his compass which was not only pointing towards God but inseparably united with him. Yes, he was one with his Father, but the inferior part neither knew nor felt anything at all of this: a trial which the divine Goodness had never imposed nor ever will impose on any other soul, for no other could bear it.

You see therefore, my daughter, if God were to take everything away from us, he would never take himself away as long as we did not wish it. But there is another thing, which is that all our losses and separations are only for this brief moment of earthly time. Oh indeed, we must be patient as it is only for such a little while. Perhaps I am speaking a little too freely; but there, I am following my heart which never thinks that it is saying too much to this dear daughter.

I am sending you an escutcheon to fall in with your wishes; and since you want to have the funeral service where this girl now rests, I agree to it, but let it be without great pomp, excepting whatever Christian custom rightly demands: for what is the point of anything more? Afterwards you will make an account of all these expenses and those of her illness, and send it to me, for this is my wish; and in the meanwhile we will pray to God for her soul and as fittingly as possible give her all the little honours due to her. We shall not send an official representative to the memorial mass in a month's time. No, we must not make such a to-do about a girl who never held any rank in this world, it would be ridiculous. You know me: I like simplicity both in death and in life. I should very much like to know the name and the dedication of the church where she lies. And that is all on this subject.

34

To the Baronne de Chantal

Annecy, 1 January 1608

I am so hard pressed that the only thing I have time to write to you is the great word of our salvation: JESUS. O, my daughter, if we could only for once really say this sacred name from our heart! What sweet balm would spread to all the powers of our spirit! How happy we should be, my daughter, to have only Jesus in our understanding, Jesus in our memory, Jesus in our will, Jesus in our imagination! Jesus would be everywhere in us, and we should be all in him. Let us try this, my very dear daughter; let us say this holy name often as best we can. And even if at present we can only say it haltingly, in the end we shall be able to say it as we should. But how are we to say this sacred name well? For you ask me to speak plainly to you. Alas, my daughter, I do not know; all I know is if we are to say it well our tongue must be on fire, that is, we must be saying it moved only by divine love which alone is capable of expressing Jesus in our lives and of imprinting him in the depths of our heart. But courage, my daughter, surely we will love God, for he loves us. Be happy about this and do not let your soul be troubled by anything whatever.

I am, my dear daughter, I am in this same Jesus, most absolutely yours,

Francis, Bishop of Geneva.

35

To the Baronne de Chantal

Annecy, 24 January 1608

My Daughter,

I take up my pen to write you as long a letter as I can, and with the desire really to write at length to make up for all the time during which I only seem to have written to you in a great hurry. I have received your letters of the 18, 19 and 25 November, and of the 5, 14, and 22 December of last year, none of which I have really answered, at least I doubt if I have.

In your first letter you tell me that you feel more than usually starved for holy communion. There are two kinds of hunger: one which is the result of a good digestion, the other comes of an upset stomach clamouring for food. Humble yourself as much as you can, my daughter, and warm yourself inside with the holy love of Christ crucified, so that you can spiritually digest this heavenly food as you should. And so that she who complains of hunger should get enough bread, I say to you, yes, daughter: this Lent go to communion on Wednesdays and Fridays and on Our Lady's day, besides Sundays.

But what do you think this means, digesting Jesus Christ spiritually? People who have a good digestion feel their whole body strengthened as the food distributes itself evenly to every part of them. In the same way, my daughter, people who have a good spiritual digestion feel that Jesus Christ who is their food penetrates to every part of their soul and of their body and communicates himself to them. They have Jesus Christ in their head, heart, breast, eyes, hands, tongue, ears and feet. But what does our Saviour do in them? He straightens everything out, purifying, mortifying, quickening all things. He loves in our heart, understands in our head, inspires our actions within us, he sees in our eyes, he speaks with our tongue, and so with all the rest: he does everything in us, and then we live, not we

K   145

ourselves, but Jesus Christ lives in us. O when will that be, my dear daughter? When, O God? But in the meanwhile I am showing you what to aim at even though we must be content to get there gradually. Let us stay humble and go to communion trustfully; little by little our faculty of spiritual digestion will get accustomed to this food and will learn to assimilate it as it should. It is a great matter, my daughter, to confine ourselves to eating one dish only when it is a good one; the stomach can do its job more easily. If we only long for our Saviour, then I have every hope that our digestion will be good.

I had not thought of saying so much to you on this first point, but I am easily carried away when I am writing to you. And then I shall soon be going to this divine feast with you, for it is Thursday, and this is the day on which we keep close together, and when, as I see it, our hearts are joined by means of this holy sacrament. . . .

I should very much like to say a word to you about loving God's will, for I see that you are making a special point or exercise of it during your time of prayer, and this is not what I meant; for you should not tie yourself down to any special point in prayer. But when you are going for a walk on your own, or elsewhere, consider God's will in general, by which he wills all the works of his mercy and his justice in heaven, on earth, under the earth; and then with deep humility approve, praise and love this sovereign will which is holy, just and beautiful. Consider God's will in particular, by which he loves his own and consoles or afflicts them in various ways. And you should dwell on this for some time, considering the variety of consolations but especially of tribulations which are the lot of the upright; then with great humility approve, praise and love every aspect of his will.

Consider his will as it is manifest in your own case, in everything good and bad that can happen to you, apart from sin; then approve, praise and love all this, protesting that you want to honour, cherish and adore this sovereign will for ever, giving up yourself and all who belong to you (and I am one of them) to his mercy. Finally, end with a great act of confidence in God's will, knowing that it will do all things well for us and for our happiness.

I have said nearly all I wanted to say, but I will add that having done this exercise in this way two or three times, you can shorten it, vary it and adapt it as you think fit, for you should imprint it in your heart by making frequent aspirations. . . .

And now, God be with you, my very dear and much beloved daughter, may we belong to God for ever. I am wholly yours in him.

F.

May Jesus reign! Amen.

36

To a Lady[1]

1605–8

Some time ago I received a letter from you which I hold very dear because it shows that you trust in my affection for you, which is indeed and without a doubt wholly yours. I only regret that I hardly know how to reply to what you ask me about your difficulties in prayer. Also I know that you are in a place and among people where you can lack nothing on this subject; but charity which rejoices in interchange prompts you to ask for my views by giving me yours. So I shall say something to you.

Your anxiety in prayer together with your great eagerness to find some object to content your mind and in which it can rest, is in itself enough to stop you from finding what you seek. Your hand and eye will pass over a thing a hundred times without perceiving it when you are hunting for it too strenuously.

The only result of such vain and useless eagerness is weari-

[1] Probably Mademoiselle de Soulfour, who later entered the Carmel at the rue Saint-Jacques in Paris. Cf. Letters 1 and 2.

ness of mind, and hence your soul's coldness and numbness. I do not know what remedies you should apply, but I am inclined to think that if you could prevent this bustling eagerness you would gain a great deal; for it is one of the greatest traitors encountered by devotion and true virtue. It pretends to kindle us for our profit but all it does is to chill our fervour, only making us run so as to trip us up. That is why we must beware of it at all times but more especially during prayer.

And to help you in this, remember that the graces and benefits of prayer are not earthly waters but come from heaven, and that therefore all our efforts cannot acquire them, although it is true that we must dispose ourselves to receive them with great care but humbly and peacefully. We must hold our hearts open towards heaven and wait for the heavenly dew to fall. And never forget to carry this thought with you to your prayer: that in prayer we approach God and put ourselves in his presence for two main reasons.

The first is to render to God the honour and homage which we owe him, and this can be done without him speaking to us or ourselves speaking to him; for this duty is absolved in that we acknowledge him to be our God and ourselves his lowly creatures, and in that we stay before him, casting ourselves down before him in our hearts and awaiting his commands. How many courtiers are there who seek the king's presence over and over again, not to speak to him or to hear him speak, but simply to be seen by him and to signify by this regular attendance that they are his servants? And this aim in presenting ourselves before God, just so as to signify and protest our willingness and gratitude in his service, is very excellent, very holy and very pure, and therefore a thing of great perfection.

The second reason for which we present ourselves before God is to speak to him and to hear him speak to us by inspirations and inner stirrings of the heart; and usually this is associated with delight and pleasure, because it is of very great benefit for us to speak to so great a lord, and when he answers he pours out balm and much precious ointment to fill the soul with sweetness.

And now my dear daughter (since that is how you wish me to address you), your prayer cannot be without either one or other of these two benefits. If we can talk to Our Lord, let us talk to him, praise him, pray to him, listen to him. If we cannot speak because our voice fails us, let us nevertheless stay in his court-room and bow down before him; he will see us there, he will graciously accept our patience and look favourably upon our silence. Another time we shall be much astonished when he takes us by the hand, talks about one thing and another, and walks up and down with us in the path of his garden of prayer; and even if he never does this, let us be content with the fact that it is our duty to be in his suite and that it is a great grace for us and a still greater honour that he should allow us to be in his presence. In this way we shall not be over-eager to speak to him, because this other way of being near him is no less useful to us; indeed, perhaps more useful, although it may be a little less agreeable to our taste.

So when you come before Our Lord, speak to him if you can; if you cannot, stay there, show yourself and do not strive eagerly to do anything else. This is my advice; I do not know if it will work, but I am not worried about it; for, as I said to you, you are in a place where you cannot help getting advice that is far better than mine.

As to the fear you have that your father might make you lose your desire to be a Carmelite by making you wait too long before carrying out your wish, just say to God: 'Thou, Lord, knowest all my longings'[1] and let him do his will; he will influence your father's heart and will shape it to his glory and to your profit. In the meanwhile foster your good desire and see that the spark of it lives on beneath the ashes of humility and resignation to the will of God.

You ask for my prayers and you have them, for I could not forget you, especially at holy mass. I trust in your charity so that I may not be forgotten in your prayers either.

[1] Ps. xxvii, 10.

149

37

To Madame de la Fléchère

Annecy, April or May, 1608

I have been much consoled by the letters you have written to me and by seeing that Our Lord has let you taste the beginnings of that tranquillity with which, by the help of his grace, we must from now on continue to serve him in the rush and variety of business forced on us by our vocation. I have very great hopes for you because I think I have seen your heart firmly resolved to serve his divine Majesty and this makes me sure that you will be faithful in the exercises of devotion. And if it happens that you often fail because of infirmity you must not be in any way put out; but while hating the offence towards God, you must also cultivate a certain joyful humility which helps you to make a point of seeing and recognizing your misery.

I will tell you briefly what exercises I advise for you; you will see them set out more fully in something else that I wrote.[1] Preparation for the whole day which is done briefly in the morning, mental prayer before dinner, which can take an hour or thereabouts according to your leisure; in the evening, before supper, a short time of recollection during which by way of repetition you will make a few heart-felt aspirations to God on your morning meditation, or some other subject.

During the day and amidst your work, examine yourself as often as you can to see whether your love is not too far engaged in what you are doing, or in some way out of order, and whether your hand is still clasped in that of Our Lord. If you find yourself harassed beyond measure, calm and quieten your spirit. Imagine how Our Lady calmly used one hand to do what needed doing while she held her Child with her other hand or on her other arm, for she held him most carefully.

[1] Instructions drawn up in 1604 for the ladies at Dijon. Cf. A. XXVI, p. 165 ff.

In times of peace and tranquillity make many acts of meekness, for in this way you will tame your heart and train it to gentleness. Do not stop to fight the small temptations which come your way by contesting them or disputing with them, but simply by turning your heart back to Jesus Christ crucified, as though kissing his side or his feet because you love him.

Do not force yourself to much vocal prayer; and when you are praying and feel your heart carried towards mental prayer, always let it follow this attraction freely. And if you were to use mental prayer only, together with the Lord's prayer, the Hail Mary and the creed, that would do perfectly well.

I dedicate myself whole-heartedly to the service of your soul which will henceforward be as dear to me as my own. May Our Lord rule for ever, and I am in him your servant,

Francis, Bishop of Geneva.

38

To Madame de la Fléchère

Annecy, 19 May 1608

I remember your telling me how the manifold variety of the things you have to do presses on you; and I told you that this was a real and solid way of acquiring virtue. To have to see to a great variety of things is really a continual martyrdom; for in the same way as those who make a journey in the summer find the flies more troublesome and irritating than the journey itself, so the fact that one has to attend to a great many different sorts of things is in itself more troublesome than the actual load of business.

You need patience, and God will give it to you, I hope, if you make a special point of asking him, and if you make yourself practise it faithfully, preparing yourself for this every morning by particularly applying some point of your meditation to it and making up your mind firmly to keep patient all day every time you feel yourself slipping.

Do not lose any opportunity, however small, of showing sweetness of temper towards everyone. Do not trust in your industry to carry you successfully through all your affairs but only in God's help; and then rest securely in his care of you, believing that he will do what is best for you, providing that you for your part work diligently and yet without straining. Without straining and gently, I say, for violent effort spoils both your heart and the business in hand, and is not really diligence but rather over-eagerness and agitation.

How soon, Madam, we shall be in the realm of eternity! And then we shall see how little all the affairs of this world amount to and how little it mattered whether they did or did not succeed; but all the same, now we pursue them as though they were great things. When we were small, how eagerly we put together little bits of tiles and wood and mud to make houses and tiny buildings! And if someone smashed them, how very miserable we were and how we wept; but now we see how very unimportant it all was. One day we shall experience the same thing in heaven when we see that what we clung to in this world was nothing more than a child's fancy.

I do not want to take away the care which ought to go into all these little tricks and trifles, for God wants us to practise on them in this world, but I do want to take away the ardour and warmth which goes into our caring. Let us carry on with our childish pursuits since we are children, but do not let us take them too seriously. And if someone smashes our little houses and plans, let us not get too agitated, for here too, when evening comes and it is time for us to go to bed, I mean when death comes, all these little houses will be useless: we shall have to leave them and go into our father's house. See to your affairs faithfully, but be conscious all the time that the affair which matters most is that of your salvation and that of directing your soul's salvation into the way of true devotion.

Be patient with everyone but especially with yourself; I mean that you should not be troubled about your imperfections and that you should always have courage to pick yourself up afterwards. I am very glad to hear that you start all over again every day: there is no better way of getting there in the end in the spiritual life than always starting all over again and never thinking that you have done enough.

Recommend me to God's mercy and I pray that this same mercy may make you abound in his holy love.

Your most humble servant,

Francis, Bishop of Geneva.

39

To Madame de la Fléchère

Annecy, 28 May 1608

Madam,

Yes, of course; when you think it will afford you consolation to write to me I should very much like you to do so with all confidence.

We must learn to combine two things: great desire to practise our exercises faithfully and well in what concerns prayer and the virtues, and not being in any way disturbed or troubled or dismayed if we happen to fail; for the first point depends on our fidelity, which should always be complete and should grow from hour to hour; the second depends on our infirmity which we shall never shed during our life here on earth.

My very dear daughter, when we commit a fault, we should examine our heart at once and ask if it has kept intact its resolution of serving God; and I hope it will answer yes, and that it would rather die a hundred deaths than give up this resolution. Then say to your heart: then why are you faltering now? Why are you such a coward? It will answer: I was taken by surprise and I don't know how it happened, but I feel so heavy and clumsy now.

Alas, my dear daughter, you must forgive your heart; it has not fallen because it is unfaithful but because it is infirm. So you must correct it gently and peacefully and not make it any angrier or more upset. We ought to speak to it and say, Come

153

now, my heart, come my friend, in the name of God, be of good cheer; let us go on our way, stepping carefully, let us look on high to him who is our help and our God. Alas! dear daughter, we must be charitable in dealing with our soul, and not treat it roughly while we see that it is not offending wilfully. And this, you see, is an exercise in which we practise humility.

Whatever we do towards our salvation is done in God's service, for what did Our Lord himself do here on earth except work our salvation? Do not go out of your way to desire warfare but be bravely prepared for it when it comes.

May Our Lord be your strength. I am in him,

Your very affectionate servant,

Francis, Bishop of Geneva.

28 May, in haste.

40

To Madame de la Fléchère

Annecy, 16 July 1608

The most important thing of all is to make sure of having tranquillity, not because it is the mother of contentment but because it is the daughter of the love of God and of our own will's resignation. Occasions for practising tranquillity come our way every day; for we never lack contradictions, wherever we may be; and when there is no one to contradict us we inflict contrariness on ourselves. O my dear daughter, how holy and pleasing we should be to God if we really knew how to use the occasions for mortifying ourselves which our vocation provides, for they are certainly greater than among religious; the trouble is that we do not make proper use of them as they do.

Look after yourself very carefully while you are pregnant; do not be in the least anxious about keeping yourself to any sort of spiritual exercise, except in a most gentle way. If you get tired of kneeling, sit down; if you have not sufficient concentration to pray for half an hour, then make it a quarter of an hour or even half of that.

I ask you to put yourself in the presence of God and to suffer what pain you have before him. Do not impose force on yourself not to complain, but I would like you to complain to God in a spirit of dependence, as a tender child would speak to its mother; for provided you do it lovingly, there is no danger in complaining, nor in asking to be healed, nor in changing one's position and allowing oneself to be helped and relieved. Only do this with love and resignation in the arms of God's good will.

Do not worry because you are unable to perform acts of virtue as you would like to; for as I have told you, they do not cease to be good even if they are done apathetically and dully and are, as it were, forced. You can only give God what you have got, and in this difficult time you have nothing else to offer. At a time like this, dear daughter, your beloved is as a bundle of myrrh to you; go on pressing him to your heart. 'My Beloved is mine and I am his';[1] he will always be in my heart. Isaias calls him the Man of Sorrows; he loves sorrows and those who suffer. Do not struggle to do a great deal, but dispose yourself to meet your suffering with love.

May God look upon you with favour, Madam, and grant you the more retired kind of life of which you speak. Whether we are ill, or live or die, we belong to God, and nothing will separate us from his holy love, if his grace is with us. Our heart will never have any life except in him and for him, he will be the God of our heart for ever. I shall not cease to beseech this of him, nor to be entirely in him,

Your very affectionate servant,

Francis, Bishop of Geneva.

[1] Canticle ii, 16.

41

To Mademoiselle Clément

October 1608

Mademoiselle,

You should resign yourself entirely into God's hands, and when you have made your small contribution towards putting your plan into effect, God will be very pleased with all you do, even if it is much less than you would yourself wish to do. In short, you should go ahead with your plans very bravely since God has given you such a great desire to become a nun.

But if after all your efforts you do not succeed, you could do nothing more pleasing to God than sacrifice your will to him and live in peace, humility and devotion, complying with all your heart with his divine will and good pleasure; and you will not be left in any doubt about this if after you yourself have done all you possibly can, your hopes still remain unfulfilled. For God sometimes tests our courage and love by depriving us of things which seem, and indeed are, very good for the soul; and if he sees us ardent in pursuing an end of this kind and yet humble, peaceful and resigned in doing without the thing we desire, he gives us greater blessings in doing without the desired object than we would have had, had we attained it; for at all times and in all places God loves those who can say to him whole-heartedly and simply, on all occasions and whatever may happen: Thy will be done.

Francis, Bishop of Geneva.

42

To the Baronne de Chantal

Annecy, 28 October 1608

I cannot reply now, dear daughter, to your letter of the seventh of this month which I received late last night; for I am just setting off to say mass and I have to visit a church some distance away. I will say what I can.

My daughter, I am full of vanity, and yet I do not esteem myself as much as you do. I wish you knew me well; you would not cease to have absolute confidence in me but you would have no esteem. You would say: this person is a reed on which Our Lord wants me to lean; I feel quite safe because it is God's will, but all the same, the reed is worthless.

Yesterday after reading your letter I walked up and down in my room and my eyes filled with tears at the thought of what I am and of what people take me to be. I see how highly you esteem me and that this esteem is a source of great happiness to you: but what you are really doing, my daughter, is to set up an idol in your heart. Do not let this depress you, for God is not offended by sins of the intellect and understanding, although we should guard against them if possible. Your strong affections will calm down gradually day by day if you make frequent acts of indifference. Have another look at the letter which I wrote to you at the beginning, about liberty of spirit.[1]

God be with you, my very dear daughter. I am he whom God makes ever more yours,

Francis, Bishop of Geneva.

43

To the Baronne de Chantel

1605–8[2]

Whatever time we decide to give God in prayer, let us give it to him with our thoughts free and disentangled from everything else, resolving never to take this time away from him

[1] Letter 7.
[2] Fragments from certain letters of St. Francis copied by Madame de Chantal in her notebook, 'Le petit livret'; cf. Oeuvres, vol. II.

again, whatever toil comes our way. Let us treat this time as something which no longer belongs to us; and even if you just spend the time acutely aware of your insufficiency, do not let it upset you, even rejoice in it, thinking that you are a very good object for God's mercy.

Often ask yourself whether you can really say in all truth: 'My beloved is mine and I am his.'[1] See whether there is not some part or faculty of your soul or some sense in your body which does not belong wholly to God; and having discovered it, take it, wherever it may be, and give it back to him, for you are all his, and everything that is in you is his. Our Lord does not want you to think either about your progress or about your improvement in any way whatever; but to receive and use faithfully the occasions of serving him and of practising the virtues at every moment, without any reflection either on the past or on the future. Each present moment should bring its task, and the only thing we have to do as we turn towards God is to abandon ourselves utterly to him and long for him to destroy everything in us that opposes his plans.

People should love the virtues which accord with their vocation and are suitable to their state. A widow's virtues are humility, despising the world and herself, simplicity. She should exercise herself in loving her abjection, serving the poor and the sick; her place is at the foot of the cross; her rank is to be the very last of all; her glory is to be despised; her crown should be her neediness: all these are little virtues. For as to matters like ecstasies, insensibilities, divine union, elevations, transformations and so on, and considering it a distraction to serve Our Lord in his humanity and in his members, and spending all one's time in the contemplation of the Divine Essence— we must leave all that to exceptional souls who are far advanced and worthy of it. We ourselves do not deserve such a high rank in God's service; we must first of all serve him in lowly offices before being drawn into the inner sanctuary.

[1] Canticle, ii, 16.

Look at your Abbess in all the circumstances of her life. In her room at Nazareth she shows her modesty in that she is afraid, her candour in wanting to be instructed and in asking a question, her submission, her humility in calling herself a handmaid. Look at her in Bethlehem: she lives simply and in poverty, she listens to the shepherds as though they were learned doctors. Look at her in the company of the kings: she does not try to make any long speeches. Look at her at the time of her purification: she goes to the temple in order to conform to church customs. In going to Egypt and in returning she is simply obeying Joseph. She does not consider she is wasting time when she goes to visit her cousin Elizabeth as an act of loving courtesy. She looks for Our Lord not only in joy but also in tears. She has compassion on the poverty and confusion of those who invited her to the wedding, meeting their needs. She is at the foot of the cross, full of humility, lowliness, virtue, never drawing any attention to herself in the exercise of these qualities.

God rewards his servants according to the dignity of the office they exercise. I do not say that we may not aspire to these outstanding virtues, but I say that we must train ourselves in the little virtues without which the great ones are often false and deceptive. Let us learn to suffer humiliating words gladly, and whatever leads to the disparagement of our opinions and ideas; after that let us learn to suffer martyrdom, to annihilate ourselves in God and to hold all things as nothing. David first of all learnt how to hunt animals and afterwards how to defeat armies. We know what Abraham's servant did in order to see whether Rebecca was fit to be the wife of his master's son: he asked her for a drink of water, to see whether she would give it willingly, and also to his camels. A little courtesy, a humble virtue, but the sign of a much greater one.

I do not exclude the upraising of your soul, mental prayer and interior conversation with God, a constant lifting up of your heart towards Our Lord; but do you know what I mean, my daughter? I mean that you should be like the valiant woman of whom the Wise Man says: 'She hath put out her hand to strong things: and her fingers have taken hold of the spindle.'[1] Meditate, lift up your mind and let it rise up to God, that is to say, draw God into your mind: those are the strong things. But with all that, do not forget your distaff and your spindle: spin the thread of little virtues, do humble works of charity. Anyone who tells you differently is making a mistake and is himself deceived.

Leave the care of your other desires to me, I will keep them very carefully for you; have no anxiety about them, because I may never even give them back to you, as it may not be expedient; but have confidence that I shall not make bad use of them. I must render an account of them to God and I hold myself responsible for them.

Go straight on, and always in God's sight. God takes pleasure in seeing you make your little steps; and like a good father who holds his child by the hand, he will conform his steps to yours and will be quite happy not to go any faster than you. What are you anxious about? Whether you are taking this road or that other way, going fast or slow? All that matters is that he is with you, and you with him.

Never argue with the enemy or give him any quarter whatsoever when he suggests things to you which are against faith, chastity, vowed obedience or against your resolution to aim at perfection. Your heart is impregnable, and these are the things on which its strength is founded. What need is there to argue? No, not a single word is to be said in answer, unless the words of Our Lord: 'Get thee behind me, Satan, thou shalt not tempt the Lord thy God.'[2]

Go on your way with joy, my daughter, with very great confidence in the mercy of your Spouse, and believe that he will lead you aright; but leave it to him.

The practice of the presence of God taught by Mother Theresa in chapters 29 and 30 of *The Way of Perfection*[3] is excel-

[1] Prov. xxi, 19.
[2] Matt. iv, 7, 10; Luke iv, 12.
[3] Cf. Complete Works, translated by E. Allison Peers, vol. II, p. 121.

lent, and I think it amounts to the same as I explained to you when I wrote that God was in our spirit as though he were the heart of our spirit, and in our heart as the spirit which breathes life into it, and that David called God: the God of his heart.[1] Use this boldly and often for it is most useful. May God be the soul and spirit of our heart for ever, my very dear daughter! Courage!

44

To Madame de la Fléchère

Annecy, February 1609

I am sending back your book[2] with corrections, my very dear daughter: may it be as useful to you as I hope and wish! Undoubtedly we must resolve over and over again to unite ourselves to God if we are to remain faithful. But I do not wish you, in your fervour, to desire temptations and occasions of mortifying yourself; for as, by the grace of God, they are not lacking in your life, you need not desire them explicitly in your heart. You should rather occupy yourself in preparing your heart and putting it into the right disposition for receiving and accepting things of this kind, not when you want them, but when God thinks fit to send them.

There is no harm in rejoicing a little in divine grace when things turn out as we want them to, provided we carry on and finish what we are doing in a spirit of humility. It is permissible to try and remedy things which do not concern you personally but do concern your household and family, but you should resign yourself to await with an even heart whatever God ordains. You should in every way possible avoid complaining about your misery and misfortune; for apart from the fact that this ill becomes a servant of God, it points to a heart which is too

[1] Cf. Ps. 72, v. 26.
[2] *Introduction to the Devout Life*, the first edition of which appeared at the end of 1608 or the beginning of 1609.

downcast, and is really more the result of rebellion than of a lack of patience.

Come, my dear daughter, you must make a particular exercise of gentle acquiescence in God's will, not only with regard to extraordinary events but chiefly in those little everyday deceptions. Prepare yourself for this in the morning, after dinner when you are saying grace, before and after supper in the evening, and render yourself a strict account of it for a time. But do it with a tranquil and glad heart, and if you happen to fail, humble yourself and begin all over again.

It is a good thing to aim in a general way at the greatest perfection of Christian life but we should not philosophize about it in detail, unless to consider how we may amend ourselves and advance in the course of the ordinary, everyday happenings of our life; and from one day to the next we should entrust our general wish for perfection to God's providence; and as we look to him for this, we should cast ourselves into God's arms like a little child who in order to grow, simply eats what its father provides day by day, hoping that he will provide according to its appetite and need.

As for your temptations to envy, put into practice what I say about this in the book.[1] As holy communion is so profitable to you, go often with a fervent spirit and a pure conscience. Go on your way joyfully in spite of all your temptations. Do no other penance at present, and only punish yourself in a gentle way by putting up with your neighbour in a spirit of charity, visiting the sick; and be of good cheer. . . .

Good night, Madam, my very dear friend and daughter; your heart belongs to God, be happy that you are so well housed in him. I am with all my heart,

Your very faithful servant and friend,
Francis, Bishop of Geneva.

I will pray for my God-daughter.[2]

---

[1] *Introduction to the Devout Life* (1st edition, Part II, ch. 45, 52).
[2] Françoise-Innocente, Madame de la Fléchère's daughter.

45

To Monseigneur Pierre de Villars, Archbishop of Vienne

Annecy, about 15 February 1609

Monseigneur,

On the eighth of this month I received the letter you were kind enough to write to me on the twenty-fifth of the previous month, and I assure you that it is a long time since anything afforded me such great joy and honour; for my soul which has always revered yours with profound respect longed to find a worthy way to your favour by some such happy chance. But how could I entertain any hope of this, seeing that I am nailed and fixed to the spot among these mountains, and so unworthy of your consideration? And now in spite of all, God has been pleased to afford me this consolation for which I most humbly thank his goodness and feel obliged to you in acting with such condescension. In this way my poor little book[1] has borne great fruit, which indeed I did not expect; but on this sole account more than for any other fruit it has as yet borne, I will love and cherish it henceforth.

You will not have failed to notice, Monseigneur, that this work was not done according to a plan thought out beforehand. It is a collection of notes which I had drawn up for a lady who asked for my direction; and it was done during the busy time of Lent when I was preaching twice a week. She showed the notes to Fr. Fourier, at that time rector of the College of Chambéry and now of that at Avignon, whom she knew to be my great friend and to whom I myself often rendered account of my actions. It was he who urged me so strongly to have these notes published, that after having hastily looked through them and put them in order by means of a few little rearrangements, I sent the work to the printer: that is why it appeared before you in such poor shape. But since you favour it with your approba-

---

[1] *Introduction to the Devout Life.*

tion as it is, I am planning—if it is ever reprinted—to put it into better shape and expand it by certain additions which will, in my opinion, make it more useful for the public and less unworthy of the favour which you have shown it.

And since you exhort me, Monseigneur, to continue setting down whatever God prompts me to write for the edification of his Church, I should like to talk to you freely and openly about my intentions in this respect. There can be no doubt that I lack everything for undertaking works of great size and considerable scope, for I really have not the necessary mental equipment. And perhaps no bishop for a hundred miles around has to cope with such a tangled mass of affairs as I do; I am in a place where I have no access to books and to the personal contacts necessary for such a task. That is why, leaving great plans to great workmen, I have conceived the idea of certain small works less hard to write and nevertheless quite suited to the conditions of my life, a life which is dedicated and even consecrated to the service of my neighbour for the glory of God. I will tell you briefly what form these works are to take.

I am planning to write a little book on *The Love of God*, not to treat the matter theoretically but in order to show the practice of it by the keeping of the commandments of the first table. This book is to be followed by another which is to show the practice of the same divine love in the following of the commandments of the second table, and the two together will be combined in one volume of about the right size, and easy to handle. I am also thinking of bringing out one day a little calendar or day-by-day book for the guidance of devout souls, in which I will outline holy occupations for every week of the year for Philothea.

Besides that I have some material for introducing beginners to the exercise of evangelical preaching which I would like to follow up with a methodical study for the conversion of heretics by holy preaching. In this last book I should like to demolish, by way of a practical method, all the most obvious and celebrated arguments of our adversaries, and that not only in a style that will instruct, but also move, so that the book will not

only serve for the consolation of Catholics but for the conversion of heretics; and I intend to use towards this end some
meditations I composed during my five years in the Chablais[1]
where the only books I had to help me in my preaching were
the Bible and those of the great Bellarmine.

This, Monseigneur, is what my modest zeal prompts me to
do; and as this zeal is indeed not *secundum scientiam*,[2] time, my
scant leisure, the knowledge of my lack of capacity will all
serve to modify it; although, to tell you the truth, your
authority has considerably stimulated me by the favourable
opinion you have given me of this first little book, about which,
as I must also tell you, our Lord Bishop of Montpellier has
written to me.

He drew my attention to the fact that it is too hurried and
condensed in certain places, and that I do not state my opinions
in sufficient detail. In this I see he is certainly right; but as I only
compiled this work for a person I often saw, I wrote briefly
because I had the opportunity of expanding my remarks by
word of mouth. The other thing he says is that considering this
is a simple and first introduction, I take my Philothea too far;
and that happened because the soul I was dealing with was already very virtuous, although she had had no taste as yet of the
devout life; that is why she advanced very rapidly in a short time.

Now I can easily remedy both these faults if ever the *Introduction* is reprinted, for in order to end where I began, the
honour afforded to me by this book because it has opened up
the way to your friendship, and your opinion that it will be
profitable to souls, will be a reason for my loving it and doing
it all the good I possibly can.

But what will you say about me, Monseigneur, seeing me reveal my heart to you so freely and with so much *naiveté* and
confidence, as if I had really deserved the welcome you gave my
work and the access to you that this affords? This is what I am
like, Monseigneur, and your saintly charity gives me free trust-
fulness, and moreover makes me beg you by the mercy of our
common goal and Saviour to go on extending your kindness to

---

[1] *Controversies*, A.I.   [2] Romans x, 2.

me as you are now doing, not only imparting the sweetness of your spirit to me, but also censuring me and drawing my attention to faults in every way that your love and zeal prompt you to do. I promise you that you will encounter a heart which is capable of receiving such favours, though unworthy of them.

May God preserve you for a long time and prosper you in his grace, according to the wish of,

Your very humble and very obedient servant,
Francis, Bishop of Geneva.

46

To Madame de la Fléchère

Annecy, March 1609

I have received your two letters, dear daughter, and it is quite clear to me that your difficulty was a confusion set up in your mind by two desires which were not satisfied: one was the desire to serve God on the occasion which offered; the other, the desire to know if you had done your duty faithfully. And in each instance you were over-eager, which led to disturbance and anxiety and finally to confusion. Now there is no doubt that you really did do your duty. You are always inclined to be a little hard on yourself and this made you feel that what you had done was very little, and at the same time you were most anxious to satisfy your obligation; not being able to make absolutely sure of this you gave way to sadness and discouragement, or weariness.

Well now, my dear daughter, you must forget all that and be quite happy again, humbling yourself deeply before Our Lord and remembering that your sex and your state of life do not allow you to prevent the evil that is going on outside your own home, except by making people want to do what is right by your good example; also by simple, humble and charitable admonishment of the offenders, and by informing superiors when this is feasible; which is what I told you once before. And

I will add to this as a general reflection that when we cannot properly distinguish whether we have really done our duty as we should in some instance, and are wondering whether we have offended God, we must humble ourselves, beg God to forgive us and ask for more light on another occasion, completely forget what has happened and go on our way as usual; for curious and eager research into whether we have done right or not undoubtedly springs from self-love which makes us want to know for sure whether we are worth anything, whereas a pure love of God prompts us to say to ourselves: beggar and coward that you are, humble yourself and put your trust in God's mercy, ask forgiveness in any case; and promising God yet again that you will be faithful, just carry straight on.

I approve of not sleeping one's fill, except if one happens to be in need of rest; but so that this may not be harmful we must take some exercise instead of the sleep so as to dissipate the humours that sleep has left unused. So you can cut out an hour's sleep in the morning, not at night, and I think you will be all the better for it. As for other austerities, do nothing out of the ordinary, for your constitution and your state of life preclude this; nor do I approve of a long retreat for the present, for in order to acquire virtues it is better to exercise them amidst the ordinary contradictions of life; and we must not let them discourage us, but have recourse to constant preparation so as to take them as we should.

May God always be our only love and our whole desire, my dear daughter, and I am in him all yours.

Francis, Bishop of Geneva.

47

To the Baronne de Chantal

Baume-les-Dames, 16 November 1609

My dear daughter,

It gives me quite special consolation to talk to you in this dumb language when I have had to talk to so many other people the whole day long by word of mouth. And I want to tell you what I am doing, for that is practically all I can manage, and even then I hardly know what I am supposed to be doing!

I have just been praying, and on asking myself why we have come into this world, I understood that we are only here to receive and to carry our sweet Jesus: on our tongue, in telling people about him; in our arms, in doing good works; on our shoulders, in carrying his yoke, the dryness and sterility he sends, and thus in our interior and exterior senses. O blessed are they who carry him gently and with constancy! I have really carried him on my tongue all these days, and I carried him into Egypt, it seems to me, because in the sacrament of confession I heard a great number of penitents who approached me with great confidence so as to receive him into their sinful souls. O may God deign to keep him in their hearts!

I have also been learning a practice of the presence of God which for the time being I have locked in a corner of my memory so as to tell you about it as soon as I have read the treatise on it by Fr. Arias.[1]

Be great-hearted, my dear daughter, and open out your heart to receive the will of God. Do you know what I say as I spread out your corporal for the consecration? Thus may the heart of her who sent me this be opened out to the sacred influence of the Saviour's will. Courage, my daughter, keep very close to your holy Abbess and entreat her over and over again that we may live, die and rise again in the love of her dear Child.

May Jesus reign, he who has made me all yours, and more than I can say. May the peace of our sweet Jesus reign in your heart.

Francis, Bishop of Geneva.

[1] *Exercise of the Presence of God.* Valladolid, 1593.

48

To Madame de Boisy, his Mother

Annecy, 29 November 1609

Madam, my dear Mother,

I was much consoled by the news my young brother brought me of the improvement in your health, but nevertheless I still agree with my cousin Chaudens that Sieur Marcofredo should be consulted about your health, either by his visit to Sales or by you yourself going to Geneva for three or four days; but in this latter case you should make the journey soon, so as to get it over before the severe cold sets in.

If my brother had also been able to give me as much information about your state of mind, my consolation would have been greater; but all he was able to say was that you were fairly cheerful and sometimes sad, and that you did not want to have new shoes made, as you thought that you would not live long enough to wear them out. Well, there is no great harm in all that; and yet I wish that you could gradually shed little ideas of this kind and cast them off, because they are utterly useless and unfruitful, and moreover they take the place which should be occupied by other and better thoughts agreeable to Our Lord. You must let your mind launch out more and be more at ease with Our Lord, and not burden him with these little emotions and ideas, living as one who is free, leaving to Our Lord's providence and good pleasure what may become of you.

But with your permission I will speak frankly to you. You must not, my dear Mother, continue to dwell on certain considerations which serve no useful purpose and are of too little value to occupy the mind; and having ordered your affairs as well as you can, praise God for the result, if they go well; if they do not go as well as you wish because you cannot do better, leave it all in God's hands who in the end will make all things work together as he sees expedient for our good.

Here is my little bit of advice, my dear lady and good mother. For the love of God, try to be very brave; say a hundred times a day, but say it from your heart: God will help us, and you will see that he will do it. Command your children freely, for God wishes it.

I send you two letters from Dijon, and wishing you all the graces which Our Lord gives to his loyal servants, I remain, Madam, my dear Mother,

Your very humble son,

Francis, Bishop of Geneva.

Vigil of St. Andrew.

49

To the Baronne de Chantal[1]

Annecy, mid-December 1609

Your Anne-Jacqueline pleases me more and more. The last time I saw her she asked me after confession whether she could have permission to fast on bread and water in Advent and to go barefoot all the winter, so as to prepare and accustom herself to being a nun. O dear daughter, I must tell you what I said in answer, for I think it will be as apt for the mistress as for the servant. I said that I wanted the daughters of our congregation to have their feet well shod but their hearts quite bare and stripped of worldly affections, their heads well covered and their spirit bare, in that they had achieved perfect simplicity and completely renounced their own will.

50

To Madame de la Fléchère

Annecy, mid-December 1609

It is really true, my very dear daughter, that nothing in this

---

[1] Fragment from a letter the rest of which is lost. It concerns Anne-Jacqueline Coste, a servant whom St. Francis met in Geneva. She followed him to Annecy and was the first turn-sister of the Visitation when it was founded in 1610.

Part of a letter from St. Francis de Sales to his mother, Madame de Boisy, 29 November 1609 (see page 169)

world can give us deeper tranquillity than looking at Our Lord
in all the afflictions that beset him from the time of his birth
until his death, for we shall see so much scorn, calumny,
poverty and indigence, abjection, sorrow, torment, stripping,
insults and all kinds of bitterness, that in comparison with all
this, we shall realize that we are wrong to describe as affliction
and sorrow and contradiction the little accidents which befall
us; and that we are wrong to desire patience for things of such
small account, for a tiny little share of due modesty is enough
to help us bear all that may come our way.

I know the state of your soul very well and it seems to me
that I still see it before me with all those little emotions of sadness, disturbance and fretting which come to trouble it because
it has not yet got far enough with laying the foundations of
real love of the cross and of abjection of the will. My very dear
daughter, a heart which greatly honours and loves Our Lord
crucified, loves his death, his grief, his torment, his being spat
upon, vituperated, deprived, his being hungry and thirsty and
despised; and when some little chance of sharing in this comes
your heart's way, it will rejoice and be glad and embrace it
lovingly. Every day, therefore, not at your time of prayer but at
some other time, while you are out walking, you should pass in
review the sorrows Our Lord suffered in the course of our redemption and consider what happiness it will be for you to
have some share in them; consider on what occasion this good
thing can come your way, that is to say, the contradictions you
may experience in all your desires, but chiefly in the desires that
seem just and legitimate to you, and then, with great love of
the cross and the passion of Our Lord, you should cry out with
St. Andrew: O lovely cross, so much beloved by my Saviour,
when will you receive me in your arms?

You see, my very dear daughter, we are being too fastidious
when we describe as poverty a state in which we are neither
hungry, thirsty or cold, and suffer no ignominy but only a few
slight pinpricks as we carry out our plans. When we meet again
remind me to talk to you a little more about this fastidiousness
and shrinking in your dear heart, for what you most need for

your peace and rest is first of all to be cured of this, and to have a clear apprehension of eternity fixed in your mind; for some-one who often dwells on this thought worries very little what happens in these three or four moments of our mortal life.

As you have fasted for the first half of Advent you can carry on to the end. I agree to your going to communion even two days running when they are feast days. Have no scruples about going to mass after dinner; this is according to the ancient custom of Christians. Our Lord takes no notice of little things like that; reverence is in the heart, you must not let your mind dwell on little considerations of this kind.

Good-bye, my very dear daughter; always look upon me as all yours, for that is what I really and truly am. May God bless you. Amen.

Francis, Bishop of Geneva.

51

To the Baronne de Chantal

Annecy, 29 December 1609

And now, my very dear daughter, this past year is about to be swallowed up in the gulf which has devoured all the rest. O how desirable is eternity in exchange for this poor and passing state of uncertainty and change! May time pass on, time with which we ourselves gradually pass so as to be transformed into the glory of the children of God.

This is the last time I shall be writing to you this year, my dear daughter. What blessings I wish for you, and how ardently! I cannot possibly express what I feel. Alas, when I think how I have used God's time, I fear that he may not want to give me his eternity, since he only wants to bestow it on those who make good use of his time.

It is three months since I last had a letter from you, but I believe that God is with you and that is enough for me. My only wish for you is that you should have God. I am writing to you without leisure, for my room is full of people who are clamouring for my attention; but my heart is solitary all the same and full of longing always to live for this holy love which is its whole aim and object. And during these holy feast days, at least, I have been seized by countless longings to give you the joy you so much want for my soul as well as for your own— that of advancing swiftly in that state of holy perfection which is your aim and which you wish for me, while I in turn wish you the closest and highest union with God to be found here on earth.

That is the only wish of him whom God has given you.

Francis, Bishop of Geneva.

52

To the Baronne de Chantal

Annecy, 16 January 1610[1]

I still cannot tell, my very dear sister, my daughter, whether I shall be able to write to you at any length, because your dear nephew told me this morning that he was not leaving till the day after tomorrow, and now his servant is packing the bags and says that he has since decided to go tomorrow; this has made me change my mind about visiting Monsieur Nouvelet who is just recovering from a serious illness, and here I am writing as much as I am able.

The baron[2] and I have had several talks on the subject of steadiness and discretion, but the fault you saw in him, my dear daughter, can only be cured by experience, for this false esteem of ourselves is so strongly fostered by our self-seeking that it is not in any way accessible to reason. Alas, it is the fourth diffi-

---

[1] The authentic autograph of this letter which in the older editions had appeared as two separate and truncated letters, was discovered at the Lisbon Visitation in time to be included in the supplementary volume of letters, A. XXI, p. 89 ff (1923).

[2] Madame de Chantal's nephew, Jacques de Neufchèzes.

cult thing for Solomon and which he says he was utterly ignorant of: the way of a man in youth.[1] God gives your nephew much grace in that he has his grandfather to watch over him; may he long rejoice in this privilege!

As to your journey here, do not be in any hurry because of my projected voyage to Paris, for as I have had no further news after what I showed you, it seems that it will not take place; and I think that it would be very hard to take your children on a journey during Lent, quite apart from the fact that your good father and your brother had in mind for you the time immediately after Easter.[2] Perhaps your heart will say: look how this man keeps postponing things! O dear daughter, believe me that I am longing as ardently as you are for the day of your consolation; but I am having to do this for reasons which it is not expedient for me to put in writing. So wait, my very dear sister, 'wait' I say 'with expectation', in the words of the Bible.[3] Now 'waiting with expectation' means not to be restless while waiting; for there are many people who wait without expectation, getting anxious and fidgety.

We shall win through, dear daughter, with God's help. And although in many hidden little ways things have gone against the grain for me and tried to disturb my peace, this fills me with a more peaceful and sweeter tranquillity than ever, and seems to me to be a sign that my soul will soon be established in God. And this is undoubtedly the great ambition and passion of my heart, indeed the only one I have. And when I say my heart, I mean my whole heart and soul, including the one which God has indissolubly united to it.

And since I am on the subject of my soul I want to give you some good news about it. I am really doing and shall go on doing what you asked me to do for it, and I am grateful to you for the zeal you have for its welfare, which is undivided from the welfare of your own soul, if we can distinguish yours and mine in this respect. I will also tell you that I find it a little more to

[1] Prov. xxx, 18, 19.
[2] She in fact reached Annecy on Palm Sunday that year.
[3] Ps. xxxix, 1.

my liking than usual because it does not seem to cling to the things of this world as it did, and is more conscious of the things of eternity. How happy I should be if the strength and power of my attachment to God were as great as my complete alienation from the world! And how pleased you would be, my daughter! But I am referring to what is within and what I feel; as to the exterior, and what is worse, my outward behaviour, it is full of a great many different imperfections, for the good which I would, I do not; all the same I know that I really and truly with an unchanging will want to do what is good. But then how is it possible, my daughter, that I can combine so much good will with so many imperfections showing and growing in me? No indeed, this does not happen with my will or by my will, although it appears to form part of my will. It seems to me that they are like mistletoe which grows and shows on a tree, although it is not part of the tree, on the tree but not of it. O why am I telling you all this? Surely it is because my heart always opens and pours itself out with complete freedom when it is near yours.

Your way of praying is good; just be very faithful in staying near God in this gentle and still attention of the heart, in this sweet sleep in the arms of his providence and in your gentle acquiescence in his holy will, for all this is agreeable to him. . . . I reread your letter late last night. Go on doing just as you say in your letter: avoid forcing yourself to use your understanding, because this is harmful to you, not only in general but especially in prayer; let your affections dwell as simply and as gently as possible on the object of your desire. The understanding will of course make efforts to apply itself from time to time; this cannot be avoided and you should not be anxious to guard against it as this would serve as a distraction. When you become aware of this you must be content simply to return to acts of the will.

Keeping in God's presence and placing yourself in God's presence are, to my mind, two different things; for in order to put yourself there you have to withdraw your soul from every other object and actually make it attentive to this presence, as I have explained in the book.[1] But after you have done this you continue in his presence while you are using either your understanding or your will to make acts to God, either looking upon him or looking upon some other thing for love of him; or not looking at anything at all but speaking to him; or neither looking at him nor speaking to him, but simply staying where he has put you, like a statue in its niche. And if, as we simply remain before God, we also feel in some way that we belong to God and that he is our All, we should render great thanks to his goodness.

If a statue that has been put into a niche in some room were endowed with speech and one were to ask it: 'Why are you here?' It would say, 'Because my master, the sculptor, put me here.' 'Why are you not making any movement?' 'Because he wants me to stay quite still.' 'What use are you? What do you gain by being here like this?' 'I am not here to gain anything for myself but to serve and obey the will of my master.' 'But you do not see him.' 'No,' it would say, 'but he sees me and is pleased that I should be where he has put me.' 'But would you not like to be able to move so as to get closer to him?' 'No, indeed, unless by his command.' 'Do you not want anything at all, then?' 'No, for I am where my master has put me, and the only thing that can make me happy is to do what he wants.'[2]

Dear daughter, what an excellent way of prayer this is, and what a good way it is of keeping in the presence of God, doing what he wants and what pleases him! It seems to me that Mary Magdalen was a statue in her niche when she listened to what Our Lord said, sitting at his feet, without saying a word, without moving and perhaps without looking at him. When he spoke she listened to him; when he stopped speaking she ceased to listen, and yet she was still there. A little child that is at its mother's breast while she is asleep is really in its right and proper place although both are silent.[3]

Dear God, my daughter, how happy I am to talk to you for a

---

[1] *Introduction to the Devout Life*, Pt. II, ch. 11.
[2] This passage is the first rough draft for the dialogue in book 6, ch. 9 of the *Treatise on the Love of God*, A. IV, p. 341 f.
[3] Cf. A. IV, p. 332.

little while about these things! How happy it makes us to want to love Our Lord! Let us then really love him, my daughter, without trying to go into minute details about what we do for love of him, as long as we know that we never want to do anything that is not done for love of him. For my own part, I think we keep in the presence of God even while we are asleep, because we fall asleep in his sight, at his will and pleasure, and he puts us on our bed like a statue into its nook; and when we wake up we find that he is there, close to us; he has not moved and neither have we, so we can say we have kept in his presence but with our eyes closed in sleep.

But here is your baron urging me to finish my letter. Good night, my dear sister, my daughter; you shall have news of me as often as I can manage it. Believe me that the first word I ever wrote to you was absolutely true—that God had given me to you;[1] this feeling grows stronger in my heart every day. May God in his greatness ever be our All. Stand fast, dear daughter, cast out all doubt; God holds us in his hand and will never abandon us. Glory be to him for ever and ever. Amen. May Jesus reign and his very holy Mother. Amen. And praise be to our good father St. Joseph! May God bless you with countless blessings.

53

To Madame de la Fléchère

1609 or 1610

Indeed, dear daughter, it is not that my heart does not feel tenderly towards you but that I am so harassed by crowds of things to see to that I cannot write when I want to. And then your suffering, which is nothing but dryness and aridity, cannot be remedied by letter; I should have to listen while you tell me all the little things that have been happening, and even then, patience and resignation are the only possible source of healing.

[1] Cf. Letter 3.

After this winter-time of coldness, a blissful summer will come and we shall be consoled.

Alas, daughter, we always hanker for sweetness, happiness and delicious consolation; but bitterness and dryness are really more fruitful. And although St. Peter loved the mount of Thabor and fled from the mount of Calvary, the latter was nevertheless of greater profit than the former, and the blood that is shed on the one is more desirable than the radiance shed on the other. Our Lord is already treating you as being stronger and more grown-up; try to live up to this. It is better to eat bread without sugar than sugar without bread.

The anxiety and grief you feel from realizing your nothingness is not pleasant; for although the cause is good the effect is not. No, my dear daughter, this knowledge of our nothingness should not trouble us but should have a soothing, humbling and chastening effect; it is self-esteem which makes us impatient at seeing ourselves vile and abject. Come now, I entreat you by the love of him whom we both love, of Jesus Christ, to live consoled and peaceful in your infirmities. I glory in my infirmities, says our great St. Paul, so that the power of my Saviour may dwell in me. Yes, indeed. for our misery is as a throne to make manifest the sovereign goodness of Our Lord.

I wish you a thousand blessings. O Lord, bless the heart of my dear daughter, make it burn like a holocaust of sweetness in honour of your divine love; may it not seek any contentment but in you, nor ask for any other consolation than that of being most perfectly consecrated to your glory. May Jesus be the centre of this heart for ever, and may this heart be for ever in the centre of Jesus; may Jesus reign in this heart, and this heart in Jesus.

I am in him, more than you could believe possible,

Your very affectionate servant,

Francis, Bishop of Geneva.

54

To the Baronne de Chantal

Annecy, 11 March 1610

My very dear daughter, must we not everywhere and in all things adore this supreme providence? For its counsels are holy, good and most lovable. And now it has pleased God to take my very good and dear mother out of this unhappy world, to hold her, as I firmly hope, in his presence and in his right hand. Let us confess, my dearly beloved daughter, that God is good and that his mercy is everlasting. All his ways are just and all his decrees are righteous, his good pleasure is always holy and his ordinances very gracious.

And for myself, my daughter, I own that the pain of this parting has gone very deep (for I must confess my weakness after confessing God's divine goodness); but nevertheless, my daughter, the pain has been peaceful, though keenly felt, for like David I have said: 'I was dumb, O Lord, and opened not my mouth, because thou hast done it.'[1] Of course, if it had not been God's doing, I would have cried out aloud beneath this blow; but I do not think I could dare to cry out or presume to murmur beneath the blow of that fatherly hand which, thanks to his goodness, I have learnt to love so truly and tenderly from my youth.

But you would perhaps like to know how this saintly woman ended her days. So here is a brief account for you, to you whom I have given my mother's place in my memento at mass, without robbing you of yours. I could not do this, for you are established so firmly in the place you already hold in my heart; so now you come first and last. My mother, then, came here in the winter, and during the month she spent here, she made a general review of her soul and with very great love renewed her desire to do everything as well as she could; and she went away entirely content with me, saying that she had derived

[1] Ps. xxxviii, 10.

more consolation from me than ever before. She continued in this happy frame of mind till Ash Wednesday when she went to the parish of Thorens where she made her confession and communion with very great devotion, heard three masses, and vespers; and in the evening when she had gone to bed and could not sleep, she asked her maid to read her three chapters of the *Introduction* so as to occupy her mind with good thoughts, and she had the 'Protestation'[1] marked in the book so as to make it the next morning. But God took the will for the deed and disposed otherwise; for when morning came and she had got up and was combing her hair, she suddenly fell down in a seizure and lay as one dead. My poor brother, your son,[2] who was still asleep, was called and came running in his night clothes. He had her lifted up and made her walk, gave her cordials, essences and other remedies judged expedient in such circumstances, so that she was roused and began to speak, but almost unintelligibly, because her throat and tongue were both affected by the stroke.

I was sent for and I set off at once with the doctor and the apothecary who found her lethargic and paralysed on one side of her body; but the lethargy was such that she was nevertheless very easy to rouse, and in those moments of awareness she showed full possession of her mental faculties, this being proved either by the words she tried to say or by the movements of the hand she could still use. For she spoke very coherently about God and her soul, and her hands groped for the cross (for she had gone blind) and kissed it. She never took anything from us without having made the sign of the cross over it, and in this way she received extreme unction. When I got there she fondled me tenderly, blind and drowsy as she was, saying: 'He is my son and my father,' and she kissed me and put her arm round my neck, first kissing my hand. She continued in this state almost two and a half days, after which it was hardly possible to rouse her properly; and on the first of March she gave up her soul gently and peacefully to God, and with a

[1] *Introduction to the Devout Life*, Part I, ch. xx.
[2] Bernard de Thorens who had married Madame de Chantal's eldest daughter.

dignity and beauty greater perhaps than it had ever been, she
remained in death as beautiful as anyone I have ever seen.

I have still to tell you that I had the courage to give her the
last blessing, to close her eyes and her mouth and to give her
the last kiss of peace at the moment of her death. After that my
heart swelled within me and I wept more for my good mother
than I have ever wept since I became a priest; but I wept without any bitterness of spirit, thanks be to God. This is all that
happened.

Well, my dear daughter, we must resign ourselves and always
praise God even if it should please him to visit us yet more
severely. If then you find it can be done, you can travel so as to
be here on Palm Sunday. I say you can come here, to town, for
it would not do for you to spend these great days in the
country. Your little room will be ready for you, our simple
meals, our simple and modest entertainment will be given and
offered with a good heart. I mean it will come from my heart
which is so very much yours. . . .

Now about the precepts of prayer which have been given to
you by the good Mother Prioress;[1] I will not say anything
about them for the moment, I would only ask you to learn as
much as you can about this prayer and its principles. To tell you
frankly, although last summer it did happen two or three times
that having put myself in the presence of God without preparation and without forethought, I found myself very happy with
His Majesty, with a single very simple and continual movement
of love that was almost imperceptible but very sweet; all the
same I have never dared to leave the high road and to make a
practice of this. I do not know how it is, but I love the common
way of the saints who have gone before us and of simple souls.
I do not say that when we have made our preparation and are
drawn to this sort of prayer while we are actually praying, we
should not follow it; but I do find it rather hard to take that one
should make a regular point of not preparing oneself and of
leaving God without any sort of act of thanksgiving, without
any offering, without any set prayer. All this can indeed be

[1] Mother Louise de Jésus of the Carmel at Dijon.

done, and usefully, but I confess that it fills me with slight re-pugnance to make a rule of it. Nevertheless (I speak simply before Our Lord, and to you to whom I can only speak quite openly and candidly) I do not consider myself so expert as not to be very happy, I say, extremely happy, to give up my own feelings in this matter and to follow the opinion of those who have every reason to know more than I do; and I do not only mean this good Mother Prioress, but anyone of much less account. So please find out what she thinks about it and all her reasons, but do it quite gently and without eagerness and so that she does not think you are submitting her to an examina-tion. I honour this soul with all my heart, and also her monastery.

May God be with you, my dear daughter, until we meet again soon, with the help of Jesus; may he live and reign for ever in our spirit. Amen.

55

To Madame de Travernay

Annecy, 21 July 1610

While our body is in pain it is very difficult for us to raise our hearts to the perfect consideration of our Saviour's goodness; this can only be done by those who as the result of long habit have their mind entirely turned towards heaven. But we who are still quite young in prayer, find that our souls are easily dis-tracted by the body's toil and pain; therefore it is not surprising that you should have dropped your mental prayer while you were ill. At such times it is enough to use ejaculatory prayers and holy aspirations; for as our pain often makes us sigh, it costs no more to sigh in God and to God and for God than to sigh and complain without making good use of it.

But now that God has given you back your health, you should take up your prayer again, my dear daughter, at least for half an hour in the morning and for a quarter of an hour in the evening before supper; for since Our Lord has given you a taste for this heavenly honey, it would be a matter of great reproach to you if you lost the taste of it, and especially as he made you taste of it with much facility and devotion, as I very well remember your admitting to me. So you must make a really brave effort and not allow talk and the pointless tyranny of social contacts to deprive you of such a rare treasure as that of speaking heart to heart with your God and maker.

You oblige me greatly by giving me news of your soul, for mine loves yours dearly and cannot help wanting to know in what state it is; but your husband's change of plan about bringing you here or else making you stay in the country prevented me from asking you for news of yourself. So please do me the kindness of writing to me from time to time, and I can assure you that I shall always answer and by a very sincere affection in serving you, correspond faithfully to the honour you do me of wishing me well.

May God always be in the centre of your heart so as to fill it and make it overflow with his holy love; this, Madam my dear daughter, is the daily wish of,

Your most humble friend and servant,
Francis, Bishop of Geneva.

56

To Madame de la Fléchère

Annecy, 19 September 1610

My very dear daughter,

I have heard about your many difficulties and I have put them before God, asking him to deign to give them his holy blessing as he blessed the difficulties of his dearest servants, so that they may be used for the sanctification of his holy name in your soul.

I must confess that although in my opinion afflictions which

183

concern people and those close to them personally are more distressing, the difficulties connected with lawsuits nevertheless arouse my compassion in a higher degree because they are more dangerous for the soul. How often do we see people in peace amidst the thorns of illness and the loss of friends, and then watch them lose their inner peace when caught up by the worries of a lawsuit. And this is the reason, or rather the cause which has no foundation in reason: we find it hard to believe that God is using the evil of lawsuits as an exercise for us, because we see that it is men who are prosecuting us; and not daring to kick against providence which we know to be both good and wise, we kick against the people who are afflicting us and we upbraid and blame them, not without great danger of losing charity, the only loss we ought to fear in this life.

Well now, my very dear daughter, when are we going to make up our minds to prove our fidelity to our Saviour if not on occasions like these? When are we going to learn to rein in our heart, our judgement and our tongue, if not along these rough roads so near to the edge of the precipice? For God's sake, my very dear daughter, do not let a time so favourable to your spiritual advancement slip by without really gathering the fruits of patience, humility and gentleness and the love of abjection. Remember that Our Lord never said a single word against those who condemned him; he did not in any way pass judgement on them; it was he who was wrongfully judged and condemned, and he remained in peace and died in peace and his only revenge was to pray for them. And we, my very dear daughter, we pass judgement on our judges and on our opponents, we arm ourselves with complaints and reproaches. Believe me, my very dear daughter, we must be strong and constant in our love for our neighbour; and I say this sincerely and with all my heart, without considering your opponents or what they mean to me, and I believe that the only thing which actuates me in this whole business is my jealous desire for your perfection.

But I must stop; indeed I had not really intended to say so much. You will always have God when you yourself want him;

and is this not riches enough? I entreat him to make his will
your peace and his cross your glory, and I am for ever,

Your very humble and unchanging servant in him,

Francis, Bishop of Geneva.

57

To Mère de Chantal[1]

Annecy, 28 November 1610

You would like to have a few good thoughts, my very dear
daughter, to help our Sisters spend Advent with as much devotion as they would like to feel. What shall I tell you, my
daughter, except that the Holy Roman Church, our mother, today conducts her children to the church of S. Maria Maggiore
to make the station there and to begin the season of Advent.
Let us do the same thing, my very dear daughter; let us enter in
spirit into the intention of Holy Church and in union with her
join the sacred Virgin, our good mother and mistress.

In the course of this month we shall see three things which
are not only capable of occupying our soul but which should
ravish our hearts in holy love. The first is Mary conceived
without sin; the second, St. John, the child of grace, crying in
the desert to make the rough ways smooth for the Spouse who
is about to come to us; the third, this same Spouse and Saviour
coming among us by his holy birth which makes us rejoice and
sing Emmanuel, or God is with us, at Christmas.

Here you have enough matter for meditation, daughter, until
I see you with the dear little flock on which may God bestow
his blessing.

[1] This is one of the earliest letters addressed to 'Mère de Chantal': the first
Visitation convent was established in the Maison de la Galérie at Annecy on
Trinity Sunday, 6 June 1610. Madame de Chantal had been in Annecy since
March. From now onwards the correspondence between the two saints neces-
sarily changes in character as they were able to see one another every day. It
takes the form of notes, sometimes of meditations, rather than of the longer
letters of earlier days. These return in later years when Mère de Chantal was
travelling and making foundations, visiting the convents of the rapidly spreading
order all over France.

58

To Monsieur Celse-Bénigne de Chantal

Annecy, 8 December 1610

Sir,

So you are at last about to hoist sail and launch out on to the high seas of the world: you are going to court. May God be gracious to you and keep you ever in his holy hand.

I am less apprehensive about this way of life than many other people and I do not consider it one of the most dangerous for men of noble spirit and of manly heart, for there are only two main reefs to guard against in these deep waters: vanity which is the ruin of sensual, slothful, effeminate and vacillating characters, and ambition which ruins those who are foolhardy and presumptuous. And in the same way as vanity is a defect of courage which, lacking force to win true and solid approbation, seeks and is satisfied with empty praise; so ambition is a surfeit of boldness which makes us pursue glory and honour regardless of reason and even running counter to it. Thus vanity leads us to fritter away our energy in idle frivolity designed to curry favour with women and other people of slender intellect, while earning the disapproval of men of great heart and minds of real distinction. Ambition, however, makes us grasp at honours before we have done anything to deserve them, making us want others to look upon the excellence of our ancestry as our own and putting it forward as a claim on the world's esteem.

Now, Sir, to strengthen you against all this, since you want me to advise you, continue to nourish your mind with spiritual and divine fare, for this will make it strong to withstand vanity and right-minded in your attitude towards ambition. Be faithful to frequent communion and believe me that you could do nothing more certain to make you firm in your practice of virtue. And in order to make sure of keeping faithful to this exercise, put yourself under the guidance of some good confessor and ask him to assume authority over you, calling you to account in confession for any failure on your part in this exercise, supposing such a thing were to happen. Always be humble in confession and have a real and express purpose of amendment. Never forget (and I entreat you to make a special point of this) to ask Our Lord's help on your knees before you leave your lodgings in the morning, and ask him to forgive your faults before you go to bed at night.

Above all, beware of bad books, and not for anything in the world allow your mind to be carried away by certain books which captivate people of feeble brain-power because of certain subtleties which they savour, as for instance in the writings of that infamous man Rabelais and certain others of our age who profess to throw doubt and contempt on everything and jeer at all the maxims and precepts we venerate of old. On the contrary, have about you books of solid doctrine, and especially Christian and spiritual books, so as to find sound recreation in them from time to time.

I should like you to cultivate a gentle and sincere courtesy which offends nobody but wins everyone, which seeks to gain love rather than honour, which never jests at anyone else's expense, and never hurts, which never affronts anyone and is itself never affronted; and should this happen, it happens rarely, for courteous people are very often honourably advanced.

Take care, I beseech you, not to get involved in flirtations and not to allow your affections to run away with your judgement and reason in your choice of those on whom you fix your affections; for once affection is given free rein it drags judgement along with it like a slave and impels it to very unsuitable choices, fully deserving the repentance which soon follows.

From the beginning I should like you to make open and unambiguous profession in your bearing and your conversation of wanting to live virtuously, judiciously, and in a steadfast and Christian way. I say virtuously, so that no one makes any attempt to draw you into debauchery; judiciously, without exaggerated outward demonstrations of your intention, but contenting yourself by behaving in a way which is in accordance with your condition and cannot be censured by wise people;

steadfastly, because unless you give constant witness of an equal and inviolable intention, you will expose your resolutions to the designs and assaults of a number of mean souls who attack others so as to reduce them to their own way of life. And finally I say in a Christian way, because a whole number of people profess to a desire for virtue attained by means of philosophy, and they are nevertheless not virtuous and cannot in any way achieve this object; they are nothing but shadow-figures of virtue, and from those who are not closely associated with them they hide a bad life and evil inclinations by graceful manners and speech. But we who are well aware that we are incapable of the least little act of virtue except by Our Lord's grace, must live virtuously with the help of piety and holy devotion, otherwise all our virtue will prove imaginary and insubstantial. Now it is infinitely important to let it be known at once what we mean to be always, and in this matter there must be no shilly-shallying.

It is also extremely important for you to make some like-minded friends so that you can be strengthened and fortified in one another, for it is eminently true that the society of disciplined people is of inestimable value in helping us to keep our own souls disciplined. I should think you might find some worthy and gracious friend among the Jesuits, Capuchins or the Feuillants, or even outside a religious order; someone who will be happy for you to go and see him from time to time for your spiritual recreation and in order, as it were, to draw spiritual breath.

But you must allow me to stress a particular point. You see, my dear Sir, I am afraid that you may return to gaming, and I dread it because it will do you very great damage; in the space of a few days this would dissipate your heart and make all the flowers of your good desires wither and die. It is the occupation of an idler; and those who seek to attract social renown and favour among the great by gaming, calling this the quickest way of getting known, show that they are men of inferior merit because they have recourse to methods only fit for those who have a lot of money and are willing to risk losing it; and there is no great merit in being known as a gambler, but if, on the other hand, they lose heavily, it is clear to everyone that they are fools. I am not for the moment considering the consequence of quarrels, despair and acts of violence from which not a single gambler is exempt.

I wish you further a vigorous heart so that you may not flatter your body too much by being finicky about food, sleep and other indulgence, for surely a generous heart always has a little contempt for mere luxury and delight of the body. Our Lord says: Those who are arrayed in soft garments are in the houses of kings,[1] that is why I mention it to you. And Our Lord does not mean that all those who are at court must be dressed in soft garments, but he is only saying that those who do dress in soft garments are in fact found at court. Now I am not speaking about the outside appearance of your clothing, but of your inner attitude; for, as to the exterior, you know so much better what is fitting that it is not my business to discuss the matter. What I mean is that I should like you to be hard on your body sometimes by making it feel some sort of rigour and difficulty, by despising softness and by often renouncing things which are agreeable to the senses; for reason should indeed sometimes assert its rightful superiority, and the authority proper to it of commanding the sensual appetites.

Indeed, I am writing too diffusely, and if this is so, I scarcely know what I am trying to say, for it is being done without leisure and at odd moments. You know my heart and will take everything in the right spirit. But I just want to add this. Imagine that you were a courtier of St. Louis: this saintly king (and your king is at present holy by innocence)[2] liked the people about him to be brave, courageous, generous, cheerful, courteous, affable, frank, polite; but above all he wanted them to be good Christians. And if you had been with him you would have seen him laugh merrily when occasion offered, speak out boldly when the need arose, maintaining a brave outward show of royal splendour and dignity, like another Solomon; and the

[1] Matt. xi, 8.
[2] Louis XIII was then nine years old.

next moment you would have seen him serving the poor at the hospitals, and in short marrying civil virtue to Christian virtue, and majesty to humility. And this, in a word, should be your aim: to be no less brave for being Christian and no less Christian for being brave. And this implies being a very good Christian, that is to say, very devout, pious, and if you can, spiritual, for, as St. Paul says: the spiritual man discerns all things,[1] he knows the right time and order to practise every virtue.

You should often call to mind this good reflection: that in this world we are poised between paradise and hell, that our last step will land us in our eternal dwelling place, and that we do not know which will be the last; and in order to make the last step a good one, we must go on trying to make all the others good too. O blessed and endless eternity! Blessed are they who often think of you! For is not all we do here on earth for a brief, uncertain time but as a child's play and pastime? It would amount to nothing at all, if it were not the passage to eternity. That is why we must give careful heed to our time here on earth and to all our occupations, so as to use them to win our lasting good.

Love me always as belonging wholly to you, for I do belong to you, in Our Lord, wishing you all happiness in this world and above all in the world to come: may God bless you and keep you ever in his holy hand. And to end where I began: you are taking to the high seas of worldly life, but do not on that account change your captain, your mast, your sails, your anchor, your fair breeze. Always keep Jesus as your captain, his cross for your mast on which to spread the sails of your good resolutions; let your anchor be deep trust in him and then sail on happily. May the favourable breeze of heavenly grace fill your sails more and more and carry you safely and joyfully into the haven of a blessed eternity, which is the true and heartfelt wish, Sir, of,

Your most humble servant,
Francis, Bishop of Geneva.

[1] 1 Cor. ii, 15.

59

To the Présidente Brûlart

Annecy, April 1611

My very dear Sister,

As I am writing to your husband to introduce a friend of mine, a canon of Lyons, I am enclosing a little message for you, simply to greet you with all my heart, not only in my own name but also in that of your dear and good sister, Madame de Chantal, who is going from strength to strength in her recovery, and whose sanctity, let this be said only between ourselves, is increasing in the same way; for tribulation and illness are very fitted to advance sanctity because they lead to so much solid resignation of ourselves into Our Lord's hands.

Live for God alone, dear daughter, and because you are exposed to much talk and social life, make yourself useful to your neighbour in ways which I have often described to you. And do not think that Our Lord is any further away from you while you are caught up in the worries attendant on your state of life than he would be if you were enjoying the delights of a tranquil life. No, my very dear daughter, what brings him near to our hearts is not the tranquillity but the faithfulness of our love, not the feeling we have of his sweetness, but our free consent to his holy will; and it is more desirable that his will should be wrought in us than that we should follow our own inclinations in him.

Good day, my very dear sister, my daughter. I pray that this sovereign goodness may give us the grace of seeking him in a spirit of love, and I am all yours in him, Madam,

Your very humble servant,
Francis, Bishop of Geneva.

60

To Mère de Chantal

Annecy, Whit Sunday, 22 May 1611

'Arise, O north wind, and come, O south wind: blow through my garden, and let the aromatical spices thereof flow.'[1] O my very dear daughter, how I wish you this gracious south wind of divine love, the Holy Ghost who gives us the grace to long and yearn for him!

How I should love to give you some gift, my dear daughter; but apart from the fact that I am so poor, it is not fitting that we should be concerned with giving presents of our own on the day on which the Holy Spirit brings us his gifts; all we need to know on this day of magnificent generosity is how to receive. Dear God! How sorely I need the spirit of fortitude, for indeed I am feeble and infirm, although I glory in this so that the strength of my Lord may live in me. I prefer to be weak rather than strong before God, for he lifts up the weak in his arms and leads the strong by the hand. May the eternal Wisdom dwell in our hearts for ever so that we may savour the treasures of the infinite sweetness of Jesus Christ crucified.

Tell my daughter, Soeur Marie-Jacqueline Favre, that like me she should glory in her weakness which is so fit to receive the gift of strength; for to whom should strength be given if not to the weak?

Good night, my very dear daughter. May this sacred fire which changes all things in its flames transform our heart so that nothing may remain except love, and we may no longer be loving, but love itself, no longer two, but a single self, since love binds all things in a sovereign unity. May God be with you, my dear daughter. Let us persevere in our desire for this unity which God has made us taste even now, in so far as our infirm condition can understand it, and may he then give us a more perfect enjoyment of it in heaven.

Francis, Bishop of Geneva.

[1] Canticle iv, 16.

61

To Mère de Chantal

Annecy, 10 June 1611

Good morning, my very dear daughter. I have got to judge a cause this morning between two of our clergy of Gex, and this deprives me of the consolation of going to see the dearest sheep of my flock and of myself feasting them on the Bread of Life. I am sending you M. Rolland[1] to make up for my absence. All the same, he is not a sufficiently good messenger to bring you the thought which God sent me during the night: that our house of the Visitation is, by his grace, noble and important enough to have its own coat of arms, its escutcheon, its device and its battle cry. So I have thought, dear Mother, if you agree, we should take as our coat of arms a single heart pierced by two arrows, the whole enclosed in a crown of thorns, and with the poor heart serving to hold and support a cross which is to surmount it; and the heart is to be engraved with the sacred names of JESUS and MARY.[2]

Dear daughter, the next time we meet I shall tell you a great many little thoughts which I had on this subject; for indeed, our little congregation is the work of the hearts of Jesus and Mary. Our dying Saviour gave birth to us by the wound in his sacred heart; it is therefore perfectly right that by constant mortification our own heart should always remain surrounded by the crown of thorns which once rested on our master's head while love held him pinned to the throne of his mortal sufferings.

Good morning to you again, my daughter; I see that one of our plaintiffs has just come in to interrupt the peace of my thoughts.

[1] Georges Rolland (1576–1641) entered St. Francis's service in 1595 as his servant and secretary. He was ordained in 1605 and remained his most trusted servant and the steward of his household to the end.

[2] In 1611, June 10 fell on the Friday after the Octave of Corpus Christi, which ater became the feast of the Sacred Heart.

62

To Madame de la Fléchère

Annecy, 17 August 1611

Come now, what do you want me to say to you, my very dear daughter, if not that when your troubles return or your enemy makes his appearance, you must take up your arms and your courage again to fight harder than ever. I can see nothing very dreadful in your letter. But do be careful not to be in any way faint-hearted, for God's heavenly goodness does not let you fall into these faults in order to abandon you, but so as to humble you and make you take a firmer and tighter hold on the hand of his mercy.

You are pleasing me very much by going on with your exercises in spite of the dryness and interior languor which have returned; for as we only want to serve God for love of him, and the service we render him in the difficulty of dryness pleases him more than that rendered in a state of interior sweetness, we should also, for our part, prefer it, at least in the superior part of our will. And although our taste and self-esteem finds sweetness and tenderness more pleasing, dryness is more profitable, more to God's taste and to his love; just as dry food is better for those suffering from dropsy, although they always prefer the opposite.

As to your temporal difficulty, since you tried to straighten it out and failed, you must now be patient and resigned, willingly embracing the cross which is your lot; and as occasions present themselves, you will practise the advice I have given you in the past.

Live in peace, my dear daughter; often say to Our Lord that you want to be whatever he wants you to be, to suffer whatever he wants you to suffer. Fight your impatience faithfully by exercising a holy compliance and sweetness towards those you find most troublesome, not only in case of need but even when you can see no special reason, and God will bless your endeavour.

Good night, my very dear daughter; may God be your only love. I am in him with all my heart all yours.

F.

63

To Mère de Chantal

Thonon, 10 September 1611

Here I am at Thonon, my very dear daughter. I got here three days ago, travelling very happily and without feeling any fatigue. My very dear daughter, I hardly know which road I took—did I go to Thonon or to Burgundy?[1]—but I know that I am more in Burgundy than here. Yes, my daughter, because it is his divine pleasure, I am inseparable from your soul, and to speak with the Holy Spirit, we now have only one heart and one soul;[2] for what was said of all Christians in the Infant Church is now, thanks to his grace, a reality between us. So let us stay thus in Our Lord, my well beloved.

I am still waiting for news of the progress of your journey, which I hope was a good one, though I am not without apprehension because you are not well and it has been excessively hot these last few days; but I should like to think that in the heat of the day you will have rested and travelled in the mornings and evenings when there was always a little breeze. I pray God that he may look after you in love and holiness as after my own soul.

I entreat you, my very dear daughter, to keep very close to Jesus Christ and to Our Lady and to your good angel in all your business, so that the multiplicity of your affairs may not make you anxious nor their difficulty dismay you. Do things

---

[1] Mère de Chantal left Annecy for Burgundy on 6 September, together with Soeur Favre, to see to business resulting from her father's death.
[2] Acts iv, 32.

one by one as best you can, and apply your mind loyally but gently and sweetly. If God gives you good issue we shall bless him for it; if this is not his pleasure, we will bless him all the same. And it will be enough for you that you did your best in complete good faith, since Our Lord and reason do not demand results in the things we do, but only our faithful and whole-hearted co-operation, endeavour and diligence; for these do depend on us, whereas success does not. God will bless your good intention in undertaking this journey, and your attempt to put the affairs of this house in order for your son, and he will reward you either by a good issue or by holy humiliation and resignation. In the meanwhile my heart will have thousands upon thousands of good wishes and desires for your heart as it would for itself, and I shall not cease to implore the prayers of the most holy Virgin in this place which is wholly consecrated to her honour. . . .

May Jesus and Mary reign! May God bless you, my very dear daughter. I am in him what only he knows.

64

To Mère de Chantal

Gex, 7 December 1611

Very dear daughter,

You will have to be content with a brief note, for here I am, still at Gex,[1] with so many things to do that I hardly know which way to turn, especially now that I am preparing to leave. Well now, what need is there to speak like this to a soul that knows me as she knows herself?

I am very well, thanks be to our Saviour, who is filling me with a certain new ardour to love, serve and honour him more than ever with all my heart, with all my soul and with the whole of my being; I say with my whole being, my very dear daughter, as it seems to me that till now I have not had as much ardour

[1] Huguenot territory in St. Francis's diocese.

and zeal in the service of his immense Goodness as I should
have had.

Alas! I see these poor lost sheep here, I have dealings with
them and am aware of their palpable and manifest blindness.
Dear God! The beauty of our holy faith shines out all the more
clearly so that I am consumed with love of it, and realize that I
must guard this precious God-given gift in a heart made
wholly acceptable by devotion. My very dear daughter, thank
his sovereign brightness which so graciously shines in my heart,
so that when I am right amongst those who have no faith, I see
his greatness and his lovable sweetness all the more clearly and
luminously. Make acts of thanksgiving for this heart as for
your own.

May God bless you with his great blessing; this is the continual and unchanging wish of him whose heart is yours in
Jesus Christ.

At Gex, 7 December, the day before the anniversary of my
consecration.

65

To a Lady

1610–11

My dear Daughter,

Let us leave meditation for a little while (we are only retreat-
ing so as to be able to advance even more rapidly later on), and
let us practise that holy resignation and pure love of Our Lord
which is never more complete than when we are harassed; for
even little children can love God when everything is sugar and
sweetness, but loving him when all is wormwood and bitterness is the result of our loving faithfulness. When St. Peter was
still crude and unformed he had plenty of courage to say, 'May
Jesus reign,' but only his Mother and his faithful lover who was
given her as her child were ready to say this on Mount Calvary.

I am beseeching God, my dear daughter, to give you this
holy patience; and the only thing I can ask of him on your be-

half is that he may fashion your heart entirely according to his liking so that he may live and reign there eternally; that he may fashion it, I say, either with a hammer or with a chisel or with the stroke of a brush: it is for him to do as he wills, don't you agree, my dear daughter? Surely this is the attitude we should take?

I know that your pain has increased recently, and my grief about this in the same measure; although together with you I praise and bless Our Lord for showing his divine pleasure in you, giving you a share in his holy cross and crowning you with a crown of thorns.

But you are unable, you tell me, to fix your mind on the pain Our Lord suffered for you while you yourself are in the grip of pain. Well, my dear daughter, nor is it necessary that you should; just lift up your heart to your Saviour quite simply as often as you can and make these acts: firstly, accept the pain from his hand as if you yourself saw him laying and putting it upon your head; secondly, offer to suffer even more; thirdly, beg him by the merit of his torments to accept your little ailments in union with the great pain he suffered on the cross; fourthly, assure him that you not only want to suffer but even love and cherish these afflictions as coming from such a kind and gentle hand; fifthly, invoke the martyrs and the many men and women who served God and who now feel great joy in heaven because they were sorely tried in this world.

There is no danger in wanting remedies, indeed, you must do your best to obtain them; for God, who sent you the illness is also the author of the healing remedies. So you must make use of them, resigning yourself of course, so that if his Divine Majesty wants the illness to prevail, you acquiesce in this; if he wants the remedy to conquer, you will bless him for it. There is no danger in remaining seated while you are doing your spiritual exercises. None at all, my daughter; and I would say this even in the case of a much slighter indisposition.

Oh, my dear daughter, how happy you will be if you remain humble, gentle and supple beneath God's hand! Oh how I hope that the pain in your head will be of much profit to your heart;

your heart, I say, which mine cherishes with a special love. At a time like this, my daughter, more than ever and without illusion, you can show our sweet Saviour that you said and will go on saying, 'May Jesus reign,' with all the affection of your heart.

May Jesus reign, my daughter, and may he reign over and in your pain, for we can neither reign nor live except by the pain of his death. I am wholly yours in him,

Francis, Bishop of Geneva.

66

To Mère de Chantal

Annecy, 25 January 1612

The great wonder-worker, St. Paul, woke us up very early in the morning, my very dear daughter, by his cry in the ears of my heart and of yours: 'Lord, what wilt thou have me do?'[1] My very dear Mother and so very dear daughter, when will the time come when we shall be dead before God and alive to that new life, no longer having any will of our own but letting God will for us whatever we have to do, allowing his living will to act on our dead will?

Keep very close to God, my dear daughter; consecrate your difficulties to him, wait patiently for the return of your life's lovely sun. Ah, God has not shut us out from enjoying his sweetness, he has only withdrawn for a little while so that we may live for him and not for his delights; so that our sisters who are in need may find compassionate help in us and tender, loving support; so as to receive a sweet odour from the holocaust of a heart that has been burnt, consumed and brought low.

O Lord Jesus, by your incomparable sadness and the terrible desolation which filled your heart on the Mount of Olives and on the cross, and by the desolation of your dear Mother when she was deprived of your presence, be the joy or at least the

---

[1] Acts ix, 6.

strength of this daughter of mine when your cross and passion dwell deep in her soul. I am sending you this cry from my heart, my very dear daughter, and may the great St. Paul bless my prayer for you.

67

To Mère de Chantal

Chambéry, 25 March 1612

Although I have a great deal to do how could I help sending greetings to my very dear daughter on the day of the happiest of all greetings! I beg the glorious Virgin, hailed by an angel today, to beg for us some of the holy consolation bestowed on on her. May God bless you and fill you with his graces; God be with us, my very dear daughter; but I have no leisure for more, thanks to Our Lord who shows us the favour of using us continuously in his holy service; for it is by his work that I am being kept busy in many ways, which will please my very dear daughter's heart as well as my own. Very dear greetings to all our daughters and to my dear little sister[1] to whom I will write at my first leisure.

This morning, feast of the Annunciation.

68

To Mère de Chantal

Chambéry, 28 March 1612

Well now, my very dear and only daughter, it is high time for me to write some sort of answer, if I can, to your long letter. But alas, my very dear daughter, it will have to be done in haste, for I have very little time; I have got to preach in a little

---

[1] Baronne de Thorens, St. Francis's sister-in-law, Madame de Chantal's daughter.

while, but as I have already got the gist of the sermon in my head I can just let you have this little note.

Let us talk about the inner trial of which you wrote in your letter. It is quite simply a real insensibility which prevents you from feeling any joy in consolations and inspirations and even in faith itself, and hope and charity. All the same you have these virtues and they are in a very sound state, but you are deprived of the joy of them. You are like a child whose guardian deprives it of the use of its whole fortune, so that though the money really belongs to the child, it cannot handle it, nor does the child seem to possess or have anything of its own except life. As St. Paul says, 'he differeth nothing from a servant, though he be lord of all';[1] and so God does not want you to feel your faith, my very dear daughter, your hope and your charity, nor does he want you to have the enjoyment or use of them, except just what is needed for your bare existence and on occasions of absolute need.

Alas, my very dear daughter, how happy we are to be thus constrained and held short by our heavenly Guardian! And what we are to do is quite certainly nothing more than we are already doing, which is to adore the lovable providence of God and to throw ourselves into his arms and into his keeping. No, Lord, I want no more joy in my faith, nor in my hope nor in my charity, than to be able to say in very truth although without tasting or feeling it, that I would die rather than give up my faith, my hope, my charity. Alas, Lord, if it is your good pleasure that I should find no pleasure in the practice of the virtues which your grace has bestowed on me, I agree to this with all my will although against what my will feels.

It is the highest point of holy resignation to be content with naked, dry and unfelt acts made only by the superior part of the will, as it would be the highest degree of abstinence to be satisfied with never eating except with distaste, against one's desire, and not only without enjoyment and savour.

You have given me a very good description of your suffering, and you do not need to do anything further as a counter-

[1] Gal. iv, 1.

measure than what you are already doing, assuring Our Lord, even out aloud, and sometimes even in a song, that you are even willing to live on death, and to take nourishment as though you were dead, without tasting, feeling and knowing. In short, our Saviour wants us to belong to him so completely that there is nothing left to stop us from giving ourselves up entirely and without reserve to the mercy of his providence.

Go on like this, then, my very dear daughter, in the darkness of the Passion. I say, in the darkness, and I leave you to think this out: at the foot of the cross, in the strange and dreadful darkness which came down on earth, Our Lady and St. John no longer heard our Saviour, no longer saw him and felt nothing except bitterness and distress; and although they had faith, that too was in darkness, for it was necessary that they should share in the Saviour's dereliction. How fortunate we are to be the slaves of this great God who made himself a slave for us!

But it is time for my sermon. Good-bye, my very dear Mother, my daughter in this same Saviour. May his divine goodness reign! I have the very greatest ardour for the advancement of our heart, for the sake of which I resign all other happiness into the hands of his sovereign and fatherly providence.

Good evening once more, my very dear daughter. May Jesus, our sweet Jesus, the only heart of our heart, bless us with his holy love. Amen.

Francis, Bishop of Geneva.

69

To Mère de Chantal

Annecy, 1 August 1612[1]

Our great St. Peter, roused from sleep by the angel, says good morning to you, my very dear Mother. How many lovely things there are in the story of his deliverance, for his soul is so

[1] Feast of St. Peter in Chains.

startled that he does not know whether he is dreaming or not dreaming. May our angel touch our side today, waking us to loving attention to God, delivering us from all the chains of self-seeking and consecrate us for ever to this heavenly love, so that we may say: 'Now I know in very deed that the Lord hath sent his angel and hath delivered me.'[1]

How happy was our dear St. Peter, for it was an excess of tenderness that made Our Lord ask him so often: 'Peter, lovest thou me?' Not that he had any doubt of it, but he takes great joy in hearing us say over and over again that we love him. My dear Mother, do we not love our sweet Saviour? Ah, he surely knows that if we do not love him, we at least want to love him. Now if we love him we must feed his sheep and his lambs: this is the sign of faithful love.

But what are we to give these dear, small lambs? Love itself, for either they live on love or do not live at all: there is no middle course between death and love for them; they must either die or else love, for 'he that loveth not' says St. John 'abideth in death'.[2]

But let me tell you a happy thought. Our Lord will say to his dear St. Peter: 'When thou wast younger, thou didst gird thyself and didst walk where thou wouldst. But when thou shalt be old, thou shalt stretch forth thy hands, and another shall gird thee and lead thee whither thou wouldst not.'[3] Young apprentices in the love of God gird themselves: they take on the mortifications which they themselves think good, they choose their penance, their form of resignation and devotion and do their own will along with God's will; but the old masters of the trade suffer themselves to be bound and girt by others, submitting to the yoke imposed on them, and go along the kind of roads which they would not choose by their own inclination. It is also true that they stretch forth their hands; for although their inclinations resist, they willingly allow themselves to be governed against their will, and say that obedience is better than burnt-offerings: and this is how they give glory to God, crucifying not only their flesh but their spirit as well.

[1] Acts xii, 11.   [2] 1 John iii, 14.   [3] John xxi, 18.

Yesterday while the invitatory was being sung and I heard the words, 'The King of apostles, come let us adore him,' I really had a very great feeling of sweetness and love, and was seized with a longing that it should fill our heart completely. May our Saviour for ever be all things to us. Keep your heart on high, in the loving arms of the divine goodness and providence, for it is the place of our repose. It is he who made me all yours, and you all mine, so that we should be more purely, perfectly and wholly his. So be it.

70

To Madame de Travernay

Annecy, 29 September 1612

Madam, my very dear Daughter,

You will hear from the very worthy lady who is bringing you this letter how harassed I am as I write to you, and this will serve as an excuse if I do not write to you as fully as I should wish.

You should arrange the length of your prayer according to the number of things you have to do; and since it has pleased Our Lord to give you the sort of life which involves constant distractions, you must get used to making your prayers short, but also so habitual that you will never omit them except for some great necessity.

When you get up in the morning I should like you to kneel down before God to adore him, make the sign of the cross and ask his blessing for the whole day; this can be done in the space of time needed for one or two Our Fathers. If you are able to hear mass it will be enough for you to listen attentively and reverently, as described in the *Introduction*[1], saying your rosary. In the evening, before supper or at about that time, you can easily say a few fervent prayers, casting yourself down before

[1] Part II, ch. 14.

Our Lord for the length of time one would take to say an Our Father; for no amount of business can tie you down to such an extent that you cannot slip away for such a short while. In the evening before you go to bed, even while you are busy doing something else and wherever you happen to be, you can think over in general what you did during the day, and when you go to bed you can kneel down briefly, ask God's pardon for any wrong you have done and beg him to watch over you and give you his blessing. And this you can do briefly, in the space of a Hail Mary. But the chief thing I ask is that in the course of the day you should continually recollect yourself and lift your heart up to God to say a few short words telling him of your faithfulness and love.

As to the afflictions of your heart, my dear daughter, you can easily see for yourself those for which there is a remedy and those for which there is none. Where a remedy is possible you must try and apply it gently and peacefully; where there is none, you must bear it as a mortification sent by Our Lord to try you and make you all his.

Be careful not to give way to complaining; make your heart suffer in stillness. If you are seized with any sort of impatience, restore peace and gentleness in your heart the moment you become aware of what is happening. Believe me, my dear daughter, God loves the souls that are tossed about by the waves and tempests of the world, as long as they receive their hardships as coming from his hands, and like valiant warriors, try to keep faithful in the thick of the attack and fighting. If I can I will try to say a word or two to this dear friend of yours so that she can pass it on to you by word of mouth; I must leave you now to see whether I can settle a bitter dispute which must be prevented.

I am with all my heart, Madam,

Your humble and very affectionate friend and servant,
Francis, Bishop of Geneva.

71

To Madame de Peyzieu

Annecy, 26 October 1612

Madam, my very dear Mother,

Your letter which was so full of words of honour, love and confidence would win me to you completely if I had not wholly dedicated myself to your service long ago. But you are a little too sparing, my very dear Mother, in calling me your son, a name which comes from the heart; and instead you address me respectfully by a name which indeed also comes from the heart but not from a mother's heart, the heart which is all my delight. . . .

Speaking to you freely, my very dear Mother, as we have arranged, may I tell you not to be annoyed or astonished to see your soul still full of all the various imperfections you have told me about in confidence. Indeed, I entreat you, my dear Mother, do not do this; for although we must reject them and detest them so as to correct our faults we must not feel angrily distressed but sorry in a steadfast and peaceful way; this leads to a firm and settled determination to improve. A resolution of this kind, taken peacefully and in a spirit of quiet reflection, will make us find the real way to put it to effect. I must confess that moderating your attachment to things connected with your home and household would be very useful in this respect. I do not say that you should give up your attachment altogether, but that you should moderate it; for this moderation gives us a chance of finding a few free hours for prayer, for a little spiritual reading, for lifting up our hearts to God at various times; and this will let our heart find its way back from time to time to an attitude of peace, meekness, humility. But the great secret is to enlist everything we do in the service of our aim and object.

Give yourself seven or eight days to calm down your soul and make it take these resolutions in real earnest. Above all, my dear Mother, we must fight resolutely against hating and spurning our neighbour, being careful to abstain from an imperfection we are not aware of but which is very harmful and of which few people are free; I mean that when we happen to censure our neighbour or complain about him (which ought to be a rare thing), we never leave off but begin the story over and over again, repeating our complaints and grievances endlessly. This is a sign of touchiness and of a heart that is not really healthy as yet. Strong and staunch hearts only complain when there is really something important to complain about, and even then they do not harbour resentment, at least they do not succumb to fuss and agitation.

Your good parish priest whom I like very much has spoken to me about your desire and I have told him what I think. Take heart, my very dear Mother, and with God's help make these little years which still remain to us here below, as good and as profitable as possible for eternity. In the meanwhile I shall always be, Madam, my very dear Mother,

Your very humble son and most faithful servant,

Francis, Bishop of Geneva.

72

To Madame de la Fléchère

Annecy, March 1613

I have just been told, my very dear daughter, that this dear sister of ours has departed and has left us here below, a prey to the passion of sadness which generally attacks those who are left behind when people are separated. Indeed, my very dear daughter, I shall not tell you not to weep, for it is right and reasonable that you should weep a little; but only a little, my dear daughter, as a sign of the sincere affection in which you held her, in imitation of our dear Master who wept a little for his friend Lazarus; and yet not a great deal, like those whose thoughts are entirely centred on the short moments of this miserable life, not remembering that we too are bound for eternity, where, if we live well in this world, we shall be united with our dear dead again and never have to leave them. We cannot prevent our poor heart from grieving over the condition of this our life on earth and the loss of those who were our delightful companions while it lasted; all the same, we must not be disloyal to the solemn profession we made to unite our will indissolubly to God's will.

How fortunate our dear sister was to have seen the hour of her departure approaching gradually and from afar off, for in this way she prepared herself to die a holy death. Let us adore Providence and say: yes, be you blessed, for everything you ordain is good. My very dear daughter, how meekly our hearts should accept these little accidents, for our heart should henceforth have more longing for heaven than attachment to earth. I shall pray to God for that soul and for the consolation of her family.

Do not be troubled about your prayer nor about the variety of your desires, for variety in this is not wrong nor is your desire to have various virtues. As to your resolutions, you can particularize them in this way: I want to be more faithful in practising the virtues which I need, and on this or that occasion I will get ready to practise this or that virtue; and so on with the others. There is no need to use words, even interior ones; it is enough to raise up your heart or to rest it in Our Lord. It is enough to look lovingly at the divine lover of our souls, for among lovers eyes speak more eloquently than the tongue.

I am writing to you without leisure and in the servant's presence. So good night, my very dear daughter; pour your sister's death into the Saviour's and let them mingle, do not look at her death except as within that of the Redeemer. May his will be glorified for ever. Amen. May Jesus reign!

Your humble servant and friend,

Francis, Bishop of Geneva.

73

To Mère de Chantal

Annecy, end of June 1613

I shall be the first, if I can, to announce the arrival of your beloved Celse-Bénigne[1] to you, my very dear daughter. He arrived quite late last night and we had difficulty in preventing him from going and seeing you in bed where you must all have been by that time.

I am distressed not to be able to watch the caresses he will receive from a mother who is insensible to everything connected with natural love, for I believe that these caresses will be terribly mortified. Ah, no, my dear daughter, do not be so cruel! Let this poor lad Celse-Bénigne see how very happy you are to have him with you; we must not show outwardly all of a sudden that our natural passions have died within us!

Of course I will come and see you, if I can, but without wanting to draw any attention to myself; for how could one hope to be noticed in the presence of so lovable an object?

May God be our all, for friendship goes down rather than up as time goes on. I shall be quite happy if I can go on loving you as dearly as my daughter as you love him as your son; and I defy you to outdo me in this matter!

74

To Mère de Chantal

Annecy, 12 August 1613

Let us lift our heart on high, my very dear Mother, and look upon God's heart which is so good and so loving towards us; let us adore and bless all that he wills for us: let him cut and

[1] Her son. Cf. Letter 58.

shape us as he wishes, for we are his for ever. You will see that in spite of the fact that the road twists and turns we shall get there in the end and that Our Lord will lead us by way of the desert to his promised land; and from time to time he will give us something that will make us prize the desert more than cultivated ground where the corn grows in due season but where no manna falls.

When you wrote to me, my very dear Mother, and said that you were like a poor bee, I thought that I did not want this for you while your dryness and interior affliction last; for this little animal which is so diligent and busy in health, loses heart and does nothing at all when it falls ill. But since then I have changed my mind and said: 'O yes, I do indeed want my Mother to be like a bee, even when she is suffering spiritually; for this little animal knows of no other remedy when it is ill than to expose itself to the sun and to wait for warmth and healing from its bright rays.' Oh my daughter, let us put ourselves before our crucified Sun in this way and then say to him: 'O lovely Sun of our hearts, the rays of your goodness pour life into everything; here we are before you, half dead, and we shall not stir from here till your warmth gives us life, Lord Jesus.'

My dear daughter, death is life when we die in God's sight. Lean your spirit against the stone which was represented by the one Jacob had beneath his head when he saw his beautiful ladder, for it is the same stone against which St. John the Evangelist rested on the day of the exceeding great charity of his Master Jesus. May our heart and the Heart of our heart watch lovingly over you.

May peace be with you always. May God always be in the centre of our heart; may he make it ever more uniquely his. May Jesus reign! Amen, amen.

Francis, Bishop of Geneva.

EMBLEME XLIV.

Sa parfaite conformité à la volonté de Dieu.

Ie cherche son aspect, par tout ie le veux suivre;
Et s'il ne luit sur moy, ie dois cesser de viure.

Emblem to illustrate St. Francis de Sales's conformity
to the will of God (see page 34)

75

To Monseigneur Jean-Pierre Camus,
Bishop of Belley

Annecy, 14 August 1613

Monseigneur,

It is about a month ago since I received the letter you were pleased to write to me on the 2 July; since that time I have been either away or else ill, and so I have not been able to send you the answer you want; or rather, the answer you do not want, if I have rightly guessed what was in your mind when you favoured me with your letter.

And now you may judge whether I shall be able to comply with your request: the extraordinary feebleness of my body as a result of the exhaustion of fever has now been added to my usual feebleness of mind and this makes me more stupid than ever. But someone who understands as readily as you do will see enough of what I mean, although it is badly put.

First proposition.[1] Wanting to lay down the burden of a bishop's office for reasonable motives is not only no sin, but even an act of virtue, or modesty or humility or justice or charity.

Second proposition. A person may be said to be inspired by serious motives if he is prepared in good faith to submit to the counsel of wise men, or at least to the judgement of his superiors, his personal opinion about laying down his bishopric, his desire and the reasons for his desire; and if he is at the same time prepared to fall in with equal readiness either with one side or the other.

Third proposition. If the idea or desire to lay down this office does not in any sense constitute a sin in the way I have said, a plan of this kind is usually not without grave temptation, and very often the devil has his share in it. And this is why:

---

[1] The propositions are in Latin, no doubt for reasons of discretion in a matter of conscience.

while one is spending time trying to get rid of one's burden, it is unlikely, indeed very unlikely that one will devote enough attention to sustaining it. Thus a man who is thinking of leaving his wife will hardly give her all the love he should in the meanwhile. So that if you think you have not done your work as you should it is better to throw yourself more intensively into the task than to give up completely. Yes, it is far better to lift up our eyes to the hills from whence help shall come to us, to hope in the Lord and willingly glory in our infirmities so that the strength of Christ dwells in us, than to turn back on the day of battle as did the sons of Ephraim. For those who put their trust in the Lord shall take wings like the eagle; but whoever loses heart shall come to nothing and vanish like smoke. The soldier who leaves the field trembling with fear no doubt finds rest but no greater safety than he who goes on fighting.

Fourth proposition. It seems to me that I hear Christ saying: 'Simon, son of John, Simon Peter, lovest thou me?' and Simon Peter answering: 'Thou knowest that I love thee.' And then I hear the Lord saying gravely: 'Feed my lambs.'[1] There is no better proof of your love than carrying out your ministry.

Meanwhile a young woman of Chambéry who has allowed herself to be carried away by her love for a young man of your town, and is now afraid that his father and mother will raise some objection to the marriage which is essential for the preservation of her honour and for the fulfilling of the mutual promises beneath the cover of which she declares that she ran the risk of losing her reputation, now begs me to intercede on her behalf with you, Monseigneur. She begs you to exert your charity towards the said father and mother, to dispose them to consent to an honourable conclusion to the love between herself and the young man. I may point out that she belongs to a most worthy family and is daughter to the sister of Monsieur Boursier, former secretary to His Royal Highness.[2] Her first cousin (the gentleman who is bringing you this letter) will be able to describe the situation more clearly to you than I could

[1] John xxi, 15–17. Cf. *Treatise on the Love of God*, Bk. 9, ch. 10; A. V, p. 140.
[2] King Charles Emmanuel of Savoy.

explain it in writing; and as I think her intentions good and reasonable I make no difficulty about begging you to intercede for her, as I beg you to intercede for me, especially in your Holy Sacrifice, since I am more than anyone else in the world, Monseigneur,

Your very humble and most obedient brother and servant,

Francis, Bishop of Geneva.

76

To the Duc de Bellegarde

Annecy, 24 August 1613

Sir,

While I was still feeling the lassitude and other bad effects of an illness, I composed the 'Mémorial'[1] which you were pleased to ask of me. I added a summary which would be more convenient for you to carry when you actually go to confession, while the fuller version can be kept in reserve for you to consult in case of difficulty and to enlighten you on any point which might be obscure in the summary. The whole thing is written straightforwardly and in good faith, without art and colour, for these matters require none; their beauty lies in their simplicity, as does God's, who is their author. You will see signs of my illness, Sir, for if I had written this little work while in good health, I should no doubt have taken more trouble to make it less unworthy of its recipient. Nor was I able to write it in my own hand, but the person who wrote it does not know the use for which I intend it.

May God be blessed eternally for the goodness he is showing to your soul, Sir, inspiring you so strongly to resolve to dedicate the rest of your mortal life to the service of eternal life, which is God himself, inasmuch as he will pour life into our souls by his glory and bliss. This is life, the only real life, the

---

[1] 'Mémorial pour bien faire la confession', A. XXVI, p. 244–66. It is detailed, clear and practical, ending with a prayer to be made before confession.

only life we should live for in this world, since all life that does not lead to living eternity is death rather than life. But, Sir, if God has so lovingly inspired you to long for an eternity of glory, he has by the same token laid a duty upon you to receive his inspiration humbly and to put it into effect with the greatest care; else you will be deprived of this grace and glory, a privation the very mention of which fills the heart with terror, if it is possessed of any real courage.

That is why, in the simplicity of my heart I entreat you, Sir, to be very careful to hold fast what you already have so that you do not lose your crown. You are undoubtedly called to a manly, brave, valiant and unswerving devotion which is to serve as a mirror to show forth to many the truth of heavenly love; and is also a worthy reparation for past faults, if ever you were ranged on the side of the vanity of earthly loves.

You see, Sir, how freely my mind holds intercourse with yours and how I am carried away by the name of Father with which you have been pleased to honour me. The reason is that the name has entered into my heart, and my affections have complied to its law of love, the greatest, the strongest and the most intense of all forms of love. In consequence of this I would now beg you, Sir, to practise diligently the exercises which I have indicated in chapters 10, 11, 12 and 13 of the second part of the *Introduction*, morning and evening, for your spiritual retreat and aspirations to God. The goodness of your heart, the noble determination which God has given you will help you greatly in this practice, which you will find all the easier to fit in as you only need to spend spare moments on it; and these you can rightly steal from your other commitments. The tenth part of an hour, indeed even less, will be enough for the morning and as much again in the evening.

Oh, if you could only gently cheat your dear soul, Sir, so that having undertaken to go to communion every month for a year (a year of twelve months, however), you could add a thirteenth month when you have got as far as the twelfth, then a four-teenth, then a fifteenth, and that you could go on from month to month in this way. What a wonderful thing this would be for your heart, for as it goes on receiving its Saviour more often it would also go on being more perfectly converted to him. And this, Sir, could be done boldly without causing any sensation or interfering in your interests or leading to comment or criticism on the part of the world. During the twenty-five years that I have been serving souls experience has given me an insight into the all-powerful virtue of the Divine Sacrament for confirming hearts in the way of goodness, preserving them from evil, consoling them, and in a word making them god-like in this world, provided that they are moved by a right faith, by purity and devotion.

But I have said enough, Sir; the influence of heaven, your guardian angel and your generosity will supply what my inadequacy does not permit me to propose to you. So I pray Our Lord to let his favours abound in you ever more freely, and I am always, Sir,

Your most humble and faithful servant,
Francis, Bishop of Geneva.

77

To Soeur de Bréchard,
Sister at the Visitation in Annecy

Annecy, September 1613

I am afraid that you would make this sore leg too dear to me, my very dear and beloved daughter, if it led to a visit from you and to my sampling the skill of your nursing.[1] Indeed, I should prize this indisposition highly if it brought me such consolation; at this rate I should never want it to get better; no, not even if your Mother had come and had brought you along with her.

But as you know, my very dear daughter, this cannot be, for

[1] In the course of their sick-calls in the town two of the Visitation nuns had called on St. Francis to dress a sore on his leg but had been so overcome with emotion that they did their work badly. Soeur Bréchard then offered her services and this is the letter she had in reply.

even though in their innocence and candour the hearts of father and daughter do not need to use so much restraint, we must conform to what is required by the rigour of other hearts. So this poor Father, in all his poverty, must do without the visit of his daughters and especially of his Mother, unless he has some serious illness which warrants so great a good. My very dear Mother and my very dear daughter will pass modestly and not too far away from the house of their poor Father, without coming in and without seeing him, and they will go straight on to serve the poor who are not really their son or their father but whom they look upon as brothers and as members of Jesus Christ. So peace be with you, my very dear daughter, till tomorrow, when I shall take this sore leg to your parlour if I can; for I do not in the least deny that my very dear Mother's care and the prescription of my clever daughter would do it good. But in the meanwhile, as you cannot dress the sore leg, do something good for your poor, feeble Father's heart; pray much for him who in his turn wishes you countless blessings.

I send greetings to our sisters. Monsieur Michel[1] is very fortunate to be able to go and see my daughters when he wants to. One day we shall all see one another together in that eternal liberty of love which shall not know any bounds or any end, nor any other limit than that of its own immensity.

78

To Mère de Chantal

Annecy (1612–14)

... I am working on your Ninth Book of the *Love of God*, and today, praying in front of my crucifix, God showed me your soul and your spiritual state in the image of an excellent musician, born subject to a king who loved him dearly, and who had

---

[1] M. Michel Favre, the saint's own confessor and ordinary confessor to the Visitation community.

shown him that he cared passionately for the sweet melody of
his lute and voice. This poor singer went deaf, like you, and
no longer heard his own melodies; his master was often away,
yet he did not stop singing, because he knew that his master had
taken him into his service for his ability to sing. . . .[1]

79

To Madame d'Escrilles

Annecy, 7 January 1614

My dear and ever dearer Sister,

I have just received the two letters which you entrusted to
Madame de Travernay,[2] as well as another from her in which
she explains the nature of your trouble[3] to me; I see that this is
very considerable because of the great number of vexatious
incidents which seem to attach to it.

My very dear sister, these mists are not so thick that the sun
cannot melt them away. Believe me, God who has led you up
till now will go on holding you in his blessed hand; but you
must throw yourself into the arms of his providence with complete trust and forgetfulness of self; now is the right time. Almost everyone can manage to trust God in the sweetness and
peace of prosperity, but only his children can put their trust in
him when storms and tempests rage, I mean put their trust in
him with complete self-abandonment. If you do it, believe me
my dear sister, you will be amazed and full of wonder when
suddenly one day you realize that all the horrors which now
trouble you have simply vanished into thin air. His divine
Majesty expects this of you because he has drawn you to him
to make you his in a very special way.

Speak little and conscientiously about the man whom you
consider partly to blame; that is to say, do not dwell on the

---

[1] Cf. the famous image in the *Treatise on the Love of God*, Book 9, ch. 9, A.V.,
p. 137.
[2] Her sister-in-law with whom St. Francis also corresponded.
[3] She had been subject to calumny of some kind.

wrong you have suffered, nor speak of it often; and when you do mention it say nothing except what you really know to be true, stressing doubt where there really is doubt, in exact accordance with the truth.

I am writing to you without leisure on the most crowded day I have had for a long while. I shall write at greater length, please God, praying for your peace and consolation. Do your best to pacify your parents. Alas, on such occasions hiding your grief heals more evil in the space of an hour than open resentment could do in a year. God must take charge of it all; that is why you must entreat him to do it.

May God always be the centre of your heart, my very dear sister, my daughter. I am indeed,

Your most humble brother and servant,
Francis, Bishop of Geneva.

80

To Mère de Chantal

Annecy, 4 May 1614

Before we meet, my very dear Mother, my soul greets yours with countless good wishes. May God fill it wholly with the life and death of his Son, Our Lord.

A year ago and at about this time I was at Turin, and while I was showing the Holy Shroud[1] to a great crowd of people, several drops of the sweat that was pouring from my face chanced to fall on to the Holy Shroud itself; and then our heart made this prayer: O may it please you, Saviour of my life,

[1] The Holy Shroud (in French 'Le Saint Suaire' i.e. sudarium) is thought to have been brought to France from Constantinople after the capture of the city by the Latins in 1204. It was eventually given to the Dukes of Savoy and deposited in 1502 at the Sainte Chapelle in Chambéry where St. Francis's mother dedicated her as yet unborn child to Our Lord. The Shroud was taken to the cathedral of Turin in 1578 where the incident here described took place. The Bishop of Belley tells us that St. Francis had a great devotion to the Shroud and called it his country's shield and greatest relic. It was his favourite devotional picture and he had many copies of it, painted, engraved, embroidered, which he put in his room, his chapel, his oratory, his study, his reception rooms, and also in his breviary.

to unite my unworthy sweat to yours, and to spill my blood, my life, my affections in union with the merits of your holy sacrifice.

My very dear Mother, the Prince Cardinal was annoyed that my sweat fell on to my Saviour's Holy Shroud; but it entered my heart to say to him that Our Lord was not so particular, and that he had spilled his sweat and blood so as to unite them to ours and give them the prize of eternal life. And may our sighs unite with his so as to rise in the odour of sweetness before the eternal Father.

But now another memory comes back to me. When my brothers were ill as children I have seen my mother wrap them in my father's shirt, saying that a father's sweat could heal his child. On this holy day may our heart be wrapped in our divine Father's Shroud which bears the marks of Christ's sweat and blood; and there may our heart lie buried as at the death of our divine Saviour in an unchanging resolution ever to remain dead to itself until it rises again in eternal glory. We are buried, says the Apostle, with Jesus Christ in his death, so that we should no longer live the old life but the new life. Amen.

81

To Mère Claudine de Blonay, Abbess of Sainte-Claire d'Evian

Annecy, 18 August 1614

My very dear Sister,

At this first time of writing to you I should like to say a few words by way of preface and these will hold good for all the letters I shall send you on future occasions.

1. Neither I nor you should use any preamble in our letters; for the love of God that you have shall be my preamble for you, and my desire to have it shall be your preamble for me. 2. By virtue of this same love, either possessed or desired, I can assure you, my dear Sister, that you and all your daughters will

always find my soul open and dedicated to the service of your souls. 3. But all this is to be without ceremony, with complete freedom, for though our vocations differ in rank, the holy love to which we both aspire makes us equal and unites us in him.

Indeed, my very dear Sister, you and your daughters are happy to have at last struck the spring of that living water which leads to eternal life and to want to drink it from our Saviour's hand, to whom together with St. Catherine of Genoa and Blessed Mother Theresa you are saying this prayer: 'Lord, give me this water.'[1] May his divine Mercy be praised for ever, for he has made himself a source of living water in the midst of your community; for when we give ourselves to him in prayer Our Lord is a fountain from which our prayer can draw water to cleanse us, to cool us, to make us fruitful and fill us with sweetness.

God knows, my very dear Sister, what the monasteries are like where this holy exercise is not practised; God knows what kind of obedience, poverty and chastity is observed there in the face of his divine Providence, and if these assemblies of women are not rather communities of prisoners than of true lovers of Jesus Christ. But we do not need to consider this abuse as much as we need to weigh up fairly the great good that comes to souls in holy prayer. You are not deceived in having embraced this life, but souls which do not give themselves to prayer when they might are deceived indeed.

And nevertheless, in a certain way, as I see it, the gentle Saviour of your souls has deceived you with the cunning of love in order to draw you into a more special relationship with him, binding you in ways which only he could have thought of and leading you by paths only known to him. So be full of courage, following his attraction with holy diligence, and while real meekness and humility of heart reign among you, have no fear of being deceived.

Brother N. is an ignorant man of the right kind, for in his ignorance he knows more than many learned men; he is truly

[1] John iv, 15.

grounded in the spiritual life and anything he says to you cannot help being useful. I feel sure that his superior will not refuse you the benefit of his instructions as long as you call on his service with discretion and do not cause him too much distraction.

I have not yet been able to read the books you sent me but will do so at the first moment of leisure that comes my way. You have done well to make yourself familiar with the writings of Blessed Mother Theresa for her books are indeed a treasure of spiritual teaching.

Above all let unfeigned spiritual love reign among you, a perfect community spirit, so lovable and so little loved in this century, even in monasteries which the world admires; also holy simplicity, gentleness of heart and love of your own abjection. But work towards this constantly and firmly, my very dear Sister, not in fits and starts.

I am writing to you without leisure, my very dear Sister, but not without infinite affection for you and all your daughters; I beg them to recommend my soul to God's mercy, as I for my part will not cease to wish you blessing upon blessing, and I pray that the source of all blessing may live and reign for ever in the centre of your hearts. Amen.

I am, with heartfelt love,
Your very humble brother and servant in Our Lord,
Francis, Bishop of Geneva.

82

To the Duc de Bellegarde

Annecy, 12 September 1614

I have no greater glory in the world, my son, than that of being called father by such a son, nor have I a sweeter consolation than seeing the pleasure you derive from it. But I do not want to say any more on this subject because it cannot be put into words; it is enough that God has bestowed this grace on me, an increasing source of joy when everyone tells me that you are living for God although in the midst of the world.

O Jesus my God, how happy I am to have a son who by some miracle knows how to sing the songs of Sion in the land of Babylon! The Israelites long ago said they could not do it because they were captives and slaves of the Babylonians as well as living in their land; but the man who is not a slave of the court can adore the Lord and serve him in sanctity at the court itself. No indeed, my very dear son, although you may change the place where you live, the work you do and the people you talk to, you will never, as I hope, change your heart, nor your heart change its love, nor your love its object, since you could never choose a worthier love for your heart nor a worthier object for your love than the One who is to make you happy for ever. In this way variety in the aspect of the court and of the world will never change your own aspect, for your eyes will always be fixed on heaven to which you aspire, and your tongue will always be invoking the sovereign good which is the object of your hope.

I beg you to realize what very great pleasure it would have given me had I been able to go and see you on the occasion of the States Council, and to speak to you with that new confidence conferred by our mutual names of father and son. But as God does not want this, permitting me to be tied down here, neither you nor I should want it either. So you will be my Joshua who will fight God's cause in person, and I shall be here like another Moses, lifting up my hands to heaven, imploring the divine mercy for you so that you may overcome the difficulties in the way of your good intentions.

I will no longer entreat you now to love me, because I can say to you more briefly and clearly: be my real son with all your heart, Sir, because I am with all my heart, not only

Your very humble and obedient servant,
but your infinitely affectionate father,
Francis, Bishop of Geneva.

83

To Soeur de Chastel,
Sister at the Visitation in Annecy

Annecy, 28 October 1614

Indeed, my very dear daughter, you give me much pleasure by calling me your father, for I love your heart as a father does, seeing it still a little defenceless in the face of ordinary, slight contradictions which come its way. But I go on loving it although it sometimes thinks it will lose courage because of the little reproofs it gets from time to time; all the same it has never yet actually lost courage, this poor heart of yours, for God has upheld it in his strong hand and according to his mercy he has never abandoned his puny creature. O my very dear daughter, he will never abandon you, for although you are troubled and full of anguish about these impertinent temptations to vexation and spite, yet you never want to leave God or Our Lady, or our congregation which belongs to her, or our rules which are his will.

You are right in what you say, my poor dear Peronne-Marie, my daughter: there are two persons, two women in you. One is a certain Peronne who like her godfather Peter long ago is a little touchy, resentful and liable to flare up when approached too closely; this is the Peronne who is Eve's daughter and who is therefore bad-tempered. The other is a certain Peronne-Marie who is full of good will and wants to belong to God, and in order to belong to God she wants to be quite simply humble and humbly gentle towards all her sisters; and this is the one who would like to imitate St. Peter who was so good after Our Lord had converted him; the one who is the glorious Virgin Mary's daughter and is therefore good-tempered. And these two daughters of different mothers fight against one another, and the worthless one is so spiteful that the good one sometimes has a hard time defending herself, and then she imagines that she has been beaten and that the spiteful one is the stronger of the two. But no indeed, my poor dear Peronne-Marie, the spiteful one is not stronger than you, but she flaunts herself more, she takes you by surprise and is wrong-headed and obstinate; and when you are about to burst into tears she is very pleased because this is so much waste of time, and she is satisfied with making you lose time when she cannot make you lose eternity.

My dear daughter, lift up your heart bravely, arm yourself with the patience we ought to show towards ourselves. Rouse your heart often so that it is rather more on its guard against being taken by surprise; look out for this enemy; think of her wherever you go, if you like, for the spiteful girl goes with you everywhere and if you do not think of her she will think out something against you. But when she happens to attack you unawares, even though she makes you falter and stumble a little, do not get annoyed; just invoke Our Lord and Our Lady: they will reach out a holy helping hand to you, and if they leave you to suffer for a little while, it will be in order to make you invoke them yet again and call more loudly for their help.

Do not be ashamed of all this, my dear daughter, any more than St. Paul who confesses that there were two men in him, one rebellious to God and the other obedient. Be very simple and do not get upset; humble yourself without discouragement, encourage yourself without presumption. Remember that Our Lord and Our Lady gave you your task of housekeeping for the community and they know and can see that it harasses you; but they love you all the same provided you are humble and trustful. But do not be ashamed, daughter, of being a little grimy and covered with dust; it is better to be dusty than covered with scurvy, and as long as you humble yourself all will be well.

Pray much for me, my dear and really well loved daughter, and may God be your love and protection for ever. Amen.

Feast day of St. Simon and St. Jude, 1614.

84

To Madame Gasparde de Ballon
Sister at the Abbaye de Sainte-Catherine

Annecy, 6 January 1613–15

Our Lord loves you, my dear daughter, and loves you tenderly. And if he does not let you feel the sweetness of his holy love it is so as to make you more humble and more abject in your own eyes. But do not on that account cease to appeal to his tenderness with full confidence, especially now, at a time when we think of him as a little child in Bethlehem; for else why, my dear daughter, should he take this sweet and lovable form of childhood unless to make us love him trustfully and entrust ourselves lovingly to him?

Keep very close to the crib throughout the octave of the Holy Kings. If you love riches you will find there the gold that the Kings left; if you love honours you will find incense, and if you love things that delight the senses there is the sweet-smelling myrrh which scents the whole stable. Be rich in your love for your dear Saviour, full of honour in the private audience you have with him in prayer, and full of delight in the joy of feeling within yourself all those holy inspirations and affections which come of belonging completely to him.

As to your little outbursts of anger—you will grow out of them, or if you do not, they will serve to try you and mortify you. You see, my dear cousin, since you want to belong utterly to God, you must not let your heart be troubled, and whatever dryness you may experience, be steadfast in staying within the arms of God's mercy.

And now for your fears—they are the work of the enemy who sees that you are now quite determined to live in Our Lord without any reserves and exceptions and will make every sort of effort to upset you and make the way of holy devotion hard for you. What you must do to counteract this is to open out your heart and often repeat your protestation never to give in,

P   225

always to keep faith, to love the hardships of God's service more than the sweetness of the world's service, and say that you will never leave your Spouse.

Be very careful, my dear daughter, not to give up prayer, for that would be playing into your adversary's hand; go on steadfastly with this holy exercise and wait for Our Lord to speak to you, for one day he will say words of peace and consolation to you; and then you will know that your trouble will have been well spent and your patience useful.

Good night, my very dear daughter. Take joy and pride in living only for God and go on telling him that you are all his. Say often: May Jesus reign!

Francis, Bishop of Geneva.

85

To Mère de Chantal

Annecy, 26 January 1615[1]

This is your father's wish, my very dear daughter: may God be with you on your way; may God keep you clothed in the garment of his charity always; may God nourish your soul with the heavenly bread of his consolations; may God bring you back safe and sound to your father's house; may God be your God for ever, my dear Mother. These are the blessings which Jacob called down upon himself when he set out for Bethel,[2] and I wish them to my own self, my very dear and only daughter, as you leave this place where you stay even when you are far away, and from which you are distant even though you remain.

Go in peace, my very dear daughter, go in peace where God

---

[1] Towards the end of January Mère de Chantal set out with Soeur de Blonay to make the first foundation from Annecy at Lyons. St. Francis blessed them before they set out and privately handed Soeur de Blonay a little packet of notes, one of which she was to give to Mère de Chantal every evening when they reached the inn where they were to spend the night.

[2] Gen. xxviii, 20, 21.

calls you; stay peacefully here in the holy peace of God in which he holds and keeps you. The souls which God has made one are inseparable, for who can separate what God has joined? No, neither death, nor any other thing will ever separate us from the unity which is in Jesus Christ; may he live for ever in our heart. Amen.

And now, my dear daughter, since God is the unity of our heart, who will ever part us from him? No, neither death nor life, nor things present nor things to come[1] will ever separate us or divide our unity. So let us go on, my very dear daughter, with but one heart, wherever God calls us; for though our roads are different this cannot make us different from one another because we are pursuing one same object and one same subject.

O God of my heart, keep my very dear daughter in your hand; may her angel always be at her right hand to protect her, may the Blessed Virgin, Our Lady, always delight her by looking on her with her kindly eyes.

My very dear daughter, heavenly providence will help you: invoke it trustfully in all the difficulties which may hedge you in. As you go on, my very dear Mother, my daughter, you should grow in courage and rejoice because you are pleasing Our Lord, and his pleasure alone pleases the whole of Paradise.

As for me, I am wherever you yourself are, since his divine Majesty has willed it so for all eternity. So let us go on, my dear daughter, happily and joyously doing the work which our Master has marked out for us.

My very dear Mother, my daughter, I have been thinking about the story of the great St. Ignatius who carried Jesus Christ in his heart and cheerfully went to serve as food for the lions and suffer the martyrdom of their fangs: and here are you, here are we, going to Lyons, please our Saviour, to render Our Lord various services and prepare souls for him so that he can

[1] Cf. Rom. viii, 38.

be their Bridegroom. What can stop us from going joyfully in the name of our Saviour, since this saint went so blithely to be martyred for our Saviour?

Blessed are the souls of those who walk according to the will of the divine Spirit and seek him with all their heart, leaving everything, even the father he gave them, for the sake of following his divine Majesty!

O Lord Jesus, save, bless, confirm and preserve this heart which it has pleased you to call wholly to your divine love; and since you have led it to consecrate itself to your holy Name, may your holy Name fill it as with the balm of divine charity, spreading in perfect unity an odour of manifold sweetness for the edification of its neighbour. Yes, Lord Jesus, fill this soul to overflowing with grace, peace, consolation and blessing as it goes forth in your holy Name to be and stay wherever your glory calls. Amen.

A thousand blessings to our dear daughters. May God who called them to live together bless them; may their holy angels always be near them, bestowing many graces and heavenly consolations on their dearly beloved hearts, and may the Blessed Virgin open her motherly heart to them and protect them by virtue of her loving motherhood.

86

To Madame de Peyzieu

Annecy, February 1615

Alas, dear God, my very dear Mother, how dismayed I was to learn quite unexpectedly from your letter how long and dangerous your illness had been! For believe me, I beg of you, that I love you as a son. But blessed be God that you are almost out of danger now.

From now onwards it seems to me that you will have to get used to illness and infirmity as all part of your declining years. Lord Jesus, what real happiness it is for a soul dedicated to God to be sorely tried by tribulation before it leaves this life! My very dear Mother, how can one get to know whole-hearted and living love except among thorns, crosses and by means of a long-drawn out illness, especially if it is wearisome as well as long. So too Our Lord showed his measureless love by the measure of intensity of his toil and passion.

My dear Mother, love your Bridegroom well on your bed of suffering, for it is on this bed that he fashioned your heart when he foresaw it in his divine plan before ever it was fashioned on earth. Alas! Your Saviour counted all your pains, all your suffering, and paid with the price of his blood for all the patience and all the love you need so as to offer up your distress meekly for his glory and your salvation. Be content with gently willing all that God wills for you. I shall never fail to pray his divine Majesty for your heart's perfection, for I love, cherish and honour you tenderly.

May God be with you, my very dear Mother and daughter; may we belong to God for ever, we and our affections, and our little pains and our great pains, and everything the divine Goodness wants for us. And on this wish, I am in him, my very dear Mother, unconditionally,

Your real son and very affectionate servant,
Francis, Bishop of Geneva.

87

To Mère de Chantal at Lyons

Annecy, 5 March 1615

I wrote to you when I went to Sales, my very dear Mother, and am writing again upon my return. Three consolations came my way and you will like to know about them, for what consoles me affects you as it does myself.

Firstly, my dear little sister[1] whom I find increasingly lovable and determined to be good and devout.

---

[1] Baronne de Thorens, daughter of Madame de Chantal and wife of St. Francis's brother.

Secondly, yesterday, Ash Wednesday, I spent the whole morning alone in the gallery and the chapel[1] where I remembered with joy the dear and desirable conversations we had at the time of your general confession; I cannot tell you what good thoughts and feelings God gave me on this subject.

Thirdly, there had been a heavy snowfall and the courtyard was over a foot deep in snow. John went and swept a little clearing in the snow and threw some corn to feed the pigeons who all came together to this refectory to eat in the most peaceful and sedate way; and I took delight in watching them. You would not believe how greatly these little creatures edified me, for they never made a sound, and those who had finished feeding before the others flew away to a place close by to wait. And when they had cleared about half of what was there, a number of small birds who had been watching from afar came to join them; and all the pigeons that were still feeding retired to one corner so as to leave more room for the smaller birds who then settled down to their meal without the pigeons disturbing them in any way.

I admired this charity; for the poor pigeons were so loath to disturb the small birds to whom they were giving alms, that they all clustered together at one end of the table. I admired the discretion of the smaller birds who did not come to beg till they saw that the pigeons had nearly got to the end of their meal and that there was still plenty left over. In short, I could not restrain my tears to see the loving simplicity of the doves and the way the small birds trusted their charity. I doubt if a sermon would have touched me so deeply. This tableau of virtue did me a great deal of good the whole day.

But here they come telling me to hurry, my dear Mother. My heart talks to you about my thoughts and my thoughts generally talk to me about your heart which is quite certainly one with mine. . . . You are most precious to my heart, my very dear Mother. May God make us ever more and more his own. I send greetings to our dear Sisters.

Francis, Bishop of Geneva.

[1] At the castle of Sales.

88

To Madame de Peyzieu

Annecy, 21 May 1615

O how deeply afflicted I am for you, my very dear Mother, for I see your motherly heart plunged in great grief, a grief, however, which is no matter for blame or wonder when one considers how lovable your son was for whose loss we feel such bitter sorrow now that he has left us a second time.[1]

My very dear Mother, this dear son of yours was indeed one of the best sons who ever lived; all who knew him acknowledged and knew him as such. But is this not our greatest comfort at present, my very dear Mother? For it seems to me that men whose life is so worthy of remembrance and esteem still live on even after their death since we take such great pleasure in recalling and describing them to those who remain behind.

Your son, my very dear Mother, had already put a great distance between himself and us, having of his own free will left and renounced the part of the world where he was born so as to go and serve his God and his king in the new world. His generosity had moved him to do this and yours had made you agree to so honourable a resolution for the sake of which you had renounced the joy of ever seeing him again in this life; and all that was left to you was the hope of having letters from him from time to time. And now, my very dear Mother, it has pleased divine Providence that he should leave this other new world to go to the oldest and most desirable of all worlds, to which we must all go, all of us in due season, and where you will see him sooner than you would have done had he stayed in that new world in the thick of the toils and conquests he was willing to undertake for his king and for the Church. In short,

---

[1] Her son, Louis de Silignieu, was killed on 18 November 1614 by the Portuguese on the island of Maragnan in the course of a French expedition to establish missionaries in Brazil.

he has ended his mortal days while doing his duty and fulfilling the obligations of his oath as a soldier. This kind of death is excellent, and we can be certain that God will have made it a happy end for him, since from the cradle he had favoured him with the grace of a most Christian life.

Take comfort then, my very dear Mother, and ease your heart by adoring divine Providence which orders all things sweetly; and although the reasons for God's decrees are hidden from us, the truth of his mild graciousness is manifest and makes us believe that he has ordered all things in perfect goodness.

You are yourself as it were on the point of going where your beloved child is now; and when you get there you would not like him to be in the Indies, for you will see that he is far better off among angels and saints than among tigers and savages. But while you are waiting for the hour when you too may set sail, assuage your motherly heart by thinking about this very blessed eternity in which he now is and which is close at hand for you. And instead of writing to him sometimes, speak to God for him, and he will at once know all you would like him to know and will receive all the help you will give him by your wishes and prayers the moment you have made and delivered them into his divine Majesty's hands.

Christians are very wrong to behave in such an unchristian manner and to violate the laws of charity so cruelly by succumbing to the laws of fear; but you must pray to God, my very dear Mother, for those who committed this great crime, and offer this prayer of yours for the soul of your dead son. This is the most pleasing prayer that we can make to him who made a like prayer on the cross, to which his most blessed Mother responded with all her heart, loving him with most ardent charity.

I cannot tell you how deeply my heart grieves for him; for was he not my dear brother who loved me greatly? I have prayed for him and I will always go on praying for him, and also for you, my very dear Mother, whom I want to honour and love all my life, also on behalf of this brother of mine whose immortal friendship calls upon me to be ever more and more, Madam, my very dear Mother,

> Your most humble, most faithful and most obedient son and servant,
> Francis, Bishop of Geneva.

89

To Mère Favre, Superior of the Visitation at Lyons[1]

Annecy, November 1615

I can indeed see with my own eyes and feel in my own heart, my very dear daughter, that you have made a great act of renunciation. But oh how blessed are they who have stripped their own heart, for Our Lord will clothe them with grace, and give them his blessing and his special protection. Poor and frail creatures that we are, we can hardly do anything good in this mortal life without suffering some ill; we cannot even, as it were, serve God on the one hand without leaving him on the other, and often we must leave God for God's sake, renouncing our delight in him in order to serve him in his pain and toil.

Alas, my very dear daughter, girls who get married have to renounce father and mother and their own country to submit to husbands whom they often do not know, or at least whose temper is unknown to them; and the object is to provide children for this world. So God's daughters, leading a holy and pure life, must show still greater courage in providing children for his divine Majesty.

And yet, my very dear daughter, we can never really be parted from one another, we whom Our Lord's own blood keeps closely joined together and united, I mean his love by the merit of his blood. Indeed, for my own part, I am so much yours that the two or three days' distance which seems to

---

[1] Mère Favre was left in charge of the new foundation at the end of October 1615.

separate us physically, unite me to you spiritually with all the more affection, as to a very dear daughter. You will be the first after our Mother in my prayer and concern: a sweet concern, however, as I have such absolute confidence in the heavenly care divine Providence has for your soul; and this soul of yours would be happy indeed if you could cast all your fears upon its infinite love.

Come now, my dear daughter, keep your eyes lifted up on high to God; increase your courage by holy humility, fortify it with meekness, confirm it by a steady effort; always make your mind rule over your inclinations and moods, do not allow fears to take hold of your heart: the effort you make one day will teach you what to do the next day. You have before now conquered many a difficulty, and you did it by God's grace; the same grace will be with you on future occasions and will deliver you from difficulties and rough roads as you come upon them, for God will send an angel to carry you over the most dangerous places.

Do not turn to look at your infirmities and insufficiency except to humble yourself, and never so as to give way to discouragement. Look often at God who is at your right hand, and at the two angels he has destined for you, one for your own person and one for the direction of your little family. Often say to these holy angels: my lords, what had we better do? Entreat them constantly to pass on to you knowledge of the divine will which they are always contemplating, and the inspirations which Our Lady wants you to receive through her own generous love. Do not look at the many and various imperfections in yourself and in the children whom God and Our Lady have entrusted to you, unless to keep alive in you the fear of offending God; but never let imperfections dismay you, for it is not surprising that every individual herb and flower in a garden needs its own particular kind of care.

I knew about some of the graces which God showed to our dear sister Marie Renée[1] when she died. She was very much my

---

[1] Madame Auxerre, one of the foundresses of the convent at Lyons, died a holy death on 14 October.

daughter; for when I was there she made a review of her whole life so as to tell me all about it and reveal herself; she did this with incredible humility and confidence, and without great necessity, edifying me in a high degree when I think of her. And there she is now, praying for us and specially for you because she died your daughter and with your assistance.

Do me the kindness, my dear daughter, of consoling me by writing to me often, and always telling me in all confidence the things you think it useful for me to know about the state of your heart, which I bless in our Saviour's name with all my own heart, and I am in God all yours.

Francis, Bishop of Geneva.

90

To the Duc de Bellegarde

Annecy, 6 January 1616

Sir,

At the beginning of the new year I would like to assure you of my good wishes and of my obedience which in no way resemble the years which perish and pass away with their vicissitudes; but the infinite affection I have for your honour and glory is firm, lasting and exempt from all change except that of constant increase. For it was fashioned by God's eternal hand, in the same way as your kindly feeling towards me; and the link between us is our concern for eternity. It is a wholly supernatural feeling, transcending the laws of nature, which has given me the happiness of having you as a son, and you, Sir, the courage and humility to own me as your father.

O how often, my dear son, has the fatherly feeling I bear you urged my heart with loving zeal to implore God's goodness which has ordained this, to fill your heart to overflowing with holy love and to establish his holy kingdom within you! I know that good children often think of their fathers; but a father's thoughts dwell on his children always.

Persevere, my very dear son, in this great courage and determination which keeps you lifted high above temporal things, making you pass over them like a happy halcyon bird lifted safely above the waves of the world which flood this age. Keep your eyes steadfastly fixed on that blissful day of eternity towards which the course of years bears us on; and these as they pass, themselves pass by us stage by stage until we reach the end of the road. But meanwhile, in these passing moments there lies enclosed as in a tiny kernel the seed of all eternity; and in our humble little works of devotion there lies hidden the prize of everlasting glory, and the little pains we take to serve God lead to the repose of a bliss that can never end. May the blood of our Saviour who made salvation so easy for us be for ever blessed!

Live for ever in God and for God, Sir, and love constantly

Your very humble and obedient servant,

Francis, Bishop of Geneva.

91

To Soeur de Chevron-Villette,
Novice at the Visitation at Lyons

Annecy, February or March 1616

I am thinking about your letter, my very dear daughter, in which you describe your imperfections and your distress so very sincerely, and I should like to meet your wish and try and tell you what you had better do. But I have little leisure, nor do I think you really need my advice; for you see, my very dear daughter, there is no other remedy for most of the things you describe except the passing of time and the exercise of your rule. It is the same with bodily illness where the cure depends on a well regulated life.

Selfishness, complacency, false liberty of spirit, these are things which one cannot well uproot from the human heart; one cannot do more than prevent them from bearing their

fruit, which is sin; for one can never altogether stop their up-
rising, their first impetus, their shoots, as it were, their first im-
pact and stirring; but one can moderate their number and fre-
quency by the practice of opposite virtues and chiefly by the
love of God. So we must be patient and amend and curb our
bad habits little by little, get the better of our aversions and
master our inclinations and moods as they come up; for in
short, my very dear daughter, this life is continual warfare and
there is no one who can say: I am not being attacked. Rest is
reserved for heaven where the palm of victory awaits us. On
earth we must fight our battle between fear on the one hand and
hope on the other, in the knowledge that hope is always the
stronger because he who comes to our help is almighty. So
never give up working constantly towards your amendment
and perfection. Charity is made up of three elements: love of
God, affection for oneself and love for one's neighbour. Your
rule leads you to practise all three. Cast your heart and mind
and care upon God again and again as the day goes on; do it
very trustfully and tell him with David: I am yours, Lord, save
me. Do not spend much time speculating about the kind of
prayer God gives you but follow the leading of his grace
humbly and simply. Because of the love you owe yourself you
should be on your guard to eradicate your wrong inclinations.
Never be dismayed to find that you are worthless and thoroughly
ill-tempered. Alas! Deal gently and lovingly with your heart,
raising it up when it falls, and longing ardently for its perfection. Above all, do what you can to strengthen the superior
part of your spirit, not stopping short at feelings and consolations but passing on to resolutions, definite purposes and pro-
jects which your rule, your Superior and your reason will inspire you to undertake.

Do not be soft with yourself: soft-hearted mothers spoil
their children. Do not be tearful and sorry for yourself, nor
dismayed by these importunate and violent reactions of yours
which you find so difficult to own up to. No, my daughter, do
not be downcast; God allows this so as to make you humble
with a real humility and abject and vile in your own eyes. You

must not try to fight against this except by raising your heart up to God, by thinking of the Creator instead of the creature, and by constantly praying for humility and simplicity of heart.

Be kind to your neighbour, and in spite of the anger which you feel rising up within you, say our Saviour's divine words as often as you can: I love these neighbours of mine, Lord, eternal Father, because you love them, and you have given them to me as brothers and sisters, and you want me to love them as you yourself love them. The main thing is to love your sisters to whom God's own hand has joined you in a divine association; bear with them, embrace them and receive them into your own heart. My very dear daughter, let me assure you that I have a very special desire for your progress as it is God's will that I should.

Francis, Bishop of Geneva.

92

To Mère Favre, Superior of the Visitation at Lyons

Annecy, 17 April 1616

I have just returned from the Chablais, my very dear daughter, where thanks be to God I left the Barnabite Fathers established as His Highness, the Prince Cardinal, commanded. Tomorrow I am going on a visit of condolence to Madame de Tournon whose husband[1] has just died, being obliged to do this no less by the relationship between us than by the honour in which I hold the memory of the deceased. This is to explain to you, my very dear daughter, why I am writing to you in haste, though I do want to answer the two questions you put to me some time ago; for I can see that it is hopeless to wait for a better opportunity, since continual pressure of affairs seems to be my fate.

[1] Count of Tournon, Governor of Savoy.

My very dear daughter, there are two sorts of good desires: those which increase the grace and the glory of God's servants, and those which have no effect at all. Desires of the first kind take this form: I should like to give alms, for example, but I do not do it because I have not the wherewithal. And desires like this greatly increase charity and sanctify the soul; thus devout souls desire martyrdom, the ignominy of the cross which is not, however, within their reach. Desires of the second kind take this form: I should like to give alms but I do not want to do it. And these desires are not impossible of fulfilment, for nothing stands in their way except cowardice, luke-warmness and lack of resolution; that is why they are useless and do not sanctify the soul or lead to any growth in grace; and so St. Bernard says that hell is full of this kind of desire.

It is true that in order to clear up your difficulty completely you must understand that there are desires which seem to belong to the second group but really belong to the first, and similarly the other way round. For example, no servant of God could be without this desire: O how I long to serve God better! Alas! When shall I serve as I ought? And because we can always do better it seems to us that these desires only remain ineffective because we do not try hard enough; but this is not true, for they remain ineffective because of the condition of this mortal life in which it is less easy for us to act than to desire. That is why these desires are as a rule good and make the soul better, kindling and stirring it to progress.

But when some specific occasion which we might use presents itself, and if we then stop at our desire without putting it into effect, as when for example we have an opportunity of forgiving an injury, of renouncing our own will in some instance, and we then instead of forgiving or renouncing just say to ourselves: I should like to forgive but I cannot, I should like to give up my own will but it is impossible; very well then, who could fail to see that this sort of desire is empty and even increases my guilt in that I have such a strong impulse to do the right thing and yet do not translate it into action? And desires that take this form seem to belong to the first category but in fact belong to the second. And now I think you will be able to solve your problem without difficulty, though should any remain, do write and tell me about it, and sooner or later I will answer with all my heart, which is indeed all yours, my very dear daughter.

Those who are liable to be pursued by unseemly ideas while meditating on the life and death of our Saviour should, as far as they are able, simply represent the mysteries to their minds by faith without using their imagination. For example: My Saviour is crucified is a proposition of faith; it is enough for me to apprehend this quite simply as a fact of faith without my picturing how his body hung on the cross. And as soon as the wrong kind of pictures want to appear in our imagination we must dodge our enemy and take our revenge by means of aspirations grounded on faith: O my crucified Jesus, I adore you, I adore your torment, your affliction, your agony! You are my salvation. For you see, my very dear daughter, it would be playing into your enemy's hands to want to give up meditating on the death and life of our Saviour on this account; this is precisely the way in which the enemy tries to deprive us of our greatest happiness. So what we have to do is to swerve and turn aside, relying on faith alone.

God be with you, my very dear daughter, and may we belong to God for ever so as to love him and bless him without end.

93

To Soeur Marie-Aimée de Blonay,
Novice Mistress at the Visitation at Lyons

Annecy, April or May 1616

How right and reasonable it is, my very dear daughter, that I should spend a little while writing to you and how very happy I am to do it! Please God I may be able to say what you need for your consolation.

To live according to the spirit, my beloved daughter, means

to think, speak and act according to the virtues which reside in the spirit and not according to the senses and feelings which reside in the flesh. We must use and master the latter and not live according to them; but the spiritual virtues must be nurtured and all the rest made subject to them.

But which are the virtues of the spirit, my dear daughter? There is faith which shows us the truths which are not accessible to the senses; hope which makes us strive for things invisible; charity which makes us love God above all things and our neighbour as ourselves, not with a sensual, natural, selfish love but with a love that is pure, firm and changeless, being grounded in God.

You see, my daughter, when we go by human reason rooted in the flesh it happens over and over again that we do not abandon ourselves sufficiently to God, since we imagine that as we are worthless God cannot think much of us; for men who live according to worldly wisdom despise those who are not useful. But the spirit, on the contrary, which relies on faith, grows in courage when it is hemmed in by difficulties, for it knows well that God loves, supports and helps those who are weak and needy, provided they fix their hope in him. Human reason wants to know everything that is going on because it imagines that nothing in which it cannot have its say is any good; the spirit, on the other hand cleaves to God and often says that whatever is not God cannot matter to it; and in the same way as charity makes it able to understand what is revealed to it, so abnegation and humility make it willing to renounce insight into whatever is hidden from it.

To live according to the spirit is to love according to the spirit; to live according to the flesh is to love according to the flesh, for love is the life of the soul as the soul is the life of the body. One of the sisters is very gentle and agreeable, I love her tenderly; she loves me, she goes out of her way to oblige me and in return I love her too: who could fail to see that I love her according to the senses and the flesh? For animals who are without a spirit, having only senses and flesh, love their benefactors and those who treat them gently and kindly. One of the sisters is ungracious, rough and lacking in courtesy, but apart from that she is very devout and even longs to become more gentle and more civilized; and I do everything, not for any pleasure I take in her, nor standing to gain anything, but only to please God; I cherish her, I go up to her, I serve her, I embrace her: this is love according to the spirit, for the flesh has no part in it.

I am a poor, frightened little creature, the baby of the family, timid and shy by nature and completely lacking in self-confidence; and that is why I should like people to let me live unnoticed and all on my own according to my inclination, because I have to make such enormous efforts about shyness and my excessive fears. Who can fail to see that this is not living according to the spirit? No indeed, my dear daughter, for when I was still very young and had little understanding I already lived like this; but although according to my temperament I am shy, nervous and as timid as a mole, I want to have a good try to overcome these natural passions and little by little learn to do everything that belongs to the office which obedience, proceeding from God, has laid upon me. Who can fail to see that this is living according to the spirit?

My dear daughter, living according to the spirit means doing the actions which the spirit of God asks of us, saying the words and thinking the things that he wants. And when I say thinking the things he wants, I am referring to your willed thoughts. I am miserable and so I don't feel like talking: draymen and parrots do as much; I feel miserable, but since charity demands that I should talk I will do it: that is what spiritual people say. I have been slighted and I get cross: peacocks and monkeys do as much; I have been slighted and I rejoice: that is what the apostles did. So to live according to the spirit is to do what faith, hope and charity teach us to do, whether in things temporal or things spiritual.

So live wholly according to the spirit, my very dear daughter, live sweetly and in peace. Be quite confident that God will help you, and in all that happens rest in the arms of his mercy and fatherly goodness. May God be your all for ever, and I am all yours in him, as you know well. Your father is well and so are all those who belong to you according to the flesh; so be it with all those who belong to you according to the spirit. Amen.

94

To Mère de Chantal

Annecy, 18 May 1616[1]

My very dear Mother,

I know that I shall have to go on being alone and silent today and perhaps tomorrow: if this is so, I shall prepare my soul as you are doing and as I told you.

I agree that you should continue your exercise of complete self-renunciation, leaving yourself to Our Lord and to me. But include some acts of your own, my very dear Mother, some ejaculatory prayers expressing your renunciation, as for example: I really want this, Lord; take away, take away everything that clothes my heart. O Lord, no indeed, Lord, I except and withhold nothing; tear me away from myself. O self, I put you away for ever, until my Lord commands me to take you up again. You must say this firmly from time to time, but calmly.

Furthermore, my very dear Mother, you must not keep any sort of nurse, but as you see, you must give up even the nurse who will nevertheless still be there; and you must remain before the throne of God's mercy like a poor, needy little creature, quite naked, never asking for any action or affection for this creature. At the same time you must practise indifference with regard to all things of this kind which it may please God to prescribe for you, without stopping to consider whether it is I who am to serve as your nurse. As you see, if you took a nurse to your own liking you would not be going out of yourself but

---

[1] In May 1616, during the week before Whitsun, Mère de Chantal made a retreat, and as St. Francis was ill there was an interchange of letters. Three letters which she wrote in answer to his at this time escaped the holocaust she made after his death of all her letters to him. They are printed in the appendix to A. XVII and in her own works, Vol. 4, p. 109 ff.

still have your own way; but this is what you must chiefly avoid.

Renunciation of this kind is admirable: that of your own esteem and even of what the world thought you (which really amounted to nothing, except in comparison with people who are indeed worthless), of your own will, your pleasure in all creatures and in natural love, and in short, renunciation of the whole of yourself which is to be buried and abandoned for ever. We must neither see it nor know anything about it and act as though we had never in fact seen or known it, until such time as God orders us to do otherwise in whatever way he decides. Write and tell me what you think about this. May God make me all his for ever. Amen. For I am his here and also where I am in you, most completely, as you know; for we are inseparable except in the exercise and practice of our complete self-renunciation for God's sake.

95

To Mère de Chantal

Annecy, 21 May 1616

All is going very well, my very dear Mother. You are right, and you must remain stripped bare of all things until God clothes you again. Our Lord told his apostles to wait 'until you are clothed with power from on high'.[1] Your solitude should not be interrupted until tomorrow after mass.

My very dear Mother, it is true that your imagination is wrong in trying to persuade you that you have not relinquished and given up your care about yourself and your spiritual state; for have you not left and forgotten everything? This evening say that you renounce all virtues, only wanting them in the measure in which God gives them to you, and that you do not want to be in any way anxious to acquire virtues except in so far as his Goodness will use you in this way as he thinks fit.

[1] Luke xiv, 49.

244

Our Lord loves you, my Mother; he wants you to be all his. From now on rely only on his arms to carry you, on his breast and his providence for your repose; do not let your eyes stray elsewhere nor your spirit rest except in him; keep your will simply united to his in everything that he is pleased to do with you, in you, by you and for you, and in everything outside yourself too, so that nothing whatever stands between you and God. Think no longer about the friendship in which God has joined us, nor about your children, nor your body, nor your soul, nor indeed anything whatever; for you have consigned everything to God. Clothe yourself in our crucified Saviour, love him in his suffering, offer up aspirations on this subject. No longer do what you have to do because you want to do it but solely because it is God's will.

I am very well, thanks be to God. This morning I began my review of conscience and I shall finish it tomorrow. Without feeling it, I know that in the depths of my heart there is renewed confidence to serve God better in holiness and justice all my days; for I too am stripped bare, thanks to him who died stripped bare for us so as to give us the courage to live in this state for him. Live happily and in peace, my very dear Mother, and be clothed in Jesus Christ Our Lord. Amen.

Francis, Bishop of Geneva.

96

To Soeur de Bréchard,
Superior at the Visitation at Moulins

Annecy, 22 July 1616[1]

You are about to render to Our Lord and to his glorious

---

[1] On this day four sisters, among them Soeur de Bréchard and Soeur Humberte (see next letter) set out from Annecy to make a foundation at Moulins. Before they left, St. Francis gave them his blessing and, '. . . this holy and kind prelate gave each of them a letter in which he had written devout instructions, to each according to her particular need.' (Mère de Chaugy, *Histoire de la Fondation*.) This is the letter to the new superior.

Mother a service which can be called apostolic; for you are going to gather together a number of souls in one congregation, my very dear daughter, with a view to leading them in a new band into spiritual warfare for God's glory and against the world, the devil and the flesh; or rather, you are going to collect a new swarm of bees in a new hive to do God's work of divine love, which is sweeter above honey.

So go forth very bravely with perfect trust in the goodness of him who calls you to this holy task. When has anyone ever hoped in the Lord and been disappointed? Mistrust of your own powers is good as long as it is the groundwork of confidence in God's power; but if you are ever in any way discouraged, anxious, sad or melancholy I entreat you to cast this away as the temptation of temptations; and never allow your spirit to argue or reply in any way to any anxiety or down-heartedness to which you may feel inclined. Remember this simple truth which is beyond all doubt: God allows many difficulties to beset those who want to serve him but he never lets them sink beneath the burden as long as they trust in him. This, in a few words, is a complete summary of what you most need: never under any pretext whatsoever to yield to the temptation of discouragement, not even on the plausible pretext of humility.

Humility, my very dear daughter, may refuse office but it does not persist stubbornly in its refusal; and being employed by those in power, it does not enter into any further argument about its unworthiness, but believes all things, hopes all things, endures all things, as does charity; it is always simple. Holy humility is the great partner of obedience, and in the same way as it never presumes to think itself capable of anything whatever, it always believes obedience capable of everything; and as true simplicity humbly refuses office, so true humility simply does what it is told.

Your body is feeble, but charity, which is your wedding garment, will cover up all that. A person of feeble constitution makes all who know her want to help her and even inspires special tenderness and love, provided she shows that she is bearing her cross devoutly and lovingly. You must be as simple and frank in taking and asking for remedies as you are gentle and brave in enduring your infirmity. A person who can keep calm in spite of pain and weakness, and peaceful when harassed by a great many different things to do, is very nearly perfect; and although there are few people, even among religious, who have attained this degree of happiness, they do exist and have always existed, and we must aim at this high degree of perfection.

Almost everyone finds some virtues easy to practise and others harder, and everyone extols the virtue which they find easy and tries to exaggerate the difficulty of the others. There were ten virgins and only five had enough oil of merciful and meek kindness. An even temper, gentleness and sweetness are more rare than perfect chastity but no less desirable for that. I commend these virtues to you, my very dear daughter, because the flame of good example depends on them as on oil in a lamp; nothing edifies others more than a loving good temper.

Keep the scales of justice well balanced between your daughters so that natural gifts do not make you partial in giving your affection and help. How many people who are outwardly surly are very agreeable in God's eyes! Beauty, a pleasant manner and speech often make people who are still living according to their inclinations most attractive; charity looks for real virtue and for beauty of heart, and gives itself to all without partiality.

Go forth, then, my dear daughter, to do the work for which God has elected you. He will be your right hand so that no difficulty shall move you; he will hold you by his hand so that you may walk in his path. So be of great courage, and may your courage endure. And the way to get it is to keep on asking him who alone can give it to you; he will give it to you if you follow the leading of his grace with a simple heart. May the love, peace and consolation of the Holy Spirit be in your soul for ever. Amen. You are my daughter and I give you my blessing with a father's love. May God bless you as you set forth and where you are now to live, as you serve him, as you serve your neighbour, as you humble yourself to your very nothingness, as you lift yourself up to your All; and may God always be your all, my very dear daughter. Amen.

Francis, Bishop of Geneva.

97

To Soeur Humbert of the Visitation at Moulins

Annecy, 22 July 1616

To my very dear daughter, Sister Marie-Avoye Humbert.

Do not allow yourself to be in the least troubled by those tricks of your imagination, those strange or terrible thoughts which come to your mind, for I really know your heart and I assure you before Our Lord that you do not run any risk of sin thereby. And in order to strengthen you in this belief, when you have finished your morning prayers, disown by a brief and simple act every kind of thought that is contrary to divine love, saying: I renounce all thoughts that are not for you, O my God; I disown them and cast them off for ever. And then when they attack you, you do not have to do anything except say from time to time: O Lord, I have rejected this, you know I have. Sometimes you will kiss your crucifix or show by some other outward sign that you confirm your repudiation of them. And do not get upset, do not torment yourself, because all these ideas not only cannot separate you from God but are even the cause for your ever closer union to his mercy.

So go forth calmly and sweetly in peace to serve God and Our Lady where you have been summoned by their will, and may the grace and consolation of the Holy Spirit be with you for ever. Amen. My very dear daughter, live calmly and simply in God, always loving your own abjection and being courageous in the service of him who died on the cross to save you.

98

To Mère de Chantal

Annecy, 1616

What more can one say to a soul which God has for so long drawn to complete repose in him and in his providence except just this: stay where you are, my daughter, hidden in the most secret place of this holy tabernacle, giving yourself up completely to the will of him who deigns to take care of you. Your only care should be to please him by depending utterly on his love and trusting him, by your calm vigilance in helping his dear brides to advance in ever purer service of heaven, by exact observance, paying special attention to kindness and helpfulness without ever fearing to exceed in these holy virtues. Do this generously, cheerfully and sweetly and you will find God's graces abounding in you. I pray for this with all my soul which loves yours perfectly. Pray for him who is unconditionally yours. Blessed be God. Amen. Ever be joyful with that peaceful and devout joy which is grounded in love of your own abjection, and cultivate a calm and peaceful humility of heart, accepting all sorts of suffering and abjection, not deeming yourself worthy of anything else.

99

To the Présidente Le Blanc de Mions

Annecy, 7 April 1617

I assure you, my very dear daughter, that this is my first free moment, and even then I am stealing it from among a host of affairs so as to write to you at some length in reply to your letter concerning your dear soul. Now I beg you to talk kindly to your heart telling it what mine is going to say to you. How

happy you are, my dear daughter, to have got out of the
clutches of the world and its vanities! As far as I am able to
judge in the short time I have known you your heart is made
very specially for divine love and not for love of earthly things.

Immolate all your affections to God by often renewing your
resolution to use every moment of your life in the service of the
divine Bridegroom's holy love. . . . You should spend some
time in prayer every day unless urgent business prevents it; for,
as you have told me, when you persevere with this holy exercise
you feel a great increase of recollection which is not the case
when you give it up. But so as to suit this useful exercise to
your quick and very prompt mind it will be enough if you
spend a short half-hour at it every day, or a quarter of an hour;
for this, together with aspirations, recollecting your heart in
God and ejaculatory prayer made in the course of the day, will
be ample to keep your heart united with its divine object; and
this prayer could even be made during mass so as to gain
time. . . .

And since you tell me that you have as yet prayed and meditated very little at home, your mind being so active and restless
that it cannot concentrate, I tell you that you must try all the
same to make it stop and think, to slow down its pace gradually
so that it may go about its business calmly and tranquilly in all
circumstances. And do not imagine that calmness and tranquillity will make you less prompt in your work; on the contrary,
it will be more successful.

This is how to set about it. For example: in accordance with
the misery of our human condition you sometimes need to eat;
you should sit down quietly and stay in your chair until you
have really restored yourself by a proper meal. You want to go
to bed; undress without haste. You have got to get up; do it
peacefully, without throwing yourself about, without calling
and hurrying your maid. And in this way you must, as it were,
cheat your natural impulsiveness and gradually moderate it and
teach it a holy love of the middle way. To those who are
naturally flabby and lazy we should say: make haste, for time is
valuable; but to people like you we say: go gently, for peace,

tranquillity and a calm mind are precious things, and time is more usefully employed when you use it peacefully.

I tell you, my dear daughter, and I say it firmly, that you must do God's will faithfully in the matter of your old temptation, agreeing in all humility and sincerity to God's decree by which you find yourself in your present state of life. We must stay in our own ship to make the journey from this life to the next, and stay there willingly and lovingly. Even if it is not God's hand that has put us there but some human agency, we are there and we must stay put without fuss or protest. O how many ecclesiastics embarked on their particular ship for the wrong sort of reasons or by pressure brought to bear on them by relations to enter this state! They make a virtue of necessity and love makes them stay where force has put them. Or else what would become of them? Where there is less of our choice there is more submission to the divine will.

So let my dear daughter assent to the divine will and often say with all her heart: Yes, eternal Father, I want to be in this walk of life because it has seemed good in your sight. And moreover, my very dear daughter, I entreat you to be very faithful in practising this assent to your state of life and your dependence on it; thus you must sometimes when occasion offers, my dear daughter, call that particular person[1] by the name which repels you, and in speaking to him you should not only remonstrate but also speak with deference and regard. This point is so important for the perfection of your soul that I would willingly write it in my own blood.

How are we to show our love of him who suffered so much for us if not when we are beset by circumstances we loathe and abhor and which go against the grain? We must thrust our head among the thorns of difficulty and let our heart be pierced by the lance of contradiction; drink the gall and swallow the vinegar, eat wormwood and bitter aloes as it is God who invites us. In short, my dear daughter, since you courted and preferred temptation in the past with all your heart, you must now court and prefer this assent with all your heart. And if you

[1]Her husband.

find yourself in some extraordinary difficulty on this subject by the fault of this person, do not undertake anything without having considered eternity, made an act of indifference and taken the advice of some worthy servant of God, if the matter is urgent, or even writing to me, if time permits, because I am your father; for I think that the enemy, seeing you overcome this temptation by our assent to the divine will, is sure to think out all sorts of manœuvres to trouble us.

For the rest, may a most holy and divine humility live and reign in all and above all: your clothes should be simple but in accordance with what is properly fitted to your rank so that you do not put off younger women from following in your footsteps but rather attract them. Your speech should be simple, courteous and quiet, your gestures and conversation neither too constrained and guarded nor yet too free and relaxed, your face clear and clean. And to sum up, let sweetness and modesty be the order of the day, as is fitting to any daughter of God . . .

100

To the Présidente Le Blanc de Mions

Annecy, 26 April 1617

This is in reply to your letter of the 14th, my very dear daughter. Tell dear Barbe-Marie[1] who loves me so much and whom I love still more, that she can talk freely about God wherever she thinks this may be useful, cheerfully giving up any fear of what those who are listening may think or say about her. In short, I have already told her that she should not say or do anything so as to win praise, nor yet leave anything undone or unsaid for fear of being praised. And one is not hypocritical if one's actions are not as good as one's words; for goodness me, where on earth should we be? I should have to be silent for fear of being a hypocrite, because if I were to talk about perfection it would mean that I considered myself perfect. No indeed,

[1] Herself.

my very dear daughter, I don't think I am perfect because I talk about perfection any more than I think I am an Italian because I talk Italian; but I think I know the language of perfection because I have learnt it from people to whom I have talked and who really knew the language.

Tell her to powder her hair, since her intention is upright; for speculations on this sort of topic are idle. Do not let your mind get tangled up in these cobwebs. Barbe-Marie's mental hair is even more unruly than the hair on her head and that is why it gets tied up in knots. She must not be so fussy and waste her energy on little details which Our Lord does not worry about. Do tell her to go on in good faith, keeping to the middle way of the lovable virtues of simplicity and humility, and not rushing to extremes with so many subtle arguments and considerations. Let her boldly powder her hair; don't pheasants, those pretty birds, powder and dust their plumage so as not to risk getting lice? Tell her to pray either by using points of meditation, as we agreed, or as she used to pray, it doesn't matter which; we seem to remember telling her that she should only prepare the points and try to keep to them at the beginning; if she relished meditation it was a sign that this was the method she was to follow, at any rate for the moment. If however God's sweet presence occupied her later on, she was to yield to it and to the colloquy she makes by God's own power, there being nothing wrong with this as it is described in your letter; all the same, she must sometimes talk in her own person to this great All, as though desiring her own nothingness to do something. Since you read my books I will add nothing further, except to tell you to go on your way simply, straightforwardly, openly and with a child's naïveté, sometimes carried in your Father's arms, sometimes led by his hand. . . . I am very happy that my books have found a welcome in your mind which was brave enough to think it could get along all on its own; but are they not your father's books? And you the dear daughter of his heart, by God's grace, to whom be honour and glory for ever. . . .

101

To Madame Louise de Ballon,
Sister at the Abbaye Sainte Catherine

June 1617

My dear, really very dear Daughter and Cousin,

You certainly must get this poor woman away and protect her from her fate, for the relaxed style of living at the place where she is now staying is so dangerous that it is a miracle any of them escape downfall. Alas, my poor child, you are rightly astonished that a creature should want to offend God, for this is astonishing beyond measure; nevertheless it does happen, as one can unfortunately see any day. And what dooms these poor idle women is their ill-starred beauty and attractiveness which they attribute to themselves because evil men persuade them of it; they are so preoccupied with their body that they cease to have any care for their soul. Well, my dear daughter, you must do whatever you can, but without losing your own peace of mind.

As to yourself, my dear cousin and daughter, do not lose heart; for you should be so much in love with God that even if you can do nothing whatever when you are in his presence, you should be very happy to appear before him even if you only catch a glimpse of him from time to time. And a little while before you actually go to pray you should settle your heart in peace and stillness, making an act of hope that you will pray well; for if you go to it without hope and full of distaste before you even begin you will find it hard to keep up your desire for it.

Courage then, my little cousin, tell Our Lord that you will never leave him, even if he were never to send you any sweetness; tell him that you will not leave his presence until he has blessed you. When your heart roams or gets distracted lead it back very gently, softly putting it close to its Master; and even if you spend your whole hour doing nothing except gathering up your heart quite calmly and putting it close to Our Lord, and even if your heart does nothing except turn away as soon as you have led it back, your hour will have been very well spent and you will have done something very agreeable to your dear Bridegroom, to whom I commend you with my own heart which is all yours.

102

To Soeur Marie-Aimée de Blonay, Novice Mistress of the Visitation at Lyons

Annecy, 18 February 1618

It would have been a very great consolation to me to see you all in passing, but as it was not God's will, I will not pursue the thought any further. Meanwhile, my very dear daughter, I am very happy to read your letter and answer it.

O Our blessed Lady! You are wondering, my very dear daughter, if Our Lord can be thinking of you and looking at you lovingly? Yes, my very dear daughter, he is thinking about you and not only about you but about every hair of your head: this is an article of faith and you must not have the slightest doubt about it. I know of course that you do not really doubt it but that this is just your way of expressing the aridity, dryness and insensibility which you feel at present in the inferior part of your soul. Indeed, God 'is in this place and I knew it not',[1] said Jacob; that is to say, I did not see it and I could not in any way feel it, it did not seem possible to me. I discussed this in the book about the love of God, when describing resignation and the death of the will—I cannot remember in which section.[2]

And you have no cause to doubt that he is looking upon you with love; for he looks lovingly upon the most horrible sinners in the world, even if they have very little real desire for conversion. And tell me, my very dear daughter, is it not your intention to belong to God? Do you not want to serve him faith-

[1] Gen. xxviii, 16.   [2] Book 9, ch. 3.

fully? And who gives you this desire and intention if not he himself in the look of love he casts upon you? You must not examine whether your heart is pleasing to him but whether his heart pleases you; and looking at his heart is the same as rejoicing in it, for his heart is so gentle, so sweet, so gracious, so much in love with his poor, feeble creatures, provided they acknowledge their need, so good to the needy and the penitent! And who could fail to love this royal heart which mothers us in such a fatherly way?

You are right in saying that this is a temptation, my very dear daughter, in that your heart has no tender feeling towards God; for tenderness would mean consolation and consolation would mean the end of your unhappiness. But love of God, my daughter, does not consist either in consolation or in tender feelings; else Our Lord would not have loved his Father when he was sad unto death and cried out: 'My Father, my Father, why hast thou forsaken me?'[1] And it was then that he was making the greatest act of love we can possibly conceive.

In short, we always want to have our food sweetened with consolation, that is to say we want to feel love and tenderness, and thus consolation. And in the same way we should like to have no imperfections; but we must patiently accept the fact that our nature is human, my very dear daughter, and not angelic. Our imperfections should not please us and we should say together with the apostle: Unhappy that I am, 'who shall deliver me from the body of this death?'[2] but on the other hand they should not dismay or discourage us. We should rather make them a cause for submission, humility and being on our guard against self; but not for discouragement or affliction of heart, and even less for a lack of confidence in God's love for us; for though it is true that God does not love our imperfections and venial sins, he loves us very much in spite of them. Thus a child's weakness and infirmity does not please a mother but she nevertheless goes on loving her child, even tenderly and with compassion; and so too, although God does not love our imperfections and venial sins, he goes on loving us tenderly.

[1] Cf. Matt. xxvii, 46.　　　[2] Rom. vii, 24.

That is why David was quite right when he said: 'Have mercy on me, O Lord, for I am weak.'[1]

Come now, my very dear daughter, this is enough for today. Live joyfully: Our Lord's eyes are on you and he is looking at you lovingly, all the more tenderly because you are so helpless. Never allow your will to foster contrary thoughts; and when they beset you, do not look at them in themselves, turn your eyes away from their iniquity and turn towards God with brave humility, speaking to him about his ineffable goodness which makes him love our poor, feeble and abject human nature in spite of its infirmities.

Pray for my soul, my dear daughter, and ask prayers of your dear novices, all of whom I know except Sister Colin. I am all yours in Our Lord and may he live for ever in our hearts. Amen.

103

To the Présidente Le Blanc de Mions

Annecy, 22 April 1618

My very dear Daughter of my heart,

Would you believe it, I have a daughter who writes to tell me that my being far away from her rends her with bitter grief; that if she did not restrain her eyes they would rain down as many tears to weep at my departure as the sky holds water; and more rhapsodies of this kind. But she goes even further and says that I am not a mere man but some divinity sent from heaven to be loved and admired, and, what is more, she says she could say even more if she dared.

What do you think of that, my very dear daughter? Don't you think she is wrong to talk like that? Is this sort of language not excessive? Nothing can excuse it except the love she bears me which is certainly irreproachable and holy, if only it were not expressed in such worldly terms. Now tell her, my very dear daughter, that she is never in any way whatsoever to apply the

[1] Ps. vi, 3.

word divine to a mere man and created creature; and that it shows an ill-regulated mind, or at best a confused manner of expression, to imagine that she could praise even more extravagantly, if she would; that she must take even more pains to avoid vanity in her speech than in her clothes and hair-style; that in future her language is to be simple and not elaborately waved! But all the same, you must tell her all this gently, lovingly and calmly so that she can understand and accept this reproof which comes from a heart full of fatherly love for her, a heart which you as its very dear daughter know well, a daughter in whom I have put a great deal of trust and confidence.

May God be our love for ever, my very dear daughter, and may you live in him and for him to all eternity. Amen.

104

To Madame de Granieu

Annecy, 8 June 1618

I cannot refuse you anything, my very dear daughter, and so the two portraits you want shall be painted.[1] Why have I not done more to keep our Father's image faithfully mirrored in my heart? I ask you to help me beg for the grace to restore it within me.

Your kind of prayer is very good, and better than if you made considerations and discourse, since their only aim is to rouse the affections; so that if God is pleased to give us affec-

---

[1] Madame de Granieu of Grenoble persuaded St. Francis and Mère de Chantal to sit for their portraits. The portrait of St. Francis is the Turin portrait, the original being at the Turin Visitation, and is probably the one best known. Madame de Granieu said that she never looked at this picture without receiving new lights and a very special impression of the mystery of the Holy Trinity. Writing of her appreciation of this picture, St. Francis says: 'What will it be like, my very dear daughter, when we see the face of the eternal Father for ever, if even the dead and dumb portrait of a poor mortal has such power to gladden the heart of a daughter who loves him? But from what you tell me this portrait is not dumb, for it speaks to your spirit, saying holy things. Well, I think that only your ears with their delicate perception are capable of hearing this silent speech, recalling to your imagination what I said in the pulpit when I was talking about the will of God which is your sanctification.' (A. XVIII, p. 251, letter of July 1618).

St. Francis de Sales in 1622; from the painting at the Monastery of the Visitation, Thurnfeld, Bad Hall, Austria

tions without discourse or considerations we may call this a great grace. The real secret in prayer is to follow one's attraction with a simple heart. Take the trouble to read or to have read aloud to you if your eyes are tired, the seventh book of the *Treatise on the Love of God* and you will find there all you need to know about prayer.

I remember quite well that one day when you told me in confession how you prayed, I said that this was perfectly all right and that although you should take some prepared point to your prayer, you should not try and pursue it if God drew you on to some affection as soon as you came into his presence, but rather follow where he led you. And when the affection becomes simpler and more tranquil it will be all the better because then it will attach the spirit more closely to its object. But since you have made up your mind to this, my very dear daughter, spend no more time while you are actually praying wondering what exactly you are doing and how you are praying; for the best kind of prayer is that which keeps us so fully occupied with God that we stop thinking about ourselves and what we are doing. In short we must set about our prayer simply, trustfully and naturally, wanting to be near God, so as to love him and unite ourselves to him. Real love has no set method.

Live in peace, my very dear daughter, walk faithfully along the road which God has marked out for you; take great care to make your partner in life happy; be like a small bee which carefully makes the honey of devotion but is just as careful to manufacture the wax of household affairs; for if he who ate butter and honey[1] when he was in this world is pleasing to Our Lord, the other also serves for his honour, as it makes candles which are lit for the edification of our neighbour.

God who has taken you by the hand to put you in the way of his glory will be your guide, my very dear daughter. I shall never cease to beg this of him, for believe me, my very dear daughter, that I cherish tenderly and in a most fatherly way both your heart and soul which I entreat God to make ever more his. Amen. May Jesus reign!

[1] Isaias vii, 15

105

To a Nun

Paris, about 6 January 1619

Believe me, my dear daughter, for me too it is a very special consolation to have your letters and to send you mine.

It is good for you to be close to the manger where the Saviour of our soul teaches us so many virtues by his silence. How much he tells us by saying nothing! Our own hearts should be kindled by his little heart panting with love for us. See how lovingly he has written your name in the depths of his divine heart as he lies on the straw for your sake, longing lovingly for your progress; no sigh goes up to his Father in which you do not share, no thought that does not include your happiness. A magnet attracts iron, amber attracts straw and hay: now whether we are hard in heart as iron or feeble and helpless as straw we should follow the attraction of this sovereign little Child, the real magnet of hearts. Indeed, my daughter, let us not return whence we came, and leaving Arabia and Chaldea behind us for ever, let us stay at our Saviour's feet, saying with the heavenly Bride: 'I have found him whom my soul loveth, I hold him and I will not let him go.'[1]

Alas! my dear daughter, do you envy me because I preach the praises of God before the world? Sometimes we are indeed happy to be able to proclaim God's goodness and speak of him whom we love. But if you want to preach with me, there is nothing to stop you, my dear daughter: just ask God to give me words according to his heart and as you would wish them to be. How often we say good things because some good soul is praying for us! And is this not preaching enough, with the added advantage that the soul knows nothing about it and cannot run the risk of self-satisfaction or conceit? We are like the organ where nothing can be done without the wind, and yet the person who does the pumping gets no praise. So pray for me often, my dear daughter, and you will be preaching with me;

[1] Cant. iii, 4.

and my soul, believe me, joins with yours every day in the most holy sacrament which I receive with you and for you. And many and many times a day, my dear daughter, raise your heart to God telling him that you are all his, absolutely and for ever and ever. May Jesus live, for he is our life. May his holy love for ever live and reign in our hearts.

106

To Madame de Veyssilieu

Paris, 16 January 1619

It seems to me, my very dear daughter, that you are so sure in your heart of the unchanging affection I have for you that you can no longer be in any doubt about it: what God does is well done. And if I have delayed writing to you, please put it down to the unbearable rush and bother of life here, where one has to do more than one is able or willing to do, and cannot do what one wants to do, even if one were able.

I was afraid you might be anxious about your father's illness but now that, thanks be to God, he is regaining strength and health, I am much relieved on this score. Dear God, my very dear daughter, how worth-while it is really to understand that we are only given this life so as to attain eternal life! Without this knowledge we fix our affections on what is in this world through which we are passing; and when it comes to leaving it we are dismayed and full of fear. Believe me, my dear daughter, if we are to live happily during this pilgrimage we must keep alive before our eyes the hope of arriving in our homeland where we shall stay to all eternity; and meanwhile we must firmly believe (for it is true) that God who calls us to himself is watching to see how we are faring and will never allow anything to happen to us which is not for our greater good. He knows who we are, and will hold out his fatherly hand to us when we stumble, so that nothing may stop us. But to reap the full joy of this grace we must trust him utterly.

Do not forestall the accidents of this life by worrying about them beforehand but forestall them by perfect hope that as and when they are actually upon you, God to whom you belong, will save you. He has watched over you till now; all you have to do is to keep a tight hold on the hand of Providence and God will help you in all that happens and where you cannot walk he will carry you in his arms. What need you fear, my very dear daughter, since you belong to God who has told us so firmly that 'to them that love God all things work together unto good'.[1] Do not think about what is going to happen tomorrow, for the same eternal Father who is watching over you today will watch over you tomorrow and always: and either he will not send you misfortune, or if he does, he will give you unfailing courage to bear it.

Live in peace, my very dear daughter; put away from your imagination whatever is likely to trouble it, and often say to Our Lord: O God, you are my God, and I will put my trust in you; you will stand by me and be my refuge, and I shall fear nothing, for not only are you with me, but you are in me and I am in you. What can a child fear in the arms of such a Father? Really try to be a little child, my very dear daughter; and as you know, children don't have a lot of things to worry about because they have others to think for them; they are really strong if they stay close to their father. So do this, my very dear daughter, and you will have peace. Amen.

Your very humble servant,
Francis, Bishop of Geneva.

107

To Madame Angélique Arnauld, Abbess of Port-Royal at Mabuisson

Paris, 25 May 1619

Madam,

No, I beg you never to fear that your letters will weary me;

[1] Rom. viii, 28.

for I can really and truly assure you that they will always afford me great consolation, as long as God gives me the grace of filling my heart with his love, or at least of making me long to have it. Allow me to say this once and for all.

It is of course true that if I had never come to this city you could hardly have discussed your spiritual affairs with me; but since it has pleased divine Providence that I should be here there is no difficulty whatever about your making use of this opportunity if you see fit. And do not believe that you are seeking out excellence of person and rank, for although a thought of this kind might be very natural to my unworthiness, the fact is that I do not have it on such occasions; on the contrary, perhaps nothing is more likely to put me in the way of humility than my astonishment that so many servants of Our Lord, both men and women, can have such great confidence in a spirit as imperfect as mine. And this makes me take heart greatly and hope that I may one day become what people think me, and that as God gives me his children's holy friendship, he may one day give me his own, according to his mercy, after he has made me do penance as I deserve. But I really should not be saying all this. It is the evil spirit, then, who being for ever deprived of holy love wants to prevent us from enjoying the fruits of the Holy Ghost's love that is to grow between us, so that in our mutual holy communications we may find a means of growing in love of his holy will.

It is difficult, my very dear sister, to find people of all-round discernment who can see clearly to an equal degree in all matters: nor is it essential to have people of this kind so as to be well directed, and there is no harm, it seems to me, in gathering from many flowers the honey which we cannot find in one alone. Yes; you go on to say, but in the meantime I am cleverly indulging my inclinations and fancies. My dear sister, I see no great danger in this since you do not want to follow your inclinations unless they are approved; and although you make a point of seeking out favourable judges, as long as you find good, sensible and learned ones, you cannot go wrong in following their opinions even if it happens to be what you yourself want, provided of course that you explain your affairs and difficulties with childlike candour. It is enough, my very dear sister, to submit to advice, and it is neither necessary nor expedient to desire that this advice should go against our own inclinations, but only that it should conform to heavenly law and doctrine. For my part, I think that we should not ask for bitter suffering to come to our heart as Our Lord did, for we cannot deal with it as he did; it is enough for us to suffer patiently should the time come. That is why it is not necessary for us always to go against our inclinations provided they are not evil and have been scrutinized and found good.

There is no great harm in listening to people talking of the affairs of the world when our intention is to add to the sum of good, and we must not be punctilious in our examen on this point; for it is morally impossible always to keep to the exact point of moderation. However, my very dear sister, I should not like you to miss your prayer, at least half an hour a day, unless something very out of the ordinary happens or illness prevents you.

As for the rest, I shall do one of two things: either I shall write to you again at greater length before I leave, or I shall go and see you on the day I told your good and honest porter. And believe me, I beg you, that nothing shall stop me except if it really proves impossible, and that I shall give you all the time you want; for I have a very great desire to fall in with your wishes and a special affection for your heart which I pray God to bless abundantly. And then we shall talk as long as you please about your conduct and everything you want to put before me, nor shall I fail to try and deal with all your points unless I have not the light required to guide you. Dwell wholly in God, my very dear daughter, and in him I shall be for ever with all my soul,

Your humble brother and always your servant,
Francis, Bishop of Geneva.

108

To Madame Angélique Arnauld

Paris, 15–20 June 1619

So I shall no longer be 'Monseiur' for you, nor you 'Madame' for me; the time-old, cordial and loving names of father and daughter are more Christian, sweeter and at the same time of greater power in that they bear witness to the holy love which Our Lord wants us to have for one another. And I say boldly: which God wants us to have for one another, for I feel it strongly and do not believe that this feeling could come from any other source. And moreover I know that it is of profit to me and encourages me to do better, which is why I shall cultivate it carefully. I shall not tell you to do the same, for God will inspire you to do it if it pleases him, and I cannot doubt he will. . . .

And now, my very dear daughter, often think of what I told you: God has cast his eyes upon you to make use of you in matters of consequence and to draw you to an excellent sort of life; so you must honour his election and faithfully follow his intention. Let your courage always be informed with humility, your humility—that is to say your poverty and your longing to be humble—informed with confidence in God so that your courage is humble and your humility courageous. Let all your conduct, both within and outwardly, be sincere, gentle and cheerful, according to the apostle's advice: 'Rejoice in the Lord always: again I say, rejoice. Let your modesty be known to all men.'[1] And if possible, be even-tempered and let all your actions reflect your resolution always to love God's love.

This good bearer for whom I have very cordial feelings because he is devoted to you, is bringing you the book by Dom Sens,[2] General of the Bernadines, a book marked by a profound

[1] Phil. iv, 4, 5.
[2] Dom Sens de Sainte-Catherine, *Les Exercices spirituels distribués en vingt Méditations*, Paris 1619. In the 10th meditation he says: those are deceived who 'think they have done nothing which they need confess . . . seeing that there is

sense of spiritual doctrine and full of important maxims. If you feel it counteracts that state of holy joy which I so strongly advise for you, believe me that this is not his design; he only wants to make this joy rather more serious and grave, which is as it should be. And when I say grave I do not mean gloomy, or affected, sombre, disdainful or haughty, but I mean holy and charitable.

This Father puts forward an opinion, founded on his virtue and humility, that it is not possible to pass a single day without venial sin of a kind providing matter for confession. But experience has proved the contrary to me, for I have known several souls who had examined themselves well and had not been able to report anything which I was able to call sin, amongst others the happy servant of God, Madame Acarie. I do not say that venial failings were wholly absent, but that she could not discover them in her examination of conscience nor I recognize them in her confession, so that I saw cause to make her repeat some former sin. You will not pass this on to anyone, please, my very dear daughter; for I have such a high regard for this good Father and all he says that I should not like him to know I differ from him even on this one point. Moreover I do not know exactly how he stated this matter as I have not yet read it in his book; but I have heard him say this. I am speaking to your heart in confidence.

Do not burden yourself too heavily with vigils and austerities (and do believe me, my very dear daughter, for I know what I am talking about in this matter), but go to the Royal Port of religious life by the royal road of the love of God and your neighbour, of humility and meekness. If ever you write and tell me news of your heart there is no need to sign your name or to say where you are writing from or speak about yourself; you need only say that you are writing about the person I commended to your special care. . . . May God be at

no man on earth, however just, who passes days or hours without sinning venially'. Madame Arnauld had probably asked St. Francis to send her this book which he says he had not read and would therefore not be sending her of his own accord. But knowing his penitent's tendencies, confirmed by her Jansenism later on, he thought he ought to put her on her guard.

the centre of your heart for ever, my very dear daughter, and I
am with all my own heart invariably,

Your father and servant,

Francis, Bishop of Geneva.

109

To Madame Angélique Arnauld

Paris, 25 June 1619

I am not really writing to you today, my very dear daughter,
because I have no time this morning; there is someone coming
to make his general confession in secret and wanting to get
back to the country. So all I can do is to send greetings to your
dear soul which my own poor soul loves more than I can say,
never ceasing to wish it the perfection of divine love. And of
course I shall see you before I go if I can, so that knowing you
even better I may the better serve your soul, please God,
according to its desire.

Meanwhile tell this beloved daughter whom I commended to
you and whose welfare is so close to my heart, that I continue
to tell her that God wants to draw her to an excellent kind of
life, and that she should bless that infinite Goodness which has
looked upon her so lovingly. But I also tell her that the way
along which she is to follow this vocation is not an extraordinary one; it is one of gentle, peaceful and strong humility,
my dear daughter, a very humble, strong and peaceful gentleness.

Tell her, my very dear daughter, that she is not under any
circumstances to speculate about whether she will have a high
or a low place among souls, but that she is to follow the road I
have pointed out to her and that she is to rest in God; that she is
to walk before him simply and humbly, not looking where she
is going but in whose company. Now I mean that she is in her
King's company, with her Bridegroom, her crucified God; so

wherever she may go she will be happy indeed. To go with her crucified Bridegroom is to be lowly, humble and to despise self even to the death of all passions and I say even to the death of the cross. But note, my dear daughter, I repeat that this lowliness, humility and self-annihilation is to be practised gently, peacefully, with an even effort, and not only sweetly but with cheerfulness and joy.

Tell her to have no fear in going to communion but to go in peace and in all humility, so as to meet the desire of her Spouse who made himself lowly and sweetly humbled himself to unite himself to us, even making himself our food and nourishment, whereas we are nothing but the food and repast of worms. O my dear daughter, he who goes to communion in the Bridegroom's spirit makes himself as nothing before him and says to Our Lord: consume me, transform me, make me as nothing and change me into yourself. I do not see anything in the world which can more rightly be called our own and over which we have so much power as the food which we consume and annihilate so as to keep our body alive; and Our Lord went as far as this excess of love, making himself our food. And what should not our response be, so that he may possess us, shape and consume us, swallow us and form us anew, fashioning us according to his liking?

If people murmur against you, take it humbly and lovingly; complaints will turn into blessings. And I shall also talk to you about this when we meet. Take no pains to construct your letters to me carefully, for I am not looking for a fine edifice or the language of angels, but for the nest of doves and the language of love. Live wholly in God, my very dear daughter, and often commend to his divine Goodness the soul of him whose own soul is wholly dedicated to yours with unchanging affection. I thought I was only writing to send you a word of greeting, but without quite knowing how, I seem to have written a letter.

110

To a Gentleman

Paris, 2 July 1619

Sir,

It is very true that holy scripture contains a very clear statement of the doctrine necessary for your salvation and I never thought the contrary. It is also true that relating various passages one to another and reducing the whole to an analogy of the faith is a very good method of interpreting holy scripture; and this too I have always maintained. At the same time I most firmly believe and shall not cease to declare that in spite of the admirable and lovely clarity of the scriptures in the matter of things necessary to salvation, the human mind does not always find out their true meaning but can err and in fact very often does err in understanding those passages which are most clear and most necessary for establishing the faith: witness Lutheran errors and Calvinist books which under the conduct of the fathers of the reformation, so-called, remain in irreconcilable contradiction on the meaning of the words of institution of the Eucharist; and although each side prides itself on having carefully and faithfully examined the meaning of these words by relating and comparing them with other passages in the scriptures and adjusting the whole to the analogy of faith, they nevertheless continue to differ completely in their way of understanding words of such paramount importance.

Holy scripture is therefore clear in its words; but the mind of man is dark, and like an owl, it cannot see such a clear light. The method described above is very good, but the human mind does not know how to apply it. It is God's Spirit, Sir, which gave us the scriptures, and it is this same Spirit which gives us their real meaning, and gives it only to his Church, 'the pillar and ground of the truth'[1]; the Church by the ministry of which this divine Spirit guards and maintains his truth, that is to say,

[1] 1 Tim. iii, 15.

the real meaning of the Word; the Church which alone has the infallible help of the Spirit of Truth in finding the truth rightly, surely and infallibly in God's Word. So that anyone who looks for the truth of this heavenly Word outside the Church which is its guardian will never find it; and if anyone wants to know it except by the ministry of the Church he will be espousing a vain cause instead of truth; instead of the sure light of the sacred Word he will be following the will o' the wisp of that false angel who disguises himself as an angel of light. This is what all heretics have always done on the pretext of having a better understanding of scripture and of wanting to reform the Church, seeking the truth in vain away from the bosom of the Bride to whose keeping the celestial Bridegroom has confided it as to a faithful trustee and guardian. She will distribute it to the dear children of their rightful marriage, which is without stain and will be so for ever.

This is the substance of what I want to say to you, Sir, which does not differ in the least, look at it which way you will, from the doctrine of the Fathers advanced by M. de Mornay in his book which you were good enough to send me last night and which I return this morning, with many thanks and assuring you that I shall always long to be able to prove to you, by some happy opportunity, that I am, Sir,

Your very humble servant in Our Lord,
Francis, Bishop of Geneva.

III

To a Lady in Paris

Paris, 7 September 1619

My very dear daughter,

I say good-bye to you with all my heart. May you always belong to God in this mortal life, serving him faithfully as you follow him carrying his cross; and may you belong to him in the life eternal, blessing him for ever with the whole court of heaven. It is our soul's great good to belong to God, and its greatest good to belong to him alone. He who belongs only to God knows no sadness except that of having offended God; but then his sadness turns into deep yet tranquil humility and submission, and he lifts himself up again in calm and perfect confidence in the divine Goodness, being neither angry with himself nor resentful. He who only belongs to God seeks him alone, and because God is to be found no less in tribulation than in prosperity, he remains peaceful in adversity. He who only belongs to God thinks of him constantly in all that happens to him in this life. He who belongs to God alone does not mind if everyone knows that he intends to serve him and to practise the devotion which will keep him united to God. So belong wholly to God, my very dear daughter, and to him alone, wanting nothing except to please him and his creatures in him, in his way and for him. What greater blessing can I wish you? With this wish that I shall not cease to call down upon your soul I say good-bye to you, my very dear daughter, begging you to commend me often to his mercy, I remain,

Your most humble servant,
Francis, Bishop of Geneva.

The Eve of Our Lady, in September 1619

112

To Madame Angélique Arnauld

October or November 1619
. . . I can see quite clearly that your self-esteem fills your heart with a seething mass of inclinations, my very dear daughter, and I appreciate that your subtle, delicate and fertile mind contributes towards this; all the same, my very dear daughter, these are after all no more than inclinations, and since you think them importunate and your heart complains of them, it does not look as though you are in any way consenting

to them, at least by accepting them deliberately. No, my very dear daughter, as your dear soul has conceived a great God-given desire to belong to him alone, do not be too quick to believe that you are consenting to these contrary movements. Your heart may be in a flutter because of feeling these passions, but I think it rarely sins by consenting to them.

'Unhappy man that I am,' said the great apostle, 'who shall deliver me from the body of this death?'[1] He felt that an armed host consisting of his moods, aversions, natural habits and inclinations had conspired to bring about his spiritual death; and because he fears them he proves that he detests them; and because he detests them, he cannot endure them without pain; and his pain makes him cry out in this way and then give himself an answer: that the grace of God, through Jesus Christ, will save him, not indeed from fear, terror, alarm, nor from the fight, but from defeat and from being overcome.

My dear daughter, living in this world and not feeling such movements of passion—these two things do not go together. Our glorious St. Bernard said it is heresy to maintain that we can continue in the same state here below, as the Holy Spirit speaking through Job says that man never continues in the same state. This is in reply to what you tell me about the fickleness and inconstancy of your soul, for I quite believe that it is always stirred by the winds of passion and is always agitated as a result; but I believe just as firmly that the grace of God and the resolution it inspired, continues operative in the fine point of your soul where the standard of the cross is always raised on high and where faith, hope and charity are always calling out: May Jesus reign!

You see, my daughter, these tendencies to pride, vanity and self-esteem seep in everywhere and colour practically all our actions, whether we know it or not; but this does not make them the motive force of our actions. One day St. Bernard felt them bothering him as he was preaching and he said: 'Get thee behind me, Satan; I did not begin for you and I shall not end for you.'

[1] Rom. vii, 24.

There is just one thing I should like to say to you, my very dear daughter; you tell me that you allow affectation in your speech and in your letters to give fuel to your pride. It is true that affectation sometimes slips into what we say so that we hardly notice what is happening; but if we do notice, we must at once change our style of speaking. But in letters this is really rather more intolerable, indeed much more so, because you can see far better what you are doing, and if you notice some specially affected passage you must punish the hand that wrote it by making it write another letter in a different way.

For the rest, my very dear daughter, I have no doubt that in all these twists and turns on the part of your heart a few venial faults do slip in from time to time; but as they are only fleeting they do not deprive you of the fruit of your resolutions but only of the sweetness you would feel in not failing if only life were not as it in fact is.

So come now, be just: do not excuse your soul, but do not accuse the poor thing either except after careful consideration, for fear of making it insolent if you excuse it without reason, or of depriving it of courage and making it timid if you accuse it too lightly. Walk simply and you will walk confidently. And I must add something important right at the end of the page: do not burden your poor body with any austerity beyond that enjoined by the rule; keep your strength of body to help your soul to serve God whom we are often forced to leave when we have indiscreetly overburdened the body which must join with the soul in worship. Write to me whenever you like, without ceremony or fear; do not use respect as a weapon against the love which God wants us to have for one another and according to which I am unchangingly,

Your very humble brother and servant,
Francis, Bishop of Geneva.

113

To Madame Anéglique Arnauld

Annecy, 16 December 1619

I will begin where you end, my very dear and really beloved daughter; for your last letter of those which have reached me ends like this: 'I believe you know me well.' Now it is indeed true, I do know you well and I know that your heart is steadfastly determined to live entirely for God; but I also know that your great natural activity harasses you with many restless impulses. O dear daughter, you must really not imagine that the work we have undertaken to do in you can be done so quickly. Cherry trees bear their fruit quickly because they only bear cherries which keep but a short time; but the palm, the prince of trees, only begins bearing fruit a hundred years after it has been planted, it is said. A mediocre sort of life can be achieved in a year; but the perfection for which we are striving—that, my dear daughter, takes quite a few years to establish itself, I mean in the ordinary way.

And tell this person whom I have so earnestly commended to you that I really cannot forget her either day or night and that I am always calling down God's grace upon her; and say to her boldly, indeed no, I shall never be downcast by her weaknesses and imperfections. Should I not be unfaithful and cruel not to watch her struggles affectionately as she tries to practise gentleness, humility and simplicity? Let her go on faithfully in this way and I shall not cease to long and sigh for her good and her progress. But tell this dear daughter that she should try and put her heart into an attitude of humility, gentleness and tranquillity during her morning prayers, then again after dinner, during grace, at vespers and in the evening; and that she should try and call to mind in the course of the day that I told her to do it.

Tell her that I am staying here in my diocese as long as it pleases God; and that as nothing can remove me from it except for some particular eventuality which I believe to be for Our

Lord's glory, I should have no more difficulty in detaching myself from such favours than before ever they were offered to me. I am and shall be and want to be ever at the mercy of God's divine providence, I want to hold no other rank except that of a servant and a follower. You will always be told about everything, but be discreet. I am again invited to go to Paris on advantageous conditions.[1] I said that I would neither go there nor stay here unless to follow the will of heaven. This country is my home according to my natural birth; according to my spiritual birth, my home is the Church. I shall willingly go or stay wherever I can best serve the latter without attaching myself to the former. . . .

Live in peace, my very dear daughter, and often pray for my amendment so that I may be saved and that we may one day thrill with eternal joy, remembering how God favoured us by drawing us to himself and how he wanted us to have mutual consolation in telling one another about him in this world. O my daughter, may he always be our heart's only desire! Amen.

114

To Madame du Terte

Annecy, 18 December 1619

What joy, my dear daughter, for my heart to see how wholeheartedly and candidly you are making this new beginning! No, do not let your tears dismay you; for even if they are not good in themselves, their source is good. If one's resolutions were unimportant and revocable we should not feel so strongly about our abnegations and high endeavour. How greatly David wept for Saul even though he was his worst enemy! So let us

---

[1] He was asked to be coadjutor to Cardinal de Retz at Paris. According to a letter now lost but quoted at the canonisation inquiries, his only reason for leaving Annecy would have been that an influential post in Paris might have given him the chance of a journey to England to further the conversion of James I and of England in general, for which country he had a very special love.

weep a little about this dying world which is dead for us and to which we want to die for ever.

Oh my daughter, my good daughter, how happy I am to see you a little in labour with these birth-pangs! No, never did any soul bring forth Jesus Christ without pain, except the Blessed Virgin, to whom, however, he gave great pain in his dying. But you will see, my daughter, that after this sundering of the heart you will have untold consolations. And as for me, don't you think that my heart grieves with yours? Yes, indeed, I assure you it does, but my grief is tender and sweet because I can see that your pains are the pledge of much favour to come which God will show you if you persevere constantly and faithfully in your enterprise, the most worthy, the most generous, the most profitable you could ever undertake. So go on as you have begun, my very dear daughter, and keep your heart wide open to grace. As for me, have no doubt about my faithfulness; confide in me without fear, without withholding or excepting anything, for God who desires this will lead me by his hand so that I may serve you well.

This same God knows that when you went away I had in mind to tell you to cut out your use of musk and scent; but I restrained the remark, in accordance with my method which is gentle and allows spiritual exercises to have their own gradual effect on souls who give themselves up entirely to his divine Goodness.[1] For I am a great friend of simplicity, but I generally leave the pruning-hook for cutting back useless shoots in the hands of God: and here he is, cutting back this matter of powder and gilt cards.[2] May his mercy be for ever blessed, for I can see that he is treating you very mercifully. Yes, give these things to some lady of the world, whom you however know well enough to explain the reason for this little act of renunciation, and do not fear that it will give scandal; on the contrary,

---

[1] 'I noticed that he liked to leave great freedom to the working of God's spirit in souls, himself following the divine attraction, and guiding souls according to God's leading, leaving them free to act in accordance with divine inspirations rather than his own instructions.' St. Jane de Chantal's Deposition for St. Francis's canonisation, Works, III, p. 200.

[2] Probably perfumed cards, carried about the person and perfumed for greater elegance,

it will edify her, for I am taking it for granted that she is a good soul. You are right to renounce all these things; believe me, little abnegations of this kind are very agreeable to God.

I must really go on to tell you, since I have begun to speak to you so candidly, that I have never wanted to wear ornamented stockings, or washable and scented gloves ever since I vowed to belong to God, nor yet use powder or gilt cards; fashionable trifles of this kind are really not worth bothering about. Dear God, what high hopes I have for you now you are making such a good beginning!

Alas, my dear daughter, it is indeed true: our heart is saddened by our irrevocable renunciation of the world, our goodbye for ever to its friendships. Who would not tremble when the razor cuts and divides soul from spirit, the heart of flesh from the spiritual heart and self from self? But may God live and reign, for the blow has fallen, it is over: no, these will never be joined together again, by the grace of God for whose sake we have left everything else and are cleaving to him. . . .

When you are obliged to go to worldly gatherings you must put a cheerful face on it, my dear daughter. But so as to ensure that each side contributes topics of conversation, speak to people as one coming from a world which is not theirs, and they will speak to you of their own world; for if you speak to them in their own language it will not be news for them. For a month after I was consecrated bishop, when I came from making my general confession and from among the angels and saints in whose company I had made my new resolutions, I could only speak as one who was a stranger in this world, and it seems to me that I was not ungracious in my behaviour; and although the stress of affairs has slowed down a little this rush of an overflowing heart, my resolutions, by divine grace, have remained with me. Be brief in your conversation where there is no profit.

May God ever increase the reign of his holy love in us. I am in him, with very special affection,

Your very affectionate father and servant,
Francis, Bishop of Geneva.

115

To Soeur de Gérard, Sister at the Visitation of Grenoble

Annecy, 14 January 1620

My very dear daughter,

Your ideas about leaving the convent bear every sign of a genuine temptation; but blessed be God that the fortress has not yet yielded to this assault and is not likely to either, as I see it. My very dear daughter, be very much on your guard. There is nothing to choose between your leaving and your being lost, for do you not see, you would only be leaving in order to live for yourself, by yourself and in yourself? And this would be all the more perilous as your pretext would be closer union with God who, however, does not ever want such union with solitaries who single themselves out and withdraw of their own accord, leaving their vocation, their vows, their congregation through bitterness of heart, vexation, resentment, aversion for community life, for obedience to the rule and for religious observance.

O do you not see how prompt Symeon Stylites was to leave his column on the advice of the ancients? And you, my very dear daughter, refuse to give up your abstinence on the advice of so many excellent people who have no interest whatever in making you give it up except to rid you of your love of self? Come now, my very dear daughter, and from now on sing the song of love: O how sweet and good it is to see sisters living together! Be harsh with your temptation and say to it firmly: 'Thou shalt not tempt the Lord thy God; be gone, Satan; the Lord thy God shalt thou adore, and him only shalt thou serve.'[1]

Please turn this over in your mind, my very dear daughter: what could be clearer as a sign of temptation than genuflecting to the Blessed Sacrament as though out of spite? Good inspirations are humble, gentle, tranquil and holy; so how can your

[1] Matt. vi, 7, 10.

278

inclination be a good one when it is resentful, hard, cross and tempestuous? Get right away from this, my very dear daughter; treat this as one treats a temptation to blasphemy, treachery, heresy or despair. Do not enter into argument or come to terms with it, do not listen; counter it as often as possible by constant renewal of your vows, by frequent acts of submission to your Mother Superior; keep on invoking your guardian angel, and I hope, my very dear daughter, that you will then find the peace and sweetness of loving your neighbour. So be it.

I am writing to you in haste; but do what I tell you. And when you are in choir and the temptation says: stop singing! go on singing all the more perseveringly, as the blind man in the Gospel did. May the peace of the Holy Spirit be with you.

Francis, Bishop of Geneva.

116

To Madame Angélique Arnauld

Annecy, 14 May 1620

In spite of all you say in your last three letters, my very dear daughter, I continue to feel perfectly confident that the person I commended to your care and whom I really love as I love my own soul will succeed in being a great servant of God; for her faults are not deliberate nor does she really want to indulge her somewhat difficult, vain and mutinous inclinations. That being the case there is nothing to fear. Her natural hastiness is the cause of all her trouble; for it makes her impetuous, and impulsiveness makes her act hastily. Therefore you will tell her from me that her first care should be to keep her spirit controlled, gentle and tranquil, and that in order to achieve this she should even slow down her external actions, the way she stands and walks, her general behaviour, her gestures, and if she likes, even her tongue and her speech. And tell her not to think it strange that this is not done in a moment. It takes years to train a young horse to obedience and get it used to the saddle and the bit.

But you see, my very dear daughter, you are being rather hard on this poor girl; surely she means well and so you mustn't keep finding fault with her. Tell her that though she may shy back often and stumble, she is never to be disheartened or angry with herself; that she is rather to look at Our Lord who is watching her from heaven as a father watches his child, a child that is still weak and finds it hard to walk properly. And he says: steady, now, dear child go gently, child; and if she falls, he encourages her and says: you went too fast, you're really very good, so don't cry; and then he goes up to her and holds out his hand to help her rise. If this girl is really a child in her humility and understands that she is nothing but a child, she will not be upset at falling over because she will not be falling from any great height.

Ah! my very dear daughter, if only you knew how my heart loves this girl and how my eyes are upon her all the time even at this distance, you would look after her most carefully, if only for love of me, quite apart from what you yourself owe her; for you love me enough to love all that I myself love. When the great apostle commends poor Onesimus to Philemon he says so many beautiful things that we are quite carried away with love: if you love me, he says, if you have received me in your heart, 'receive him as my own bowels'.[1] This is what he calls Onesimus who had done some injury to Philemon, which is why he is angry. O my dear Philemone, my daughter I mean, if you love me, if you have received me in your heart, receive too my dear daughter Onesima, and bear with her; that is, receive her as my own bowels, for this is what she really is for Our Lord. And if she sometimes gives you trouble, put up with her lovingly for love of me but more especially for love of him who loved her so much that in order to draw her out of her nothingness 'he humbled himself, becoming obedient unto death, even to the death of the cross'.[2]

And as for you, my very dear daughter, how would it be pos-

[1] Philem. 12.   [2] Phil. xi, 8.

sible for you not to love God who loves you so much? What a proof of his love, daughter, that your father died such a good death, as you had so desired! Indeed, it fills me with wonder and joy. A thousand blessings on your heart, dear daughter, and on all our dear sisters, and on all that is yours, in you and round you; and so I shall have my share in it because I am infinitely yours in Jesus Christ and for Jesus Christ.

Francis, Bishop of Geneva.

117

To Mère de Chantal at Paris[1]

Annecy, 15 June 1620

O that I may receive and use the gift of understanding as I ought, my very dear Mother, so as to get a clearer and deeper insight into the holy mysteries of our faith! For this intelligence has a marvellous power to subject the will to God's service; our understanding is committed to him and plunged in him, recognizing him as wonderfully and perfectly good. And as the mind ceases to think anything else good in comparison with this Goodness, so too the will can no longer desire or love any goodness in comparison with this Goodness, even as when our eyes look deep into the sun we can no longer see any other light. But because we can only show our love in this world by doing good, because our love must act in some way, as I shall say in my sermon tomorrow, please God, we need counsel so as to see what we ought to do to put this love which presses us into practice; for it is heavenly love itself which urges us on to do good. And the Holy Ghost gives us his gift of counsel so that we may find out how to do good, which good to choose and in what way to express our love in action. So we can say that our soul shares in good measure in heaven's sacred gifts.

[1] It was customary in the Visitation to draw lots at Whitsun for the gifts of the Holy Ghost. Mother Chantal had written from Paris on 7 June 1620: 'Divine Providence has decided on the gift of understanding for you this year . . . counsel fell to my lot.' (Works, Vol. 4, p. 423.)

May the Holy Ghost show us favour and ever be our consolation. My soul and spirit adore him for all eternity! I entreat him always to be our wisdom and our understanding, our counsel, our fortitude, our knowledge, our piety; and may he fill us with the spirit of the fear of the eternal Father.

The holy feast of Whitsun for which you have such a very special devotion did not pass without constant remembrance of you.

118

To Mère Geneviève de Saint-Bernard,[1] Prioress of the Carmel at Chartres

Annecy, July–August 1620

My very dear Daughter,

How consoling for you that God himself made you Prioress, since it was decided in the ordinary way. This is why God is obliged to give you firm support so that you may do well what providence has ordained. Believe me, my very dear daughter, you must commit yourself trustfully to God's loving guidance and not except yourself in any way from the general rule: God who is the author of our goodness will perfect it according to his wisdom, as long as we are faithful to him and humble. What is needed is faithful service. And I tell you that you will be faithful if you are humble. But shall I be humble? Yes, if you want to be. Indeed, I do. In that case you are. But I know very well that I am not. All the better, that's the way to make sure of it.

You must not ask a lot of subtle questions but go boldly on your way; and as he has put souls in your charge, put him in charge of your own soul, so that he alone carries everything, you and your burden of office. His heart is great and he wants yours to find room in it. So rest in him, and when you fail or fall short in some way, do not be disheartened, but after you have humbled yourself before God, remember that God's

---

[1] Madame Acarie's daughter. See Index of Correspondents.

strength is made manifest more gloriously in our infirmity. In a word, my dear daughter, your humility must be courageous and valiant in trusting the goodness of him who put you in charge. And in order to cut the ground from under the arguments which human prudence, under the pretext of humility, generally puts forward on such occasions, remember that Our Lord docs not want us to ask for bread to last us a year or a month or a week, but only a day at a time, our daily bread. Try to do well today without thinking of the next day; then the next day, try to do the same; do not try to envisage what you are going to do throughout your time in office, but let the time pass, forgetting the anxiety. For your heavenly Father who is looking after you today will look after you tomorrow and the day after tomorrow, to the same degree in which you, knowing your infirmity, set all your hope in his providence.

It seems to me that I am putting all this rather too candidly, as though you did not know it all better than I do; but it does not matter, for these things make more impression when they are told us by a friend. I am yours.

Francis, Bishop of Geneva.

119

To Mademoiselle Lhuillier de Frouville

Annecy, 9 August 1620

I am extraordinarily happy, my very dear daughter, to see what the Holy Ghost has done in your heart, inspiring you with a valiant and generous resolution to give up the world. According to supernatural standards, my very dear daughter, how wisely you have acted! For so it was that Our Lady acted on that feast in the Gospel story of the day you entered,[1] going in haste straight into the hill country of Juda. Promptness in doing the will of God is a sure way of attracting great and

[1] Mademoiselle de Frouville entered on the feast of the Visitation, 2 July 1620, on the day of receiving a letter from St. Francis whose counsel she had asked.

powerful graces for carrying out any good work; and you see, my very dear daughter, after the rude shock your heart felt when it gave up its feelings, fancies and inclinations to follow a higher attraction, you are now at last perfectly still and happy, at rest in the blessed and hidden forest you have chosen as a home where you will live and sing for ever the glory of your soul's saviour and creator.

Now lift up your thoughts often, very often, dear daughter, to the eternal consolation you will have in heaven for what you have now done. It is indeed nothing (and I see you think the same), absolutely nothing in comparison with what you owe God and with the immortal reward he has prepared for you; for what are all those things we despise and give up for God? After all, they are only poor little moments of freedom of a kind which is a thousand times more restricted than slavery itself; perpetual anxieties, vain pretensions which change all the time, can never be satisfied and which would have harassed our spirit and engrossed us with a thousand useless cares: and all for a miserably short space of days, few and evil. And yet it has pleased God that whoever leaves these vain and empty pursuits of a moment gains in exchange the glory of eternal bliss where the very thought that we wanted to love God with all our heart and have increased our eternal love by a single little degree will overwhelm us with happiness.

Indeed, my very dear daughter, I should have been careful not to say to you: ride roughshod over your feelings, your diffidence, your fears, your aversions, had I not had confidence in the goodness of your divine Bridegroom who would give you strength and courage to take the part of inspiration and reason against the part of nature and disinclination.

But I must go on to tell you this, my very dear daughter: now that you are sweetly dead to the world and the world dead in you, that is only a part of the holocaust. Two things remain: the victim must be consumed, you must strip your heart of self, cut back hard all the little shortcomings prompted by nature and by the world; and the other is to burn and reduce your self-love to ashes and transform your dear soul into flames of heavenly love. Now this, my really very dear daughter, is not done in a day, and he who gave you the grace to strike the first blow will himself see to the other two matters in union with you; and because his hand is most fatherly, he will either do it without your knowledge, or if he makes you feel it, he will give you the constancy, indeed the joy of St. Lawrence the martyr, the vigil of whose feast we celebrate today. That is why you must not be afraid, for he who gave you the desire will bring it to a good issue. Be faithful in small matters and few, and he will establish you over great things. Promise me, my very dear daughter, that if you are given permission you will write from your happy retreat and tell me all that happens; and I promise you that you will be allowed to do it and that I shall receive your account with extremely great love. May God be for ever blessed, praised and glorified, my very dear daughter, and I am in him and for him, in a most special way,

Your very humble and very affectionate servant,
Francis, Bishop of Geneva.

P.S.   Your dear Cistercian uncle will be very happy to know that you have entered religion.

120

To a Lady

Annecy, 27 February 1621

I know, my very dear daughter, I really do know that you have a great many difficulties to endure, and I cannot hear about them without feeling them myself. At the same time I know that God whose divine providence has dedicated you to this sort of life here below, never fails to give you the holy inspirations you need to bear your trials in a saintly way.

As for myself, what is there I would not do to console you? But there are three things, dear daughter, which prevent me from writing to you as often as I did when we first got to know

285

one another. It seems to me that there is less need for it now that you are so used to the cross; and I for my part am burdened with years and (as I can speak freely to you) with infirmities which prevent me from doing what I should like to do. My correspondence, moreover, has increased to such an extent since those far-off days that I write less often to each person. But you are always present at my mass, my very dear daughter, where I offer his beloved Son to the heavenly Father, and in union with him I also offer your dear soul so that he may be pleased to fill it with his holy love, especially in your lawsuits and dealings with your neighbours. For it is most difficult to remain really gentle and humble both inwardly and outwardly in affairs of this kind and I have seen really good people in very great danger of sin; this is why I am so afraid for the people I love best when they are tried in this way. But now is the time, my very dear daughter, to prove that we are faithful to Our Lord, so that it can be said of us, as it was said of Job, following upon all his friends' reproaches and rebukes: that 'in all these things Job sinned not by his lips'[1] and did nothing wrong.

What sweeter blessing can I wish you than that of being faithful to Our Lord in the midst of the various kinds of adversities which beset you? For I never remember your soul without a thousand good wishes for its progress in the love of God. Love him well, my dear sister, in the retreats you make in order to pray to him and adore him; love him when you receive him in holy communion; love him when your heart is refreshed by his holy consolation; but above all, love him when you are harassed by untoward events, by dryness and tribulation; for he too loved you in Paradise but showed even more love for you at the time of his scourging, of the nails, thorns and darkness of calvary.

Pray to him to bear with me in his mercy and to make me worthy of the office to which he has called me. I am in him, with great affection,

Your very affectionate servant in Our Lord,
Francis, Bishop of Geneva.

[1] Job i, 22.

121

To Madame des Gouffiers

Annecy, May 1621

I will not dwell on the indeed more than fatherly love I feel for you, my very dear daughter, for I think that God who made my heart will tell you; and if he does not make you understand, no effort of mine will. But why am I telling you this? Because, my very dear daughter, I have not written to you as often as you may perhaps have wished, and sometimes people measure affection by the number of written sheets rather than by proofs of true inward feelings which only show on rare and well defined occasions and which are of more use.

I will come straight to the point and tell you openly and without disguise what my soul bids me tell you. How long, my very dear daughter, will you want to go on scoring other victories over the world and everything in it than those which our Saviour sought and at which he exhorts you to aim by so many clear indications? What did he do, he, the Lord of the whole world? It is a fact, my daughter, he was indeed the rightful Lord of all the world: and did he ever go to law to get even as much as where to lay his head? People wronged him in a thousand ways: did he ever go to law? Did he ever arraign anyone before a tribunal? Never; indeed, he did not even want to accuse the traitors who crucified him before the tribunal of God's justice. On the contrary, he called for mercy upon them. And this is the lesson he has instilled again and again: 'If a man will contend with thee in judgement and take away thy coat, let go thy cloak also unto him.'[1]

I do not wish to be rigid in this matter, nor do I condemn those who go to law provided they are acting in a spirit of truth, discrimination and justice; but I will say, cry aloud, write, and write in my own blood if need be, that whoever wants to be perfect and really a child of Jesus Christ crucified must follow

[1] Matt. v, 40.

this teaching of our Saviour's. Let the world rage, let worldly prudence fume and fret for all we care, and let all the wise men of our time invent as many loopholes, pretexts, excuses as they please: but against all prudence we should listen to the words: 'If a man will contend with thee in judgement and take away thy coat, let go thy cloak also unto him.'

Of course, you will say to me, this applies in certain cases. Quite true, my very dear daughter; but thanks be to God this is precisely the case in which we find ourselves, for we are striving for perfection and we want to follow as closely as we can in the footsteps of the man who said with truly apostolic love: having food and drink, and clothes to cover us, let us be content with that; and who cried out to the Corinthians: 'Already indeed there is plainly a fault among you, that you have lawsuits one with another.'[1] Now listen, my daughter, listen to the opinion and advice of this man who no longer lived in himself but Jesus Christ lived in him: 'Why,' he adds, 'do you not rather suffer yourselves to be defrauded?' And note, daughter, that he is not talking to a woman who is striving (after so many clear indications) to live a perfect life, but to all the Corinthians; note that he wants them to 'suffer wrong'; note that he says there is 'a fault among them' if they proceed against those who cheat or defraud them. But why was this sin? Because in this way they were giving cause for scandal to worldly unbelievers who said: look how Christian these Christians are! Their Master said: 'If a man wants to take away your coat, give him your cloak as well,' see how for the sake of temporal goods they will risk losing eternal possessions and the tender and brotherly love they ought to have for one another. And again, St. Augustine bids us notice that Our Lord does not say, if anyone wants to take away your ring, give him your necklace, both of which are superfluous; but he is talking about coats and cloaks which are necessities. O my very dear daughter, this is God's wisdom, his prudence, which is a most holy and adorable spirit of simplicity and childhood, and to use the apostle's words, the most holy foolishness of the Cross.[2]

[1] 1 Cor. vi, 7.   [2] 1 Cor. i, 23.

But then human prudence will return to the attack and say to me: how far do you want us to go? What! Are we to be trampled underfoot, grossly insulted, made to look fools, have our very clothes torn from our back without ever saying a word? Yes, that's right, I want just that; and if I do, it is not I who want it, it is Jesus Christ who wants it in me. And the apostle of the Cross and the Crucifix cries out and says: 'Even unto this hour we both hunger and thirst and are naked and are buffeted'; and finally, 'we are made as the refuse of this world, the off-scouring of all',[1] like a bit of apple or chestnut peel, or a nutshell. The inhabitants of Babylon do not understand this teaching but those who live on Mount Calvary follow it.

O Father, you will say to me, you are very severe all of a sudden. Indeed, this is nothing sudden; for since the time when grace was given me to know a little about the fruits of the Cross, this conviction has taken a firm hold of my soul and has never changed. And if I have not lived up to it this was due to weakness and not to lack of conviction; the world's clamour and scandal may have made me do outwardly the evil which I loathed in my heart. And might I dare to add this, to my confusion and just in my daughter's ear? I have never returned evil for evil and hardly ever harmed anyone except with reluctance. I am not examining my conscience, but roughly speaking, I think I am telling the truth; and all the more inexcusable am I.

But what do I really want to say to you? I am writing this letter very hurriedly and I have been obliged to take it up on two separate occasions; and love is neither prudent nor discreet, it forges straight ahead. You have so many honourable, wise, spiritual, friendly and devout people where you are; would it not be easy for them to persuade your sisters to some sort of settlement which would leave you enough to live on, judged by heaven's standards? Are they tigresses who cannot hear reason? What about good Father Binet, would he not be happy to serve God in this matter which really practically

[1] I Cor. iv, 11, 13.

affects the salvation of your soul, or on which, at least, your progress in the way of perfection entirely depends? And then Madame de Chantal? should she not be believed? For she is surely, I will not say only very good and kind, but also sufficiently prudent to advise you in this matter. . . .

Leave, O leave the world to worldlings: what need have you of the things people think essential for living in the world? Two thousand crowns and even less will be enough and plenty for a woman who loves her crucified Saviour. An income of a hundred and fifty or two hundred crowns is riches for a woman who believes in evangelical poverty. But if I am not a nun in an enclosed order but just living in association with some convent, I should only have barely enough to keep one or two servants to call me Madam. Well, and what of it? Have you ever discovered that Our Lady had that much? What does it matter whether people know that you are of a good house and family according to the world's standards, provided you belong to God's house? Oh, but I should like to make some pious foundation, or at least be of real help to some religious house; for my health is not good and this would make people put up with me more cheerfully. Yes, my very dear daughter, I knew very well that your piety was a prop for your self-love, and pitifully human. In short, we do not love crosses if they are not made of gold, studded with pearls and precious stones. It is a very lorldly, though most devout and admirably spiritual abjection, to be looked up to in a congregation as a foundress, or at least a great benefactress. Lucifer would have been glad to stay in heaven on a condition of that sort. But living on alms as our Saviour did, accepting other people's charity when we are ill, we who are high born and noble of spirit, this is indeed very difficult and hard to bear. True, it is hard to man, but not to the Son of God, who will do it in you.

But is it not a good thing to have a little property of one's own to use as one likes in God's service? The words 'as one likes' show where we differ. But I mean 'as *you* like', Father; for I am still your daughter, this being God's will. Very well then, what I like is that you should be satisfied with what

Monsieur Vincent[1] and Madame de Chantal think fit, and that you should let the rest go for the love of God, the edification of your neighbour and the peace of soul of your sisters; and that in this way you should consecrate it to love of your neighbour and to the glory of a truly Christian spirit. O what blessings, graces and spiritual riches will pour down on your soul if you do this, my very dear daughter! You will gain abundantly and more than abundantly; God will bless the little you have and he will make you content and happy. No, no, it is not difficult for God to do just as much with five barley loaves as Solomon did with all his cooks and caterers.

Be at peace. I am most constantly,

Your real servant and Father,

Francis, Bishop of Geneva.

122

To Madame des Gouffiers

Annecy, 2 August 1621

I am afraid that if we go on like this, my very dear daughter, without either of us saying a word, your heart might learn to cease to love me, and indeed I would not like this, for as your dear friendship for me was the result of God's will and nothing else, we must not let it die. And my friendship in God for you is ever alive and undying in my heart.

Well now, as it seems to be the fashion these days for fathers to make the first move in friendship—say what you like, my dear daughter, but the fact is you are in the wrong. My letter was surely not so bitter that a sweet-tempered daughter could not have sweetened it; it was full of fatherly confidence. And I am quite prepared to admit that it was not without a certain rustic forthrightness, but need you take offence at this? You know very well the kind of country which produced me: can

---

[1] St. Vincent de Paul who was adviser and later director of the Visitation in Paris.

you expect delicate fruit from a mountain tree, and such a poor tree at that? Oh so be it, then, think of me as you please in future, but I for my part will always be yours, I repeat, wholly yours; and if I can do nothing else for you, I shall not cease to prove this before God in the holy sacrifice I offer to his Goodness.

O my daughter, my daughter, may God make the spirit of Jesus Christ crucified reign over us both, so that we may live according to that sovereign spirit which made me and keeps me eternally yours. And believe me that this heart of mine which lives in the midst of the snow-covered mountains and ice of my own infirmities never felt any coldness for my very dear daughter's heart; my own misfortune is robbing me of this heart, but I prefer to lose it, provided God is not angered, rather than be found lacking in that holy sincerity which I vowed in the service of her soul, a soul which I could not flatter without betraying it, nor betray without causing its perdition; and this loss would be my affliction, for I love this daughter because I am,

Her very humble Father and servant,
Francis, Bishop of Geneva.

123

To Monseigneur Jean-François de Sales, Bishop of Chalcédoine, his Brother[1]

Turin, July-August 1622

O how happy I should be if in one or two years' time from now we could share my burden of office in such a way that I could have the part of Mary Magdalen and you that of Martha! Not indeed that I prefer Mary Magdalen's part because it is

---

[1] In a conversation at court it had been put to him that he should aim at being made cardinal, an idea which he completely rejected. He wrote to tell this to his brother who was also his successor, and this is the only part of the letter which has been preserved.

better, but because if I could rest a little at Our Lord's feet, I think I could learn certain things which I could very profitably leave to posterity in writing, as so many excellent people have exhorted me to do. But after saying this, I protest that I want nothing at all except to live and die in God's grace and according to his will.

124

To a Lady

Lyons,[1] 19 December 1622

A thousand thanks to your beloved heart, my very dear daughter, for the favour it has shown my soul in giving it such sweet proofs of affection. Dear God, how happy are those who are under no obligation to courts and compliments and who can live peacefully in holy solitude at the foot of the Crucifix! Not that I ever held vanity in high esteem, but I find it even more vain when I am surrounded by the feeble splendours of the court.

My very dear daughter, the further I advance in this mortality the more contemptible I find it and the more lovable that holy eternity for which we long and for the sole sake of which we should love one another most tenderly. Let us live only for this life to come, my very dear daughter, which alone deserves the name of life, and compared with which the life of the great in this world is a most pitiful death. I am with all my heart most truly all yours, my very dear daughter, and remain,

Your very humble and very affectionate servant,
Francis, Bishop of Geneva.

[1] St. Francis had left Annecy on 8 November to join the court of Savoy at Lyons for a meeting with the court of France.

125

To the Duc de Bellegarde

Lyons, 24 December 1622[1]

My dear Sir and Son,

This same solemnity of the great feast of Christmas which almost deprives me of the hope of seeing you again gives me sufficient confidence to appeal to you on behalf of this poor man whom I am bound to love in charity and also because of the good example he gave of his faith and uprightness while he lived in the Gex region where he was subject to persecution in spite of his innocence. He will explain his poverty in his appeal to you, and if you are unable to do as he begs, he presents an alternative appeal, my dear Sir and my son: that it may please your goodness to give him a post in the salt mines or else in forestry, which is his real work, or elsewhere under your authority.

Works of mercy are in season at this time which is dedicated to the sovereign mercy shown to us by the Son of God when he was born on earth for our salvation, and I beg him very humbly always to be favourable to you, Sir, according to the continual wish of my heart; and I am,

Your very humble and very obedient servant,
Francis, Bishop of Geneva.

On this, the Eve of Christmas 1622

---

[1] The Duke stayed on in Lyons after the French court left on 21 December, and St. Francis did in fact see him again on 27 December, stopping to talk to him at length after mass outside the church. It was a bitterly cold day. That same afternoon St. Francis was struck down with his last illness and he died the next day, in the gardener's cottage attached to the convent of the Visitation a little way outside the town.

Index of Letters

Index of Correspondents

(The numbers in brackets refer to the letter number)

ARNAULD, Madame Angélique Arnauld, Abbess of Port Royal, 1591–1661. By her father's wish she entered the Benedictine convent of Port Royal near Paris at the age of eight and became abbess. She reformed her own convent and the sister foundation at Mabuisson where St. Francis came to her help in 1619. She put herself under his direction, got to know Madame de Chantal and applied to Rome for permission to enter the Visitation. This was refused. In later years she came under the influence of the Jansenist, Saint-Cyran, and after a troubled life she died in heresy in 1661. (107–9, 112, 113, 116.)

BALLON, Madame Gasparde de Ballon, a cousin of St. Francis. She entered the Bernardine Abbey of St. Catherine at Annecy in about 1610 under his direction. She took an active part in the reformation of her convent and in making new foundations. (84.)

BALLON, Madame Louise de Ballon, sister of the above and a nun at the same convent. (101.)

BELLEGARDE, Roger de Saint-Lary et de Termes, Duc de Bellegarde, 1563–1646, Peer and Master of the Horse at the court of Henri IV and Louis XIII. In his earlier years he was one of the most worldly and arrogant courtiers of his time, a man of great power and influence. He first met St. Francis in 1603 but did not come under his more immediate influence until 1613 when he put himself under the bishop's direction and made a general confession to him. St. Francis called him his favourite 'Théotime', (the imaginary spiritual friend to whom he addressed the *Treatise on the Love of God*). The duke persevered in his good resolutions and died a holy death in 1646. (76, 82, 90, 125.)

BLONAY, Mère Claudine de Blonay, born 1565, became abbess of the Poor Clare Convent at Evian in 1614 and remained in office till 1622. Distantly related to Soeur Marie-Aimée de Blonay. (81.)

BLONAY, Soeur Marie-Aimée de Blonay, 1590–1649, daughter of St. Francis's friend, Claude de Blonay, who lived in the Chablais and was ordained priest after his wife's death. Marie-Aimée was the youngest of nine and St. Francis first knew her when she was a child. She entered the Visitation at Annecy in 1612, was made novice-mistress at Lyons in 1615 and later superior. In 1641 she became Madame de Chantal's successor as superior in Annecy and died there in 1649. (93, 102.)

BOISY, Madame Françoise de Sionnaz de Boisy, mother of St. Francis, born about 1552, died 1610. She was twenty-seven years younger than her husband, François de Sales, who upon marriage took the name of an estate which was part of her dowry. Francis was born when she was fifteen and she had twelve more children. She favoured her eldest son's vocation and supported him throughout in his endeavours while he, in turn, became her director and assisted her at the end. (48; cf. also 54.)

BRÉCHARD, Mère Jeanne Charlotte de Bréchard, 1580–1637. She belonged to the Burgundian nobility, lost her mother at an early age, was neglected and ill-treated by her father. She led an unhappy existence till she met Madame de Chantal in about 1600. Putting herself under St. Francis's direction she eventually joined her friend and Mademoiselle Favre as one of the first three Visitation nuns at Annecy in 1610. She was sent to make the foundation at Moulins in 1616, at Nevers in 1620 and at Riom in 1623. She died there in 1637. (77, 96.)

BRÛLART, Madame la Présidente Marie Bourgeois Brûlart, of Dijon, wife of Nicolas Brûlart who became president of the parliament of Burgundy in 1602. She first met St. Francis in 1604 in Dijon when she and her sister, the abbess Madame Bourgeois du Puis d'Orbe, put themselves under his direction. She was a close friend of Madame de Chantal. She had several children, was active in good works and died in July 1622, a few months before St. Francis. (6, 10, 19, 24, 30, 59.)

CAMUS, Jean-Pierre Camus, Bishop of Belley, 1584–1652. He was born in Paris, consecrated bishop in 1609 by St. Francis, gave up his office in 1629, retired to a monastery in Normandy but soon returned to Paris and active apostolic labour. A facile writer of long novels, a man of lively, unstable and combative temperament but of great good will, his greatest claim to fame is the love St. Francis bore him. From 1639–41 he wrote a long book of reminiscences of his friend, some of it of doubtful authenticity. The material was sifted and republished in 1727 in two volumes by Collot and this is the form in which the work is still known and can be read with delight and profit (see bibliography). The young bishop's answer to St. Francis's letter appears in Appendix I, A. XVI, p. 389. (75.)

CHANTAL, Baronne Jeanne-Françoise Frémyot de Chantal, 1572–1641. She was born in Dijon, and as her mother died young she was brought up largely by her father, President Frémyot (q.v.). She married Christophe de Rabutin, Baron de Chantal, at the age of twenty. He was killed in a hunting accident in 1600 and she survived him with four young children. Her only son was Celse-Bénigne (see below), her eldest daughter married Bernard de Sales, a younger brother of the saint. Madame de Chantal met St. Francis in 1604 when he was staying at the house of her brother, the archbishop of Bourges. She made annual journeys to Annecy, and when her children were old enough she moved to Annecy in 1610 to found the first convent of the Visitation under St. Francis's direction. After that her life was dedicated to the new order and she spent most of her time travelling and visiting, being responsible, directly or indirectly, for the foundation of eighty-six Visitation convents. She suffered all her life from the trial of temptations against the faith. After St. Francis's death in 1622 she prepared an edition of his letters (1626), his spiritual discourses (1629) and finally superintended the first collected edition of his works (1641). She was the chief witness at the two canonization processes. She destroyed nearly all her letters to St. Francis, but her correspondence in connection with her order fills five volumes of her 'Works' (see bibliography). She also wrote on prayer, a commentary on the rule of her order, and on various spiritual topics put to her by her nuns. She died while visiting the convent at Moulins on 13 December 1641 and was canonized on 16 July 1767. (3, 4, 7–9, 11–14, 17, 18, 20–3, 25–9, 31, 33–5, 42, 43, 47, 49, 51, 52, 54; Mère de Chantal: 57, 60, 61, 63, 64, 66–9, 73, 74, 78, 80, 85, 87, 94, 95, 98, 117.)

CHANTAL, Baron Celse-Bénigne de Rabutin Chantal, 1595–1627. The only son of Madame de Chantal, a brilliant and brave soldier but a man of reckless temperament, a gambler and duellist, who caused his mother much anxiety. When she left home in 1610 to enter the Visitation, this boy, with real grief but undoubtedly with an eye for drama, threw himself on the ground in her path so that it should be said she had had to walk out of her home across her son's body. He was killed at the age of thirty-two while fighting for the cause of the Church and France at the Isle de Rhé. He married Marie de Coulanges and his only child was Marie de Rabutin Chantal, later the famous letter-writer, Madame de Sévigné. (58; cf. also 73.)

CHASTEL, Soeur Peronne-Marie de Chastel, 1586–1637. Daughter of a captain in the Duke of Savoy's army. She was one of the earliest members of the Visitation at Annecy which she entered in July 1610. She was sent to Lyons in 1615, became the first superior of the Grenoble community in 1618, and then of Aix-en-Provence in 1624. She was made superior at Annecy in 1635 and died there in Madame de Chantal's presence in 1637. She had the gift of mystical prayer and St. Francis often had her in mind in describing extraordinary states of prayer in his *Treatise on the Love of God*. (83.)

CLÉMENT, Mademoiselle. Apart from the fact that she lived in St. Francis's diocese, wanted to be a nun and was in contact with the Jesuits at Chambéry, nothing is known of her. (41.)

ESCRILLES, Madame Marie de Mouxy d'Escrilles, 1582–1645, daughter of the Seigneur de Travernay. She married Louis d'Escrilles and was left a widow at eighteen. She entered the Visitation at Annecy in July 1614 and as Mère Marie-Madeleine de Mouxy became the first superior of the convent at Belley. (79.)

FAVRE, Mère Jacqueline Favre, 1592–1637, daughter of the lawyer and statesman, President Antoine Favre, a life-long friend of St. Francis with whom he at one time carried on a delightful correspondence in Latin as a humanist exercise. St. Francis had known his daughter since childhood, he called her his *grande fille*, and she was one of the first three Visitation nuns at Annecy. She was appointed superior at Lyons in 1615, later at Montferrand, Dijon, Paris and Troyes. She died at Chambéry in 1637. She had close affinities of character with Madame de Chantal whose most trusted friend she was. She was described as 'the second pillar and corner-stone' of the Visitation order. (89, 92.)

FLÉCHÈRE, Madame Madeleine de la Fléchère, 1565–1632. She married in 1602 and was left a widow in 1616. St. Francis preached the Lenten sermons at Rumilly in 1608 and lodged at her house which she later donated as a Visitation convent. He had a very high opinion of her, admired her heroic charity to the poor, her deep faith. 'With the exception of our dear Madame de Chantal' he wrote in 1616, 'I doubt if I have ever come across a more vigorous soul in a woman, a more reasonable mind, a more sincere humility.' (37–40, 44, 46, 50, 53, 56, 62, 72.)

FROUVILLE, Mademoiselle Hélène Lhuillier de Frouville, of Paris. Her early and tragic marriage was annulled in 1618. She put herself under St. Francis's direction when he visited Paris that same year. She gave her fortune to endow the Visitation in Paris and herself entered it in 1620. She was superior at various times until 1647 and was responsible for seven other foundations in the north and west of France. Henriette of France, King Charles I's widow, lived in retirement at her convent in Chaillot, and Mère Hélène-Angélique died in the presence of her royal friend in 1655. (119.)

FRÉMYOT, Président Bénigne Frémyot, Seigneur de Beauregard, the father of Madame de Chantal and of the archbishop of Bourges. He was a lawyer and magistrate, and second president of the Parliament of Burgundy. During the wars of religion he opposed the League and went into exile with the legitimate parliament, showing extraordinary courage and devotion to duty. Under Henri IV he was mayor of Dijon (1595 and 1596) but refused all the other honours which the king wanted to confer on him. He set great store by the friendship of St. Francis and supported his daughter's vocation. He died in 1611. (5.)

GENEVIÈVE, Mère Geneviève de Saint Bernard (Acarie), Prioress of the Carmel at Chartres, 1592–1644, the youngest daughter of St. Francis's friend, Madame Barbe Acarie, later Soeur Marie de l'Incarnation and a lay sister at her daughter's convent. St. Francis met Mère Geneviève when she was a child and later in the first convent of St. Theresa's reform founded in Paris. She entered in 1607 and founded the Carmel at Chartres in 1620. (118.)

GÉRARD, Soeur Jeanne-Hélène de Gérard-Réautier, entered the Visitation at Annecy in 1617 and took her final vows at Grenoble. From 1625 she was in charge of the new foundation at Embrun where she was re-elected several times until 1653.

She seems then to have gone out of office and the chronicles lose trace of her. (115.)

GOUFFIERS, Madame Elisabeth Arnauld des Gouffiers, *un terrible esprit*, in Madame de Chantal's words. Ardent, gifted, insubordinate and headstrong, she tried to the utmost the love and patience of two saints and of all her friends and relations. Without a real vocation she entered the order of the Paraclete, left it in 1613 to live at Annecy under St. Francis whom she admired, sank her fortune in the foundations at Lyons, Moulins and Paris. In 1620 she tried to retract what she had given and sued her relatives for more money. She died in peace a year later, reconciled with all whom she had persecuted, and forgiven by them. (121, 122.)

GRANIEU, Madame Laurence de Granieu, 1579–1652, daughter of a King's Counsellor, married François de Granieu, Minister of Finance, in 1595, had several children and led an exemplary Christian life. St. Francis stayed at her house when he preached at Grenoble in the Lent of 1617 and 1618. She was a friend of Madame de Chantal and a benefactor of the Visitation where at her own wish she was buried. (104.)

HUMBERT, Soeur Marie-Avoye, 1590–1657, entered the Visitation at Annecy in 1612. She was sent to Moulins in 1616 and died there after an uneventful and hidden life, distinguished for exact observance of the rule. (97.)

MIONS, Barbe-Marie Le Blanc de Mions, wife of the president of the parliament of the Dauphiné at Grenoble, a man of dissolute life. She was a friend of Madame de Granieu (q.v.) and met St. Francis when he was preaching at Grenoble in 1617. It was largely her generous effort and ardent piety that led to the foundation of a Visitation convent in that city. She died in 1619. (99, 100, 103.)

PEYZIEU, Madame Françoise de Dizimieu de Peyzieu, married and the mother of several children. St. Francis was a close friend of the whole family and he looked up to Madame de Peyzieu as to his mother, even addressing her by this name. One of her sons was killed in South America (cf. Letter 88), and a granddaughter of hers entered the Visitation at Annecy in 1620. Little is known of her life. (71, 86, 88.)

RYE, Madame de Rye, 1580–1647, Benedictine nun and niece of the Archbishop of Besançon. Later abbess of her convent. (16.)

SALES, Jean-François de Sales, Bishop of Chalcédoine, 1578–1635, younger brother of St. Francis. He was ordained by his brother in 1603, became his vicar general in 1615 and was nominated titular bishop and coadjutor in 1621, succeeding to the bishopric of Geneva on his brother's death the following year. He was distinguished for his zeal in visiting his diocese, for his goodness to the poor and for his devoted personal service to the sick in times of pestilence. He died in 1635 and asked to be buried at his brother's feet in the church of the Visitation at Annecy. (123.)

SOULFOUR, Mademoiselle Jeanne de Soulfour, daughter of Nicolas de Soulfour of Paris, translator of Louis de Blois's *Institution Spirituelle*. She tried her vocation at the Filles-Dieu Benedictine convent but left after a short period. Later she entered the Carmel at the rue Saint-Jacques in Paris as Soeur Thérèse de Jésus, persevered in her vocation and died at Riom in 1633. (1, 2, probably 36.)

TERTRE, Madame Marie-Aimée Le Gruet de Morville du Tertre, was left a widow at twenty-two and entered the Visitation at Moulins in 1619. She gave and then retracted large sums of money for the foundation at Nevers, caused endless suffering and difficulty to the order until in the end, rather like Madame des Gouffiers (q.v.) whom she resembled, she made public amends for her malicious calumnies and died peacefully in 1633. (114.)

TRAVERNAY, Madame Péronne de Montfalcon de Travernay, daughter of the Governor of Savoy. She married the Seigneur de Travernay in 1598 and one of her three children was the goddaughter of St. Francis who was on affectionate terms with the whole family. She was the sister-in-law of Madame d'Escrilles (q.v.) (55, 70.)

VEYSSILIEU, Madame Marguerite de la Croix de Chevrières de Veyssilieu, married in 1608 and lived in Grenoble, a friend of Madame de Granieu and Madame le Blanc de Mions. She met St. Francis in 1617 when he preached the Lenten sermons, and was a member of the group that founded the Visitation convent in that city. Her daughter entered it and was instrumental in establishing a second convent there in 1648 when her mother was still alive. (106.)

VILLETTE, Soeur Françoise-Jéronyme de Chevron Villette, 1595–

1665, related to St. Francis and to Mère Favre, one of the early Visitation nuns. Her father, ambassador for the Duke of Savoy, was assassinated while on diplomatic service in Switzerland. She was one of the first to enter the new foundation at Lyons in 1615, and later made numerous foundations all over France. She died at Chalon in 1665. (91.)

VILLARS, Pierre de Villars, Archbishop of Vienne, 1545-1613. Became archbishop in 1587 and resigned his office for reasons of health in 1599. He retired to Annonay and later to Lyons, devoting himself to prayer, study and writing. He was the Metropolitan of the Bishop of Geneva who admired him greatly and considered him one of the most saintly and learned prelates of his time. (45.)

Select Bibliography

I. GENERAL BIBLIOGRAPHY

BRAZIER V., and others. *Opere e scritti reguardanti San Francisco di Sales; repertorio bibliografico*, 1623–1956. Biblioteca del Salesianum, 44. Soc. editrice internazionale, Turin, 1956.

II. WORKS OF ST. FRANCIS DE SALES: EDITIONS AND TRANSLATIONS

A. Works in General

Oeuvres de Saint François de Sales. Édition complète d'après les autographes et les éditions originales. Par les soins des Religieuses de la Visitation du Premier Monastère d'Annecy. Annecy, 26 vols. 1892–1932. (Abbreviated as A. in footnotes.)
 1. *Les Controverses;* 2. *Défense de l'Estendart de la Sainte Croix;* 3. *Introduction à la Vie Dévote;* 4 and 5. *Traitté de l'Amour de Dieu;* 6. *Les Vrays Entretiens Spirituels;* 7–10. *Sermons;* 11–21. *Lettres;* 22–26. *Opuscules.* A final volume, containing indices and errata, is in preparation.
Library of St. Francis de Sales. Translated and edited by H. B. Mackey, O.S.B. London, 1883–1910.
 1. *Letters to Persons in the World;* 2. *Treatise on the Love of God;* 3. *The Catholic Controversy;* 4. *Letters to Persons in Religion;* 5. *Spiritual Conferences;* 6. *Mystical Explanation of the Canticle of Canticles; Depositions of St. Jane Frances de Chantal in the Cause of the Canonisation of St. Francis de Sales;* 7. *The Spirit of St. Francis de Sales, by his friend Pierre Camus, Bishop of Belley.* Translated by J.S.

B. Letters

Les Epistres du Bien-Heureux Messire François de Sales, Evesque et Prince de Genève, Instituteur de l'Ordre de la Visitation de saincte Marie. Divisées en sept Livres. Recueillies par Messire Louys de

Sales, Prévost de l'Eglise de Genève. Lyons, 1626. 2nd revised edition, 1628.

Lettres de S. François de Sales. Revues sur les Originaux et enrichies de Sommaires, de Citations, de Notes et de Remarques par l'Abbé Corru. Paris, 1758.

Nouvelles Lettres inédites de Saint François de Sales, publiées par M. le Ch. P.-L. Datta. Paris, 1835.

Oeuvres Complètes de Saint François de Sales, par H. de Vivès. Paris, 1856–8 (Vols. 10–12, *Epistres Spirituelles*)

Oeuvres Complètes de Saint François de Sales, par J.P. Migne. 6 Vols. Paris, 1861–2. (Vols. 5–6, *Lettres.*)

Lettres de Saint François de Sales. Nouveau Choix par E. Veuillot. 2. Vols. Paris, 1865. (Further reprints up to 1925).

Lettres de Direction et Spiritualité de Saint François de Sales, présentées par Ernestine Le Couturier. Lyons and Paris, 1951. (The first selection based on the Annecy text)

Selection from the Letters of St. Francis de Sales. By Mrs. C. W. Bagot. London, 1856.

A Selection from the Spiritual Letters of St. Francis de Sales. Translated by the author of 'The Life of St. Francis de Sales' (Mrs. Sidney Lear). London, 1871 and 1880.

Library of St. Francis de Sales. Vols. 1 and 4. (See above).

St. Francis de Sales in his Letters. Edited by the Sisters of the Visitation, Harrow-on-the-Hill, now at Castle Cary, Somerset. Introduction by Abbott C. Butler. London, 1933 and 1954.

Letters from a Saint; the great Christian guide to peace of mind and soul. Ed. by George T. Egglestone, New York, 1957.

NOTE

The most complete study of St. Francis de Sales as a letter writer, together with a full bibliography, is by the Editors of the Annecy Edition: 'Saint François de Sales étudié dans ses Lettres', the introduction of 175 pages to Vol. 21, 1923.

C. Other Works

See *Library of St. Francis de Sales,* above.

An Introduction to a Devout Life Leading to the Way of Eternitie. London, 1616.

An Introduction to a Devout Life, containing especially a prudent method for spiritual closet-exercises, and remedies against the difficulties ordinarily occurring in the conduct of a pious life. Fitted for the use of Protestants. By Henry Dodwell. Dublin, 1673.

Introduction to the Devout Life. Translated by A. Ross, new ed. London, 1943.

Introduction to the Devout Life. Translated by J. K. Ryan, New York, London, 1953.

A Treatise of the Love of God. Translated by Miles Car, Douai, 1630.

The Love of God; abridged by the Sisters of the Visitation, Harrow-on-the-Hill; foreword by Cardinal Bourne, introduction by Abbott Butler. London, 1931.

Delicious Entertaynments of the Soule. Written by the holy and most Reverend Lord Francis de Sales, Bishop and Prince of Geneva. Translated by a Dame of Our Ladies of Comfort of the Order of St. Bennet in Cambray. Douay, 1632. (*Spiritual Conferences.*)

III. WORKS OF ST. JANE FRANCES DE CHANTAL:
EDITIONS AND TRANSLATIONS

Ste. Jeanne-Françoise Frémyot de Chantal. Sa Vie et ses Oeuvres. Edition authentique publiée par les soins des Religieuses du Premier Monastère de la Visitation Sainte-Marie d'Annecy. 8 Volumes, Paris, 1874–9. 2nd edition 1893. 3rd edition 1910.

    1. *Mémoire sur la Vie et les Vertus de Ste. Jeanne-Françoise Frémyot de Chantal*, par la Mère Françoise-Madeleine de Chaugy; 2 and 3. *Oeuvres Diverses*; 4–8 *Lettres.*

Selected Letters of St. Jane Frances de Chantal. Translated by the Sisters of the Visitation, Harrow-on-the-Hill. London, 1918 and 1922.

The Spiritual Life, compiled from the writings of St. Jane Frances de Chantal. London, 1928 and St. Louis, 1928.

The Exhortations, Conferences and Instructions of St. Jane Frances de Chantal, Chicago, Loyola University Press, 1929.

IV. GENERAL

BEDOYERE, Michael de la
    François de Sales. London, 1960.

BORDEAUX, Henry
    Au Pays de Saint François de Sales. Paris 1922.
    Saint François de Sales et notre coeur de chair. Paris, 1925. English

translation by Sr. Benita: *St. Francis de Sales, theologian of love.* London, 1929.

BOUGAUD, Emile
Histoire de Sainte Chantal et des Origines de la Visitation. 2 Vols. Paris, 1863; 7th edition 1870.
English translation by the Sisters of the Visitation: *St. Chantal and the Foundations of the Visitation.* London. 1895.

BREGY, Katherine M. C.
The Story of St. François de Sales. New York, 1958.

BRÉMOND, Henri
Histoire Littéraire du Sentiment Religieux en France. 11 Vols. Paris, 1916–33. (See especially Vols. I–III and VII).
English translation of Vols. I–IV by K. L. Montgomery, London, 1928–38.

CALVET, Mgr. Jean
La Littérature Religieuse de François de Sales à Fénelon. 2nd edition. Paris, 1956.

CAMUS, Jean Pierre, Bishop of Belley
The Spirit of St. François de Sales. Translated by C. F. Kelley. New York, 1952; London 1953. (See also Vol. 7 of the Library of St. Francis de Sales.)
Le Directeur Spirituel desinteressé, Selon l'esprit du B. François de Sales par Jean Pierre Camus, Evesque de Belley. Paris, 1631.

DELPLANQUE, Albert
Saint François de Sales, humaniste et écrivain latin. Mémoires et Travaux de l'Université de Lille, fasc. 2, Lille, 1907.

DUFOURNET, Antoine
La Jeunesse de Saint François de Sales, 1567–1602. Paris, 1942.

GAMBART, A.
La Vie Symbolique du bienheureux François de Sales, comprise sous le voile de 52 emblèmes. Paris, 1664.

GUEVARA, Maria Teresa
Humanisano de S. Francesco de Sales. Mexico City, 1957.

GUERLIN DE GUER, Charles
Étude sur la Langue et le Style de Saint François de Sales. Revue d'Histoire de la Philosophie et d'Histoire Générale de la Civilisation de la Faculté des Lettres de Lille. Paris, 1934.

HÄMEL-STIER, Angela
Franz von Sales. Ein Lebensbild. Würzburg 1946.
Frauen um Franz von Sales. (Madame Acarie, Frau von Charmoisy,

Franziska von Chantal, Angélique Arnauld, Felicitas Orsini.)
Vienna, 1954.
Johanna Franziska von Chantal. 2nd edition Vienna, 1950.

HAMON, André
Vie de Saint François de Sales. Nouvelle éd. entièrement revisée par
J. F. Gonthier et G. Letourneau. 2 Vols. Paris, 1917.
English translation and adaptation by H. Burton: *The Life of St.
Francis de Sales.* 2 Vols. London, 1925.

HENRY-COÜANNIER, Maurice
Saint François de Sales et ses Amitiés. 6th edition. Paris, 1958.

HUVELIN, Abbé Henri
Quelques Directeurs d'Âmes au XVIIe Siècle. 3rd edition. Paris,
1923. Translated into English by J. Leonard, C. M.: *Some
Spiritual Guides of the Seventeenth Century.* London, 1927.

HUYBEN, Dom J.
Aux Sources de la Spiritualité Française au XVIIe Siècle. Supple-
ment to *La Vie Spirituelle,* 1930–1.

KELLEY, C. F.
The Spirit of Love. Based on the Teachings of St. François de
Sales. New York, 1951; London, 1952.
The Spiritual Maxims of St. Francis de Sales; edited and with an
introduction by C. F. Kelley. New York, 1953; London, 1954.

KÖNIGSBAUER, Ludwig
Das Menschenbild bei Franz von Sales. Studien z. Geschichte der
kath. Moraltheologie, 3. Regensburg, 1955.

LAVELLE, Louis
Quatre Saints. Paris, 1951. Translated into English by Dorothea
O'Sullivan: *The Meaning of Holiness.* London, 1954. (Includes an
essay on St. Francis de Sales: 'The Unity of Will and Love'.)

LEBERT, Antoine, and DANIELS, Joseph
Les Rapports entre Saint François de Sales et les Pays Bas. Nijmegen,
1932.

LECLERCQ, Jacques
Saint François de Sales, Docteur de la Perfection. Paris, 1948.

LE COUTURIER, Ernestine
*Françoise-Madeleine de Chaugy et la Tradition Salésienne au XVIIe
siècle.* 2 Vols. Paris, 1933.

MACKEY, Dom Henry Benedict
Four Essays on St. Francis de Sales. London, 1883. (See also his

introductions to the separate volumes of the Library of St. Francis de Sales.)

MARDUEL, M.
L'Âme ardente de Ste. Chantal. Paris, 1955.

MARTIN, Joseph
Die Theologie des Heiligen Franz von Sales, Kirchenlehrer. Rottenburg am Neckar, 1934.

MÉZARD, Denys, O. P.
Doctrine Spirituelle de Ste. Jeanne-Françoise de Chantal. Paris, 1928.

MÜLLER, Michael
Frohe Gottesliebe. Das religiös-sittliche Ideal des heiligen Franz von Sales. 3rd edition. Freiburg i.B., 1948. Translated into English (anon.). *St. Francis de Sales.* London, 1936.
Die Freundschaft des heiligen Franz von Sales mit der heiligen Johanna Franziska von Chantal. Regensburg, 1923.

RIVET, Mother Mary M.
The Influence of the Spanish Mystics on the Works of St. Francis de Sales. Washington, 1941.

RIVIÈRE, Louis de la
La Vie de l'Illustrissime François de Sales de très heureuse et glorieuse mémoire. Paris, 1624.

ROFFAT, Claude
A l'Écoute de Saint François de Sales. Paris, 1948. (A full collection of texts with a commentary.)

ROTTER, F.
Das Seelenleben in der Gottesliebe, nach dem Theotimus des heiligen Franz von Sales. Freiburg i.B., 1935.

RUSSMANN, Josef
Franz von Sales. Ein Heiliger des christlichen Humanismus. Vienna, 1948.

SALES, Charles Auguste de
Histoire du bien-heureux François de Sales, evesque et prince de Geneve, instituteur et fondatuer de l'Ordre des religieuses de la Visitation saincte Marie. Composée premierement en Latin, par C. A. de Sales et mise en François par le mesme autheur. Lyons, 1634. Modern edition. Paris, 1866.

SCUPOLI, Lorenzo
The Spiritual Combat. Translation with an introduction by Thomas Barns. London, 1909.

SEMPÉ, Louis, S. J.
Saint François de Sales, ascèse et mystique. Toulouse, 1922.

SEROUET, Pierre
De la Vie Dévote à la Vie Mystique. Études Carmélitaines, Bruges, 1958. (The influence of Carmelite mysticism on St. Francis de Sales.)

SION, Mère Madeleine-Louise de
Physionomie d'une Sainte. Jeanne de Chantal. Paris, 1950.

STEUART, R. H. J., S.J.
Diversity in Holiness. London, 1938. (Contains an essay on St. Francis de Sales.)

STROWSKI, Fortunat
Saint François de Sales. Introduction à l'Histoire du Sentiment Religieux en France au 17e Siècle. 2nd edition. Paris, 1928.

THAMIRY, Edouard
La Méthode d'Influence de Saint François de Sales. Son Apologétique conquérante. Paris, 1920.

TROCHU, Mgr. Francis
Saint François de Sales, d'après ses écrits, ses premiers historiens et les deux procès inédits de sa canonisation. 2 Vols. Lyons and Paris, 1946.

VINCENT, Francis
Saint François de Sales directeur d'âmes. L'éducation de la volonté. Paris, 1923.
Le Travail du Style chez Saint François de Sales d'après ses corrections. Étude comparative entre l'édition princeps de 'l'Introduction' et l'édition de 1619. Paris, 1923.

VISITATION
Année Sainte des Religieuses de la Visitation Sainte-Marie. 12 Vols. Annecy, 1867 ff. (Lives of the Sisters and much anecdotal material on St. Francis de Sales not available elsewhere.)
La Visitation Sainte-Marie. (Anon.) Série: Les Ordres Religieux. Paris, 1923.

WAACH, Hildegard
Franz von Sales. Das Leben eines Heiligen. Vienna, 1955.

VAN HOUTRYVE, Dom Idesbald
La Vie Intérieure selon Saint François de Sales. Louvain, 1931.
Saint François de Sales peint par lui-même. Louvain, 1952.

General Index

This index is not exhaustive but an attempt has been made to cover the main topics and persons.

185, 197, 228, 232, 276, 283, 290; *see also* 'Lady Abbess'
virtues, abject and honourable, 122 f.; easy and hard, 247; of the spirit, 241; little, 160
Visitation, feast of the, 283; Order of the, 26, 131, 170,

185, 193, 313
vocation, religious, 156, 278 f., 283 ff.

Whitsun, 192, 281
widowhood, 52, 93 f., 94, 118, 121, 122, 129, 158